MW00514523

ZOOMSCAPE

ZOOMSCAPE

ARCHITECTURE IN MOTION AND MEDIA

BY MITCHELL SCHWARZER

PRINCETON ARCHITECTURAL PRESS
NEW YORK
2004

FOR MY GRANDPARENTS

WOLF SCHWARZER (1889–1942)
AND ZOSIA GOLIGER (1900–1942)

EMIL BUCHWALTER (1898–1939)
AND PEPKA REIF (1904–1941)

PUBLISHED BY **PRINCETON ARCHITECTURAL PRESS** 37 EAST SEVENTH STREET, NEW YORK, NEW YORK 10003. FOR A FREE CATALOG OF BOOKS, CALL 1.800.722.6657. VISIT OUR WEB SITE AT WWW.PAPRESS.COM.

© 2004 PRINCETON ARCHITECTURAL PRESS ALL RIGHTS RESERVED PRINTED AND BOUND IN CANADA 06 05 04 03 5 4 3 2 1 FIRST EDITION

NO PART OF THIS BOOK MAY BE USED OR REPRODUCED IN ANY MANNER WITHOUT WRITTEN PERMISSION FROM THE PUBLISHER, EXCEPT IN THE CONTEXT OF REVIEWS.

EVERY REASONABLE ATTEMPT HAS BEEN MADE TO IDENTIFY OWNERS OF COPYRIGHT. ERRORS OR OMISSIONS WILL BE CORRECTED IN SUBSEQUENT EDITIONS.

EDITING: NANCY LEVINSON, DESIGN: DEB WOOD

SPECIAL THANKS TO: NETTIE ALJIAN, NICOLA BEDNAREK, JANET BEHNING, MEGAN CAREY, PENNY (YUEN PIK) CHU, RUSSELL FERNANDEZ, JAN HAUX, CLARE JACOBSON, MARK LAMSTER, NANCY EKLUND LATER, LINDA LEE, KATHARINE MYERS, JANE SHEINMAN, SCOTT TENNENT, JENNIFER THOMPSON, AND JOSEPH WESTON OF PRINCETON ARCHITECTURAL PRESS.
—KEVIN C. LIPPERT, PUBLISHER

LIBRARY OF CONGRESS CATALOGING-IN-PUBLICATION DATA
SCHWARZER, MITCHELL.

ZOOMSCAPE : ARCHITECTURE IN MOTION AND MEDIA / MITCHELL SCHWARZER.—
1ST ED.
    P. CM.
  ISBN 1-56898-441-3 (PBK. : ALK. PAPER)
  1. ARCHITECTURE, MODERN—20TH CENTURY. 2. VISUAL PERCEPTION. 3. ARCHITECTURE AND TECHNOLOGY. I. TITLE.
NA680 .S392 2004
720'.1'05—DC22

I GREW UP SEEING THE WIDER WORLD FROM THE WINDOWS OF A CAR
AND THE SHUFFLING IMAGERY OF THE MOVIES. THANKS TO MY FATHER,
WHO LIVED FOR ROAD TRIPS, MY EARLIEST ASSOCIATIONS OF ARCHITEC-
TURE ARE MIXED WITH EXPRESSWAYS AND ROADSIDES—THE SPREADING
PANORAMA GAINED ON THE ASCENT OF A GIANT BLUE BRIDGE, THE FLOCK
OF FACADES THAT WOULD GREET US AS WE PASSED THROUGH COUNTRY
TOWNS. DURING THOSE SAME CHILDHOOD YEARS, WHEN NOT ON THE
ROAD, I WATCHED COUNTLESS CITIES ON THE MILLION DOLLAR MOVIE.
SITTING IN THE TV ROOM WITH MY MOTHER, I SAW ARCHITECTURE FLASH BY
IN SNIPPETS, PARED DOWN LIKE MEMORIES, AND EVERY BIT AS ENCHANTING.

MY WIFE MARJORIE HAS BEEN THE COMPANION BY MY SIDE THROUGH
MY CONTINUING JOURNEYS THROUGH ZOOMSCAPES. SHE HAS SEEN ME
THROUGH EVERY STEP OF THE PROCESS OF RESEARCHING AND WRITING
THIS BOOK, IMPROVING MY IDEAS AND REPEATEDLY READING EVERY WORD
OF TEXT TO MAKE SURE IT WORKED. I AM INDEBTED TO MY EDITOR, NANCY
LEVINSON, FOR HER ENCOURAGEMENT, PAINSTAKING EDITING, AND LITERARY
SENSIBILITY.

I WISH TO THANK CALIFORNIA COLLEGE OF THE ARTS FOR GRANTING ME
THE SABBATICAL THAT GAVE ME THE TIME FOR SUCH A LARGE PROJECT.
I ALSO WANT TO EXPRESS MY GRATITUDE TO SEVERAL OTHER COLLEAGUES
WHO READ EITHER THE ENTIRETY OR PORTIONS OF THE MANUSCRIPT AND
OFFERED GREAT ADVICE, INCLUDING PETER HALES, STANFORD ANDERSON,
MICHAEL LORDY, BOB BRUEGMANN, WILLIAM LITTMANN, SANDY ISENSTADT,
AND MABEL WILSON. FINALLY, THANKS ARE EXTENDED TO THE PHOTOGRAPHERS
AND FRIENDS WHO ASSISTED ME—CAROL BUHRMANN, PHILIP GRUEN,
STEVE HARP, PAD MCLAUGHLIN, KEITH PLYMALE, JOHN SANTORO, AND
BARBARA SMITH.

—MITCHELL SCHWARZER

INTRODUCTION

I HAVE NEVER SET FOOT in scores of buildings in scores of towns, but they are familiar to me. I know thousands of buildings, streets, and cities, not from any tactile encounter, but through trips in vehicles and through images taken by cameras. Not long ago I spent an entire day viewing architecture on the run. Downtown, in a major industrial city, I boarded an elevated train that skimmed by walls, rooftops and antennae, and in sight of faraway towers. At the airport, I boarded a plane and, viewed from aloft, that same city receded into the geometries of line and plane. Airborne, I watched a film that transported me to a car chase through the streets of Mexico City. On the ground in a new city, the walk to baggage claim took me past an exhibit of sepia photos of Victorian storefronts. The cab ride from the airport wheeled me back into the present along a strip-malled highway, its signs looking like colorful tinted cellophane through the windshield. At the end of the day, in a motel, a cable news station broadcast pictures of a volcanic eruption that had destroyed the town of Goma in the Congo, red lava submerging houses on the large screen just a few feet from my bed. I was in the zoomscape all day—a largely optical mode of perception characterized by speed and surface.

Zoomscape explores the impact of mechanized transportation and camera reproduction on the perception of architecture. In the modern era, new ways of viewing buildings and cities have emerged, beginning with railroads and photography in the mid-nineteenth century, continuing with automobiles and motion pictures, and then air travel and television. Transportation and camera technologies have fundamentally altered our perception of the built environment. We have become used to seeing architecture through abrupt shifts of viewpoint and via unexpected juxtapositions. Vehicles zoom our sight across great distances at tremendous velocities. Cameras zoom our sight beyond the capacities of our bodies, and usually rupture the continuum of space and time. While transportation and camera technologies do not replace direct encounters with buildings and places, their ubiquity has altered architectural aesthetics. Perception flattens. Time spent with buildings diminishes. Seen in motion, houses and whole cities roll, break apart, and recombine. Seen in succession, images superimpose upon one another and buildings are evaluated less by their weight and presence than by their fluctuating outlines. Seen within frames, architecture is experienced as graphic and pictorial.

How do we consider architecture while looking through the windshield of a car driving along an avenue, seeing the reflections of utility poles, streetlights, and buildings on the curved surface, scrutinizing the window patterns of skyscrapers as they roll across the glass one after the other? How do we observe a cathedral that seems to dip and soar through the motions of a camera positioned in a helicopter, or watch a parking lot freeze into a single photographic image, or notice, in a film scene shot from a rushing train, a series of smokestacks that seem to float by? How do we see architecture mediated through technologies of motion and media?

Since zoomscapes encompass views of architecture modulated by the accelerator pedal or the remote control, the studio production room or the airplane flight path, they take in a mass audience. In *Zoomscape*, I adopt an expansive definition of architecture, including not only works by famous architects, but also ordinary buildings put up by craftsmen or contractors, and including as well engineering structures and infrastructures, streets and freeways, cities, suburbs, and skylines—in short, a range of cultural landscapes. I use the term "architecture" because it encapsulates these diverse environments.

While we inhabit an overwhelmingly built-up world, most works of architecture receive only passing glances. Few people understand buildings as architects do, as complex spatial and structural creations, described in technical drawings, and explained in dense theoretical and historical language. Architectural tours and travel itineraries guide visitors through historical landmarks and districts, but most people, most of the time, pass by the architectural landscape with little reflection. Or do they? Attentiveness to architecture depends upon the context of the experience. When connected to art (as in a museum exhibition), to collective history (the site of a famous event), to personal history (someone's childhood home or neighborhood), to celebrity (the home of a politician or movie star), or to a media story (the design competition for the World Trade Center site), architecture acquires a larger following. Like most things, architecture means more when it mediates the extraordinary moments of life.

Certainly, part of the appeal of buildings lies in their stillness and sculptural depth, in their implied resistance to the world of speed, surface, and image. Architecture remains the grand framework or infrastructure in which we inevitably live. Yet the building art does not exist in isolation. In 1831, in *Notre-Dame de Paris*, Victor Hugo argued that mechanized printing was usurping architecture's traditional role as the locus for societal communication. While Hugo was right to recognize the onset of the mass media, he did not realize that architecture would become part of that system of information. Not only does the built world change all the time, but, through technological mediation, so too do its perceptual contexts, coordinates, and constraints. Today, for buildings or cityscapes to be noticed, they must be viewed in states of mediated perception—energized in velocity or dazzling light and sound effects. Architecture must merge into the flow of information, into the spectacle of media. Fredric Jameson is correct to describe postmodernity as the condition in which the traditional fine arts (including architecture) are mediatized, in which they come into consciousness of themselves as media within a media system.[1]

Already by the 1960s, the cusp of the postmodern era, a host of artists were probing the mediatized landscape for cultural inspiration—writers like Thomas Pynchon, photographers like Garry Winogrand, and filmmakers like Jean-Luc Godard. Architects, too, were conceptualizing urban design in concert with the marketplace and entertainment industries; Robert Venturi and Denise Scott Brown took note of the roadside and its informative efflorescence of signage; Charles Moore looked at that same roadside for its kitschy fantasies of form. Scholarly writers on the built environment understood that aesthetic perception was changing. In *The Last Landscape*, published in 1962, William H. Whyte complains, "Of all the tons of studies done of our cities, it is rare to find any that attempt to discern the city as most people see it."[2] Whyte was concerned about a growing gulf between expert judgment and popular taste. The cartographic perspectives and quantitative analyses of the planning profession had little relevance for the myriad ways in which people actually inhabit and regard landscapes, especially while driving in a car or riding in a train. Whyte proposed redesigning transportation corridors as scenic successions of visual events, but this was a proscriptive solution, an attempt to remake emerging vehicular landscapes in the manner of eighteenth-century English landscape gardens. Still, he was onto something. Our appreciation of buildings or landscapes depends on how we see them.

1. Fredric Jameson, *Postmodernism: Or the Cultural Logic of Late Capitalism* (Durham, North Carolina: Duke University Press, 1991), 162.

2. William H. Whyte, *The Last Landscape* (Garden City, New York: Doubleday & Co., 1968), 314.

While architecture was not fully associated with the media until the late twentieth century, the study of buildings perceived in motion began a century earlier. By the 1870s, scholars of optical physiology and psychology began to examine how the perceptual faculties—eyes, brain, nerves, muscles—participate in the forming of an object. Instead of equating visual perception with the passive activity of receiving impressions of light on the retina, they associated vision with nerve and muscle movements, and aesthetics with the pleasurable or disagreeable mental sensations caused by those movements. The way the form of a building causes a person to move his eyes or head influences how he feels about the building; architectural aesthetics equates with the steady or monotonous feeling of horizontal lines, the rise and fall of verticals, the complex dynamics of diagonals and spirals. In 1893, Adolf Hildebrand linked these ideas to bodily movement through built space. Hildebrand, a sculptor and art theorist, writes that "architecture arouses in us not merely the possibility of movement, but a definite feeling of space . . . ideas of movement are stimulated and attain unity of effect through space itself being converted into visual impression."[3] Likewise, in *The Foundations of Art History*, published in 1905, August Schmarsow, a German art historian, describes architectural experience as an accumulation of sensations brought about through movement within a built space. The impression of a colonnade, for instance, has less to do with its overall composition than with our peripatetic sensation of specific rhythms of cylindrical solids and concave voids. Architecture becomes less about the building as a whole object or its historical meanings, and more about particular aspects of the building witnessed by an individual, mobile observer.

Hildebrand's and Schmarsow's theories were based on bodily sensations. Later, other theorists of perception became interested in the powers of the body acting in concert with machines. James Gibson, in *The Perception of the Visual World*, of 1950, addresses the effects of vehicles on our experience of the environment. Gibson is captivated by how rapid movement on trains, automobiles, or airplanes presents observers with a visual field dissimilar from that experienced while walking. Machine velocity induces the foreground to blur and the background to look like an outline; the direction of movement expands or contracts the visual field. Gibson also recognizes something that earlier art historians—like Alois Riegl, who traced the history

3. Adolf Hildebrand, *The Problem of Form in the Fine Arts* (Strasbourg: Heitz & Muendel, 1893), 119.

of perception from the tactile sense in antiquity to the optical sense in modernity—had been arguing for some time. The visual sense was becoming increasingly dominant in technological perception. Walking requires considerable muscular effort. In a vehicle, the muscular work involved in steering or accelerating is minimal. As Gibson says, "visual stimulation becomes proportionally more important than the bodily stimulation in these relatively passive types of locomotion."[4]

In *Techniques of the Observer*, of 1990, Jonathan Crary focuses on the emergence of a distinctly modern type of spectator. Crary maintains that during the nineteenth century the body (and not the object viewed) increasingly became the site where perceptual meaning is produced. He also recognizes the growing importance of optical devices that enhance and transform perception. Going further than earlier theorists of perception, he complicates the perceptual role of machines. While machines affirm the power of individuals to see strikingly new visual terrains, they also calibrate vision into technological measures and separate the viewer from the space of the object. Through dioramas, stereoscopes, zoetropes, and other devices, people started to see things out of context and unattached to one another—dissociated from the unified field of geometric perspective that had dominated the idea of viewing since the Renaissance. As Crary writes, "If perspective implied a homogeneous and potentially metric space, the stereoscope discloses a fundamentally disunified and aggregate field of disjunct elements."[5] Modern spectators became disconnected. The visual field acquired unprecedented autonomy and flexibility.

In a little more than a century, attitudes on the relationship between technology and perception changed a great deal. During the early industrial age of the nineteenth century, there was scant mention of machines, although the human body and its perceptual faculties were understood through mechanistic metaphors and systems. At the height of the industrial age, the middle of the twentieth century, human perception was often regarded as an extension of machines; great value was placed on the powers of this human-machine assembly. Toward the end of the twentieth century, in the midst of the information age, the human-machine assembly has been divested of some of its potency. The influence of technologies on

4. James J. Gibson, *The Perception of the Visual World* (Boston: Houghton Mifflin, 1950), 135.

5. Jonathan Crary, *Techniques of the Observer: On Vision and Modernity in the Nineteenth Century* (Cambridge: MIT Press, 1990), 125.

human perception is equated with disembodied, discontinuous experience and signification.

In coining the term "zoomscape," I am trying to describe the overall arena of transformed architectural perception brought about by industrial technologies of motion and media. My interests parallel to some extent those of the film theorist Anne Friedberg. In *Window Shopping: Cinema and the Postmodern*, published in 1993, Friedberg brings up the idea of a mobilized and virtual gaze. The mobilized gaze refers to a new way of moving in the world (including trains, planes, and automobiles) that produces a new sense of distance and time. The virtual gaze (including the media stemming from the camera) transports viewers to an imaginary elsewhere. Through investigations of shopping locales, world exhibitions, museums, and amusement parks, Friedberg locates the mobilized virtual gaze in the modern world's proliferating architectural spaces of consumption. As she writes, already during the nineteenth century, the mobilized virtual gaze led to fluid and individualized perception: "The telegraph, the telephone, and electricity increased the speed of communications, the railroad and steamship changed concepts of distance, while the new visual culture—photography, advertising and shop display—recast the nature of memory and experience. Whether a 'frenzy of the visible' or 'an immense accumulation of spectacles,' everyday life was transfigured by the social multiplication of images."[6]

During the nineteenth century, no city better exemplified these changes than Paris. At the time, Charles Baudelaire wrote some of the most trenchant observations of the city. Instead of a socially cohesive and physically integrated community, Baudelaire diagnosed modern urbanity as a proliferation of views and viewpoints, objects and events—all held together by the fleeting sensations of an individual spectator. For the most part, he observed the modernization of Paris from within its public spaces, sitting in cafes or strolling the boulevards or arcades. He thus regarded the changing city through perceptual stances that had been available for millennia, and even criticized photography's effacement of place and past. But Baudelaire's pedestrian wanderings are not unrelated to emerging technological perception. Strolling through department stores or streets, he was witness to the creation of a new space of display—mass-produced objects for a consumer

6. Anne Friedberg. *Window Shopping: Cinema and the Postmodern* (Berkeley: University of California Press, 1993), 15–16.

market, mass-produced ornaments for a middle-class city. And he was privy to experiencing a different Paris from its rail lines or to seeing, in photographs, faraway worlds he had never visited. Since his time, the perception of architecture has increasingly migrated from the sidewalk and the square to the home and the automobile. The space of media and public life have, in other words, been turned outside in.[7] We habitually observe the world through technological frames. What does it mean to see architecture not only in on-site encounters, such as walking around or through a building or finding a good vantage point and gazing for a long time? What does it mean to be a viewer who moves at machine velocities and watches through machine constructions of space and time? Looking from vehicles or at screens produces a different kind of visual field; looking via machine movement produces a different kind of architectural aesthetics.

Almost all perception involves some level of technological intervention. Vehicles and cameras are the result of technologies that reach back centuries. Humans have long perceived architecture through the intercession of an enhanced power of motion derived from water, wind, and animals. Without modes of locomotion, such as sailing ships and horse-drawn vehicles, the experience of the built world would have been limited to walking range. Most people would have known their local environments and little else. Ships and horses opened up new visual experiences—the vistas from a ship at sea or a caravan in the desert, the sweeping emptiness of water or sand that provides a frame for viewing an environment as a unified whole.

Historically, one of the most important architectural abstractions was hand drawing. Since the Renaissance, drawing has been a flexible means of representing, framing, evaluating, and comparing buildings and cities. Illustrated books and folios positioned architecture as two-dimensional expression. On paper, an eventual material reality is envisioned through lines, cross-hatchings, and other illustrative techniques only partly related to the context of place or the demands of function and structure. Maps, atlases, and city views, likewise, enable an understanding of place in larger, idealizing terms. Such urban depictions express the unity (or disunity) of building shapes and styles or the relationship of a built environment to its natural environment. The history of architectural and urban perception owes an

7. Beatriz Colomina, *Privacy and Publicity: Modern Architecture as Mass Media* (Cambridge: MIT Press, 1994), 7.

incalculable debt to the development of diverse rendering systems. As the architectural historian Robin Evans writes: "Architectural drawings are projections, which means that organized arrays of imaginary straight lines pass through the drawing to corresponding parts of the thing represented by the drawing."[8] Evans realizes that drawings differ only superficially from the pictures on a television screen, in a film, or in a photograph. These latter types of imagery consist of converging lines reflected from an object that are projected on a photosensitive surface—techniques to imagine, design, and reproduce the three-dimensional world in two dimensions. Architecture is typically seen through projecting lines within both hand drawings and camera reproductions.

In *Understanding Media*, of 1964, Marshall McLuhan makes a case for appreciating architecture through projecting lines of light. The electric lights of cities seen while standing on the ground are, he argues, akin to those seen from a rushing airplane as well as those seen on a television screen.[9] Illuminated electrically, architectural substance becomes linear information, the patterns of light we see directly, aerially, or watching a screen. To McLuhan, the linear abstraction of architectural perception demonstrates that the medium is the message—that how we see a building, from an aerial view or a televisual view, determines in large part our understanding of the building. His position has much in common with that of late-nineteenth-century aesthetic theorists, who advocated for understanding architecture through perception. But while those scholars saw architecture as the direct spatial extension of corporeal sensations, McLuhan and other twentieth-century scholars have underscored the critical intervention and mediation of technology between viewer and object.

The zoomscape that began in the mid-nineteenth century has grown larger and faster each decade, and will continue to do so. In the aftermath of the industrial revolution, mechanized innovations in transportation and image reproduction have recast the perception and understanding of the built environment. But modern technological visuality does not erase the importance of the built environment. One of my chief aims is to delineate how the new modes of architectural experience reframe architecture within today's predominantly visual culture. That the floating planes of building seen from

8. Robin Evans, "Architectural Projection," in *Architecture and Its Image: Four Centuries of Architectural Representation*, eds. Eve Blau and Edward Kaufman (Montreal: Canadian Centre for Architecture, 1989), 19.

9. Marshall McLuhan, *Understanding Media: The Extensions of Man* [1964], (Cambridge: MIT Press, 1994), 129.

a racing locomotive, or the rapid-fire sequence of international tourist locales compressed into twenty seconds on a television commercial, are so different from earlier modes of sight makes their examination all the more important. How we see is inseparable from what we see. The technologies that structure our vision are inseparable from the built environment that we apprehend.

In recent decades, many architectural theorists have claimed that a building cannot be understood as a discrete formal object, that its meaning is produced amid systems of signs and codes—textual contexts that produce an endless array of new realities and affiliations. In *Zoomscape*, I argue that this linguistic model of architecture must be supplemented by a perceptual one. In motion and media, a building is understood not as an autonomous object, but as a part of a web of routes, narratives, and milieus—a road journey, a plot-driven movie, a book of photographs. Zoomscapes not only "liberate" a building from its status as object, they also free it from its site and from our bodies. The experience of the built environment emerges on the go or in distant places, and, in either case, more and more through visual observation. The influence of place on our understanding of architecture is less pronounced than ever. The nonvisual senses, especially touch, play a diminishing role. Today, sight moves with the swiftness of vehicles or camera edits. It shifts off-site with camera images or, with vehicles, to a state one could call passing-site. Mobile perception combines one building with others, those that precede or succeed it along a rail corridor, or in a reel of film imagery.

Nonetheless, zoomscape perception cannot be easily defined. The view can be as large as that from an elevated expressway or as condensed as that of a snapshot, as blurry as that from a high-speed train or as detailed as that of a slow cinematic pan. Often, in a speeding train or car, we see buildings for brief periods, in snippets that must be pieced together. But in other instances, watching a long take in a film, we have plenty of time to observe an environment. Sometimes we see buildings in high resolution and close-up, as with photographs. Other times we see in low-resolution and distant abstraction, as in the views from a plane. Some buildings we see only once in a glance from a train's side window; others we see repeatedly on television programs or daily commutes. Much perception on the roadside or on television is conditioned by advertising and consumption, but a film or air journey can disclose views unconnected to commerce. The wide variety of zoomscape experiences can lead us to feel we are not experiencing architecture in any usual way. To a large extent this is true. We are experiencing architecture within a technologically expanded visual field—not just as objects in continuous space, but also as variable assemblages in intermittent space. To live in a world in which one's everyday perception is composed of imagistic fragments drawn from all over the globe is to participate in a profound perceptual transformation.

Theorists and historians of modern architecture have long argued that buildings must reflect the needs, methods, and materials of their time. Buildings must reflect, too, the perceptual characteristics of their time. The divisions between authentic and appropriated imagery, real and simulated places, actual buildings and their representations, are now outdated. In restless motion, in shifting identity, in a world filled with entertainment, tourism, and adventure, we now inhabit a different sort of space than that posited by traditional theories of geometric perspective. Yet while noncontinuous and nonuniversal, this new space is a technological and artistic construct, as was its predecessor. As the cultural historian Michel de Certeau reminds us: "The desire to see the city preceded the means of satisfying it. Medieval or Renaissance painters represented the city as seen in a perspective that no eye had yet enjoyed."[10] Are the modern spatial scenes designed by engineers or cinematographers all that different?

An important characteristic of the zoomscape is mobility, the chance to go to a multitude of places quickly and easily. As part our daily visual diet, we habitually down huge portions of building and landscape, gathered from dispersed geographies. From my home in Oakland, California, in a single day, I can fly to almost any point on the globe, connect to rail or automotive transport, and reach remote building sites. I can open a book of photographs, insert a disk into the television, log onto the Internet—and the world will come to me. *Zoomscape* explores worlds of architectural perception in which tourism and voyeurism play significant roles. From the zoomscape, we can trespass, cross forbidden thresholds, glimpse private lives. From trains, travelers peer into backyards; from planes, they scan rooftops. Film and video

10. Michel de Certeau, "Walking in the City," in
The Practice of Everyday Life, trans. Steven
Randall (Berkeley: University of California Press,
1984), 92.

cameras lift viewers into the sky, move them adroitly through space, slide through cracks in windows, and even penetrate solid walls. The mechanical eye of the zoomscape can burn through space, revealing that which is usually unseen.

Mobility should not be equated simply with movement. Mobility implies freedom of movement, and includes the possibility of stationary views. Important aspects of architecture unfold while a vehicle or camera proceeds slowly or remains still. Looking out from a car stopped in traffic, we feel a sense of mobility, although we are not in motion. A succession of cinema edits might transport us to radically different environs while, each time, affording serene conditions for observation. Some film directors rely on a motionless camera. And although photographers freeze buildings and cities into still images, photographs themselves are mobile, portable images that can be transported anywhere.

Still, humans have long been infatuated with velocity, the thud of steps succeeded by the swoosh of tires, the slow skip of sight accelerated into a spinning reel of images beyond the holding capacity of consciousness. Speed is about excess, about seeing more than one can process, traveling beyond the capacities of our bodies. Speed induces architectural effects both spectacular and banal. Buildings become acrobats of the skies. Towers and facades twist and turn. "The new landscape," says J.B. Jackson, "seen at a rapid, sometimes even a terrifying pace, is composed of rushing air, shifting lights, clouds, waves, a constantly moving, changing horizon, a constantly changing surface beneath the ski, the wheel, the rudder, the wing. The view is no longer static; it is a revolving, uninterrupted panorama of 360 degrees. In short the traditional perspective, the traditional way of seeing and experiencing the world is abandoned; in its stead we become active participants, the shifting focus of a moving abstract world. . . . To the perceptive individual there can be an almost mystical quality to the experience; his identity seems for the moment to be transmuted."[11]

Mobility and velocity take us not only toward things, but also away from them. The specialized compartments and frames of the zoomscape detach us from the space of architecture. In moving vehicles, the size of windows can vary considerably, from the large panoramic domes of transcontinental trains

11. J.B. Jackson, "The Abstract World of the Hot-Rodder," *Landscape* 7.2 (Winter 1957–1958), 25.

to the tiny lozenges of commercial airliners. Camera environs, likewise, enclose architecture in frames of different sizes, from the almost square to the wide and horizontal. Whether those of a vehicle or a camera, such frames hack off the tops, bottoms, and sides of the things being viewed. Unlike direct vision, which stretches to the periphery, technological frames favor straight-ahead views. And yet zoomscapes encourage us to imagine just what is beyond the frame, the parts of buildings that might come into view or remain unseen. Anticipation and succession inform the aesthetics of the zoomscape.

Zoomscapes sever not only the outer edges but also the outer atmosphere. On a kitchen television one might watch a city scene where the air swirls with fog or gets hammered by rain. Driving on a dirt road, a car can stir up clouds of dust. From the air, the view depends on cloud cover and wind turbulence. In all these situations, the immediate environment—the kitchen, the cinema auditorium, the automobile compartment, the plane cabin—excludes most atmospheric effects. The viewing experience becomes somewhat sterilized. Sound, too, is modulated. Music or talk typically takes the place of ambient noise. In a vehicle or on a video, the soundtrack frequently orchestrates the perception of visual events. Perhaps, as the quantity, speed, and complexity of visual information continues to grow, our visual sensations will become ever more dependent upon auditory rhythms.

The screening rooms of the zoomscape lead to yet more distancing from the environment being viewed. One gazes at it from a separate space with its own architectural parameters. Vehicles tend to be small and restricting; especially in cars and planes, we are constrained by seat belts, unable to turn freely. Even in spacious viewing rooms, such as galleries and theaters, the act of viewing itself inhibits motion. Gazing intently at images demands specific body postures; it gets harder and harder to see a film or photograph if we are walking away from it. A paradoxical situation emerges. Zoomscapes encourage optical mobility and hamper physical mobility. Unlike the sensation of walking through a city and taking it in with all one's senses, the moving view from vehicles and the camera is, in the end, visual. The enormous gain in optical reach and power comes at the cost or pleasure of padded seats—whether in vehicles, theaters, living rooms, or offices—where bodies rest while the field of view becomes ever more intense.

Yet another characteristic of the zoomscape is multiplicity. Photography, film, and television reproduce images of buildings indefinitely, and in the process turn architecture into a medium of popular entertainment. In books and museums, theaters and living rooms, people see architecture less as the shaper of hierarchy and class division than as the setting for commercial fashions and dramatic situations. As Walter Benjamin argues in his 1933 essay, "The Work of Art in the Age of Mechanical Reproduction," the motorized duplication of an artwork erases uniqueness in favor of an extended life in images: "By making many reproductions it substitutes a plurality of copies for a unique existence. And in permitting the reproduction to meet the beholder or listener in his own particular situation, it reactivates the object reproduced. These two processes lead to a tremendous shattering of tradition."[12] Images, as opposed to the objects that have been photographed or filmed, circulate outside of established contexts and practices. Images have unpredictable lives of their own. Although Benjamin does not mention images of architecture, clearly, the built environments seen in photographs, in films, and on television possess the qualities of the mechanically reproduced image. A photograph shows a unique building, but there might be thousands of copies of the photograph, and thus almost as many cultural and commercial contexts in which the image of the building is perceived.

Still, while camera media encourage the diffusion of two-dimensional images of architecture, they do not erase the aura of the three-dimensional original. People engage architecture on different levels, the singular building as well as the multiple images of the zoomscape. In the case of private buildings that limit public access, multiples might magnify their presence through widespread exposure. In the case of landmarks, multiples might offer a bit of a tourist experience to those unable to travel, or inspire others to take the trip. Accessible in texts, the Internet, stores, and theaters, camera images of architectures enable an aesthetic of the replay, an optical inhabitation of built settings unaffected by the passage of time or boundaries of space.

Although systems of modern transportation do not multiply the views of buildings as cameras do, their effects produce similarly standardized

12. Walter Benjamin, "The Work of Art in the Age of Mechanical Reproduction," in *Illuminations*, trans. Harry Zohn (New York: Schocken Books, 1969), 221.

views. Cities are no longer bounded places, easily distinguished from wilderness or countryside. The development of the railroad, automobile, and airplane has led to the global metropolis, a far-flung geography and a multicultural society. Within and between world cities, people travel long distances in a week, a year, a lifetime. At the same time, building practices and styles have become increasingly standardized. The modern search for progress and newness often leads to a paradoxical repetition of scenery and experience. The strange familiarity of non-places, the feeling of having traveled far and gone nowhere, is by now familiar.

The familiarity and sameness of perception, repeated again and again, can anesthetize us. Week after week, millions of us watch the same television shows, with their familiar views of urban skylines. Package tours, whether on the road or television, offer easy, predictable journeys, free of trouble, of unexpected encounters. Classic photographs and motion pictures of certain skylines—New York, London, Rio de Janeiro, Hong Kong—proliferate in the media, while panoramas of other large cities—Seoul, Lagos, Dallas, Sao Paolo—are rarely seen. Despite mobility and speed, the zoomscape can regurgitate the same views to the point of stagnation, of boredom. As the television historian Margaret Morse writes, "Television narrative often manages to combine a sense of passage with an ultimately static situation. Like itineraries in the mall or the freeway, these stories are highly segmented enchainments that have largely given up any pretense of development."[13] At times it seems as if we travel fast and far in an endlessly looping cycle.

But zoomscapes are also creative. Most film and television zoomscapes are highly edited—consisting of a flow of imagery pieced together from disparate buildings or places. Panning or tracking cameras maneuver our sight, and editors create new landscapes, new alignments of space and of time. The changes may be abrupt or seamless, but ultimately they create a new visual whole. Film and video pictures take apart buildings and cities and arrange them anew. A street in Istanbul, a facade in Cairo, and an interior in Los Angeles—all can be melded into a continuous experience. Editing also functions (somewhat differently) within transportation perception. In any journey of appreciable length, because of the quantity of places experienced, we tend to edit out large parts of the passing scene and focus on

13. Margaret Morse, *Virtualities: Television, Media Art, and Cyberculture* (Bloomington: Indiana University Press, 1998), 123–24.

selected buildings or landscape features. The faster the speed and the more distance covered, the more likely it is that our memory will consist of a few, select impressions, usually spread out over the length of the trip. Should it be startling, then, that architects have tried to capture the rising and falling tension of image flows, envisioning in their confrontations and harmonies a new theory for the discipline? In his 1981 *Manhattan Transcripts*, Bernard Tschumi writes of wanting to "offer a different reading of architecture in which space, movement, and events are independent, yet stand in a new relation to one another, so that the conventional components of architecture are broken down and rebuilt along different axes."[14]

I share this interest in recombinatory architecture. In *Zoomscape* I offer reflections on architecture seen in different modes of transportation and through the camera. The critical feature of any zoomscape is this moving or imagistic transformation of architecture from site to flow and from object to event. Architecture in a zoomscape has the potential not only to concentrate space but also to disperse and rearrange it within time, not only to fix place but also to relocate and redefine it.

The first half of the book addresses transportation. Its three chapters—railroad, automobile, and airplane—use films, photographs, literature, history, and theory as sources. Because they move, vehicles favor the long view over the close-up, and the grand sentiment over the minute observation. The scale and sprawl of the modern metropolis comes into view from vehicles as nowhere else. In each chapter, I focus on the parts and moods of a transportation journey: the spaces of arrival and departure (rail stations, airports, highway ramps); viewing corridors (tracks and rights-of-way, elevated lines, subways, city streets, country and suburban roads, expressways, and flight paths); theories of speed, angle, penetration, distance, and distraction; and political and emotional states of travel perception. Beginning with the invention of the railroad in the 1820s, I examine how mobility has enabled us to develop and experience vastly larger urban territories, and to view buildings and cities at high speeds. In the twentieth century, automobiles combined the speed of railroads with personal freedom, creating private viewing environments on road networks that reach much of the globe and dramatically affect urban form. Airplanes, ascending heights and moving at

14. Bernard Tschumi, *The Manhattan Transcripts*
(New York: St. Martin's Press, 1994), 7.

great speeds, recast the sight of urban landscape into abstract geometries; their range facilitates the emergence of a global landscape of non-places.

In the second half of the book, I look into how the camera portrays architecture and cityscape and combines them into new contexts of art and entertainment. The chapters on photography, film, and television are structured around analyses of works in each medium as well as relevant media histories and theories. As opposed to moving vehicles, the camera often comes close to works of architecture, and includes the fixed shots of photography, the long takes of cinema, and the rapid-fire editing of television. Photographers, cinematographers, and videographers constantly manipulate the look of architecture. For example, viewers experience buildings and cities under illumination of variable intensity, direction, and substance; buildings can be shaped by shadows and highlights or bathed in flat, diffused light; filters, film stock, and lamps transform colors, turning a panorama of a city at night from a whitish grid to bursts of yellow, red, and blue.

Each camera art situates architecture in different visual and cultural contexts. Photography renders buildings in a variety of stances—in frontal isolation, from angles that include context, through details, and in city portraits. The photographic experience of architecture shifts from the building site to books, magazines, museums, lecture halls, websites—situations where only the image of the building is present. In film, building and cityscape are critical elements in the creation of an alternative moving reality, experienced in a dark auditorium and through a focused visual experience. Through camera settings, movement, and editing—through the choreography of mise-en-scène—directors use architecture to establish and develop a story and express its visual qualities. In the video age, television creates a domestic culture of mass attention and distraction, where architecture becomes the background for a viewing experience centered upon lifestyle, sex, violence, and consumption. My attention here centers on the flow of news, commercials, and programming, especially comedies and police dramas.

In the camera chapters, I analyze architecture reproduced in the zoomscape, not produced for it. I am more interested in the use of existing buildings and cities than in constructed and temporary sets. Clearly, no strict line can be drawn between the realms of reality and artifice. (And in recent years, digital editing has greatly compromised claims for verisimilitude between image and reality, and it will continue to do so.) But for images shot before the 1990s (and even for a majority of images since then), I believe it is fruitful to analyze views of existing architecture. Since my discussion of camera technology emphasizes how it influences our experience of existing architecture, I do not consider digital imaging technologies used in design. Since the 1990s, many architects have realized that computer technology not only makes drawing more efficient, but also spurs the design of radically amorphous building forms. The fame of the Guggenheim Museum in Bilbao, Spain, designed by Frank Gehry, derives from its undulating curves and warped geometries, which were facilitated by digital modeling software. Similarly, the theoretical projects of the Los Angeles architect Greg Lynn envisage the construction of elastic architectures analogous to both the natural world and, I would argue, the perceptual zoomscape world. At this point, however, digital architectural design has not much engaged the general public, and so it is beyond the scope of this book.

In choosing technological perceptions of architecture, I represent historical, artistic, and cultural viewpoints, from the nineteenth century to the present. I am interested in both popular and avant-garde expressions. In the photography chapter, for instance, I analyze photographs of Chartres Cathedral taken by Henri Le Secq in the 1850s and by Charles Sheeler in the 1920s. For the film chapter, I consider Hollywood movies like *The Silence of the Lambs*, auteur works like Jean-Luc Godard's *Two or Three Things I Know About Her*, and experimental cinema such as Ernie Gehr's *Side/Walk/Shuttle*. Of course, hardly any technological creations work in isolation. In the nineteenth century, photographic reproduction and rail travel together spurred the opening up of the Western landscapes of the United States to tourism. In the twentieth century, the bird's-eye vantage point gained from a helicopter or airplane enabled the tracking and zoom shots common to the opening credits of films and television shows. Since the 1990s, the Internet has combined camera imagery with travel across computer space. On the web, users travel to websites that present text and imagery, primarily digitally coded photographs but increasingly video images as well. Never before have so many pictures been available at the touch of a finger. More than fifty years ago, László Moholy-Nagy predicted a revolution in visual understanding: "Cubism, futurism, photomontage, superimposed photographs, stroboscopic exposures and scientific graphs pave the way for this new type of communication. They are but a beginning in the perfection of visual manuscripts which will be read more quickly and precisely than verbal ones and will express things which the word, in its nature, never can."[15] The revolution that began more than a century earlier continues to develop today more than ever. We live in a world where the technologies of transportation and the camera allow us to view architecture in an astonishing range of places, discourses, and compositions.

15. László Moholy-Nagy, *Vision in Motion*
(Chicago: Institute of Design, 1947), 121.

CHAPTER 1

RAILROAD

IN 1825, THE WORLD'S FIRST RAILROAD line opened in England between the towns of Stockton and Darlington. The trip of about nine miles took two hours, slightly faster than walking, although during the final stretch into Stockton speeds of fifteen miles per hour were reached. Tracks soon spread throughout England and the industrializing world. In the United States there were twenty-three miles of track in 1830. By 1860, the figure had climbed to more than 30,000 miles, and passenger trains traveled at speeds between twenty and thirty miles per hour, three times the speed of a horse-drawn coach. Toward 1900, train speeds of more than fifty miles per hour were common. And by the late twentieth century, bullet trains routinely charged across the landscape at almost 200 miles per hour.

For millennia people had moved slowly on land. Cities evolved slowly. The biggest of them reached about a million inhabitants, and that number was only rarely achieved. During the nineteenth century, these conditions changed in a matter of decades. Railroads swept across the world like a tempest, sending storm waves through the built environment. No transportation revolution had affected architecture and urbanism to this extent before, and since then only the automobile's reshaping of city into megalopolis compares. Across the globe, railroads extended the small scale of the walking city into the vast scope of the metropolis. Longstanding boundaries between town and countryside fell away. Grids pressed outward. New commercial districts emerged around rail stations, transfer junctures, and stops. Building heights shot skyward. City populations swelled beyond any historical measure. London counted approximately one million persons in 1800; a century later its population exceeded six million. On the urban and rural landscape, rail was the epitome of the industrial revolution.

Operating on a dedicated roadbed of iron rails, using flanged wheels for its carriages, and pulled by steam and then diesel and electric locomotives, the train was an enormous advance over the horse-drawn carriage. Trains were comfortable, safe, and dependable. Most of all, they were fast. Travel times between places were cut from weeks and days to hours and minutes. Geographic space began to be understood through units of time, distance was rendered controllable, and the demands of rail schedules advanced the worldwide adoption of standardized time zones.[1] Far-flung

1. James A. Ward, *Railroads and the Character of America, 1820–1887* (Knoxville: University of Tennessee, 1986), 111.

places began to connect with each other to make larger agglomerations. Along the expanding rail lines of the nineteenth and twentieth centuries, the understanding of architecture grew from local to regional and eventually to continental scale. Gradually, the dispersed buildings and places along the rail routes fused into shared visual identities and heritages. Instead of understanding a place largely through one's ability to walk about its streets or avenues, people who rode the rails began to recognize a linear, sprawling notion of place: cities elongated into the countryside, towns reaching other towns, the buildings of one place relating to those of another through the newfound proximity afforded by trains.

Everything felt different from the fast-moving trains. No longer did people experience the built environment with their full range of senses. As with all subsequent technological revolutions, from photographs to airplanes and television, the sense of sight would dominate. In the rail car, the other senses—touch, taste, smell, and hearing—provided comparatively little information about the passing scene. And rail vision was no ordinary mode of sight. It was a new way of viewing, part human and part machine—the vision of velocity. The effects were exhilarating but also jarring. Seen from a train, works of architecture seemed to rush in and out of view like gusts of wind. Pieces of buildings or bridges, witnessed seconds apart, joined together. Features close to the train could feel perilously near to the compartment and appeared more liquid than solid. Far-off structures could seem uncannily remote. Because of its smooth horizontal trajectory, and because it separated the place of viewing from the things being viewed, the train turned the built environment into something of a moving picture show, decades before the invention of cinema. Not by accident, after 1900, many early movie theaters took the form of a railcar exploring the wide world.

Despite its speed and optical dynamism, the rail view introduced new restrictions to the visual perception of the built environment. Unlike ships or horse-drawn carriages, automobiles or airplanes, trains course along fixed lines of track. The rail view occurs along predetermined right-of-ways, a separate rail space. This space includes stations, the miles of track yards and corridor, and the long train compartments. In large cities, the sights usually include immense terminals, where a sense of distance is conveyed by destination signs, cosmopolitan crowds, and racks of foreign-language newspapers. Once on a train, passengers see the productive backsides of cities, their copious groupings of factories, warehouses, storage lots, and rear yards, all of which usually deteriorate faster than other parts of the metropolis. Yet the ordinary passenger view takes in only limited portions of these and other landscapes. Contrary to the frontal view from the locomotive or the circular vistas available on special viewing cars, the rectangular windows of seating compartments afford little sense of where the train is heading. Passengers gaze diagonally or sideways, at objects rushing by. Experienced at speeds out of sync with the human body, the rail view often finds itself out of view, searching for fixed form while the engine moves steadily forward, mile after engineered mile.

A comparison of an intercity and urban rail journey begins to reveal the varieties of railroad experience, the mechanical motion that overwhelms the human senses and contributes to the aesthetics of modernism. The first few minutes of Walther Ruttmann's 1926 film, *Berlin: The Symphony of a Great City*, charts a trip from the Brandenburg countryside to the center of the German capital. The film begins with a view of rippling water and then cuts to a shot of horizontal bands of light and dark—the rural rhythms of nature thus give way to the mechanized perceptions of the rail journey. To engulf filmgoers further in the new technologies that were transforming metropolitan life, Ruttmann cuts again, this time to views of crisscrossing lines—an effect created by flickering light penetrating the openings of a train compartment. The editing becomes faster. Down go the guardrails for a train crossing. A transmission tower looms into view. A steam locomotive thunders across the screen.

During the next few minutes, the camera moves from vantage points on the train to views of the train from points outside. From a site near the tracks, passing railcars and steel wheels flash by, disturbing the tranquility of the countryside. Positioned in front in the locomotive, the camera stares down at parallel lines of track, conveying the steady pulse of motion. From windows in the compartments, the camera bounces around the landscape, recording the kinds of visual experiences one would have in absent-minded glances up from a book and out the window. The camera also captures the separation of foreground and background. Objects close at hand whisk away into lines of speed that seem as insubstantial as shadows. We see the blur of gravel on the track bed, overhead wires rushing by like a stream, and faint masses of shimmering trees. Further from the tracks, long views open onto a discernible if changing landscape. There are transmission towers. There are farmhouses. There are patches of building, recorded in the most passing of glances.

Gradually Ruttmann slows down the editing enough for film spectators to realize that they are on a journey. The camera stops jumping every which way across the track's steel flanks and assumes the steady position of a passenger staring out a window. From this vantage, a vague impression of diagonal lines becomes the steel trusses of a bridge. A sign reads: "Berlin, 15 kilometers." More countryside flows by, the view comprised of scattered houses, leafy trees, and low hills in the distance.

Abruptly, such scenes of rural landscape yield to views of the city outskirts, where scores of small houses cluster around gardens. The train chugs by a canal and a factory, then passes pyramids of sand and coal. It sprints past apartment buildings. More buildings cram into the frame, along with storage tanks and bridges. Because of their proximity to the viewer, works of architecture enlarge and recede almost simultaneously. Then, as suddenly as it had expanded, the view contracts. The dense city closes in around the train, as buildings approach to within a few feet of the tracks.

Once more, after the sequence of lateral shots from the side windows of the train, Ruttmann's camera shifts to the front, to the perspective of the locomotive. Spectators again look down at the tracks, but this time the tracks expand, forming intricate lines, bifurcating and joining, switching and multiplying as the train approaches the station. The train felt separate from the agrarian landscape; in the city it seems part of the visual pandemonium, the multiplicity of urban experience. The characteristics of urban life—from mass transportation to mass production to mass consumption—are suggested by the harsh angles and myriad perspectives of the cinematographic rail view. And then, just as we feel the city collide with the rail camera, we hear the squeal of brakes. The machine dissolves into darkness. The train enters Anhalter Station. A large sign, "Berlin," floats into view. The journey has ended. The railroad sequence concludes outside the train, with quick shots of wheels, brake shoes, and crankshafts, the machine musculature that made possible the journey, with its exhilarating sights.

The sequence from country to city lasts about three minutes. In this brief time, Ruttmann's camera leads the filmgoer into the rail experience—the slanting, running, flickering forms, the motion of the camera that exaggerates the motion of the train that puts architecture into motion. The filmic journey does not take place in real time or in continuous space. Camera editing highlights certain sensations and views, condensing and rearranging them into a narrative of transition, anticipation, and arrival. Ruttmann has no aim to deceive the spectator. Clear breaks between shots and many spatial and temporal ellipses disrupt any illusion of seamless travel experience. The train speeds forth, the camera darts here and there, and we in the audience speed and dart along with these mechanical forces. The only constant in the film is the steady progression of the train and film toward the city.

Another journey captured on film records the very different visual experience of rail travel on city streets. The year is 1905, the setting San Francisco, as witnessed from the front of a cable car traveling along Market Street. In the ten-minute film, by an unknown filmmaker, the cable car travels along a mile and a half of the downtown thoroughfare, moving continuously toward the water, and the Ferry Building, where passengers board ferries for points around San Francisco Bay. Made shortly before the big earthquake, the film explores the rhythm of architecture along the city's principal street. Market Street is experienced as a space in motion between two great walls of building. The street is packed not only with people, but also with shifting masses and shapes. Its appearance keeps changing depending upon which buildings occupy the slanting sides of the viewing frame. Buildings appear and disappear, their facades blending together—in the rail view, we tend to focus less on their period style and more on their compositional patterns. What is accentuated are the continuities and breaks in cornice lines, the alterations of window size and spacing, the gaps in streets revealing the receding sides of other buildings, and the occasional thrust of a tall building. Even at the slow pace of a cable car, there is no time to gaze at details.

Through the straight and steady movement of the cable car, the Ferry Building is always visible. It compels our attention and dominates the film, appearing first as a small tower in the distance, and then growing in size.

From *Market Street*, 1905

The conclusion takes advantage of the dramatic momentum—as the camera progresses to a close-range shot of the ground-floor walls, the Ferry Building dissolves in blurry details. Seconds later, the cable car swirls around. The stable perspective and bay vista are gone, as the spectator looks back at the city street just traveled.

The final turnaround is not the only discordant part of the film. The traffic on the street is chaotic. Unlike trains, with their right-of-ways, cable cars negotiate city streets. Here clashing street grids create awkward intersections and turbulent traffic. Triangular intersections propel cable cars, horse cars, and streetcars in dizzying and frightening paths. And the street space is thick with horse-drawn buggies, carts, vans, wagons, and pedestrians moving in all directions. People and automobiles dart in front of the camera, circle around the filming cable car, and jockey for better position. There appears to be almost no traffic control, neither lights nor police.

Set at the front of the moving cable car, the camera commands a privileged view. The cable car neither stops nor veers out of the way of traffic. It plows through the tumult of the street, giving filmgoers a powerful position, a height for observation, a place for contemplation. The aesthetics of the zoomscape emerge through speed, but also through personal detachment and the provision of seating comfort and steady, mobile sight lines. From both the railroad and the cable car, the architectural viewer occupies a stance of engagement amid isolation. Because of the fast speeds, more is seen; yet because of the isolation from what is seen, viewers can ruminate on the passing urban environment. Perhaps ironically, the rail experience, for all its speed, affords a significant role for both memory and imagination within the act of perception.

The San Francisco and Berlin cinematic sequences illustrate characteristics of the view in motion—continuity versus fragmentation, slowness versus speed, populated versus unpopulated space. In Ruttmann's trip to Berlin, we see no people. The viewer is drawn into the perceptual sphere of the railroad and camera, transformed by speed, mobile viewpoints, and rapid editing. On the Market Street cable car, the camera and viewer occupy a fixed position, moving through the crowded city in real time. One might think that Ruttmann's approach would yield a greater sense of dynamism and isolation.

But this is not the case. During the steady spatial penetration of San Francisco's Market Street, filmgoers merge with the vantage point of camera and vehicle. Transformed into a mechanical eye, they experience a sense of isolation (even estrangement) and succumb to the spell of relentless movement and remarkable focus. Strangely, the highly edited *Berlin: The Symphony of a Great City* more closely approximates the changeable experience of rail travel. For here movie spectators are never allowed to enjoy any concentrated, continuous movement. Because of the camera's frequent changes in point of view—on the train, off the train, looking out, looking down—they experience the film as a condensation of a real rail journey, with its shifts of sight, its distractions. There is no feeling of isolation, for the movie spectator occupies no stable position within the moving landscape. If there is dynamism in *Berlin*, it is the cinematic effacement of geographic space into montage fragments, the jumbled shots of place that begin to resemble those absorbed in rail travel.

For decades after the first trains rolled down their tracks, railroad vision was as unfamiliar as railroads themselves. The train was a marvel, an object to be watched as much as a platform for watching. It inspired many metaphors, ranging from "iron horse" to "mechanical monster" to "beast of burden." In *The Octopus*, his 1901 novel about the impact of the Southern Pacific Railroad on the development of the Central Valley of California, Frank Norris portrays some of the diverse reactions to the railroad. In one passage, he describes how a locomotive sped by the protagonist "with a roar, filling the air with the reek of hot oil, vomiting smoke and sparks; its enormous eye, cyclopean, red, throwing a glare far in advance, shooting by in a sudden crash of confused thunder; filling the night with the terrific clamor of its iron hoofs."[2] For the first time in history, a mode of transportation had created a corridor excluding all other activities; rail tracks are a separate and often dangerous domain. And the sight of a racing train could bring to mind the acceleration of change in the modern era, its ruthless effacement of tradition. At the same time, trains could, paradoxically, evoke a sense of nostalgia. Later in *The Octopus*, Norris writes of how a lumbering freight train "passed slowly on its way with a mournful roll of wheels, like the passing of a cortege, like a file of artillery-caissons charioting dead bodies; the engine's

2. Frank Norris, *The Octopus: A Story of California* (New York: Doubleday, Page & Co., 1901), 49.

smoke enveloping it in a mournful veil, leaving a sense of melancholy in its wake, moving past there, lugubrious, lamentable, infinitely sad."[3] Norris's sentiments speak to the railroad's transformation of the landscape. Instead of following the cycles of the sun and seasons, the landscape built by railroads and seen from them is a place fleeting and linear, an environment in the throes of movement and change, a corridor of new and old, of invention succeeded by obsolescence. The implications for the experience of architecture were, from the start, profound. Instead of knowing buildings and cities inside out, seeing them slowly and close at hand, the rail traveler perceived only passing surfaces, glimpsed from a distance. The full-bodied, sensual and sustained relationship to building becomes a fast, flattened gaze. The view from the train can either vault into the void (and the future) that lies ahead or get left behind on the side of the tracks.

Railroads embody the modern ethos of technological progress, the promise of a new world. More than did any earlier machine, they expanded human potency. In the train, we became surveyors of the wide landscape, philosophers of insides and outsides, artists of shifting form, athletes capable of bounding over hills and across valleys. In "The Railway Train," Emily Dickinson describes the omnipotent vision and mobility a train offers its passengers.

> I like to see it lap the miles,
> And lick the valleys up,
> And stop to feed itself at tanks;
> And then, prodigious, step
> Around a pile of mountains,
> And, supercilious, peer
> In shanties, by the sides of roads;
> And then a quarry pare
> To fit its sides, and crawl between,
> Complaining all the while
> In horrid, hooting stanza;
> Then chase itself down hill
> And neigh like Boanerges;

3. Ibid., 93–94.

Then, punctual as a star,
Stop—docile and omnipotent—
At its own stable door."[4]

Dickinson famously evokes the railroad's substitution of steam power for horsepower, and the extraordinary service this iron horse will perform for humans. But she also suggests the perceptual changes brought about by the mechanical beast. Riding the rails, people will no longer traverse the land as they had for millennia. Now their movements and sight will be mechanized, and at a scale once reserved for the gods.

DEPARTURE AND ARRIVAL

The railroad station is the archetypal building of the nineteenth and early twentieth centuries, exemplifying the industrial era's rush to the future, even as it clung to the past. No wonder that the station had a split architectural personality—it had to facilitate transitions between place and journey, human locomotion and machine movement, architectural expression and engineering technology. In large cities, the station usually featured both an impressive masonry facade—with classical colonnades, towers, and ornament—and a vast open space roofed with glass and supported by iron or steel trusses. Since the nineteenth century, architects and planners have tried with mixed success to integrate railroad stations into the rest of the metropolis. Often, the new building type was pushed as deep as possible into the historic center, only to be stalled in its tracks a mile or two distant: consider, for example, the circuit of rail stations around central Paris. The huge buildings, outlying tracks, switching yards, and spurs to other industrial buildings threatened the historic city. And not only size made the station an ungainly interloper. Like seaports, rail stations were the locale of pickpockets, prostitutes, and hucksters, of pool halls, seedy bars, and cheap hotels. In most cities and towns, the station and its tracks divide good neighborhoods from bad. Railroads, the great connectors, segregate cities almost as comprehensively as walls once did and highways later would.

But rail stations also unite cities. Wherever stations locate, they install a wider, more cosmopolitan world. Here people meet and mingle, books and

4. Emily Dickinson, *Collected Poems of Emily Dickinson*, ed. Mabel Loomis Todd (New York: Random House, 1998).

5. Jeffrey Richards and John M. MacKenzie, *The Railway Station: A Social History* (Oxford: Oxford University Press, 1986), 2.

newspapers are delivered, goods and foodstuffs arrive. From here people depart for the seaside, the mountains, and the wider world.[5] Railway stations give off the scent of travel and faraway places. They are the central components of a complex, branching network extending thousands of miles and connecting thousands of places. The global erasure of boundaries, which would intensify with the airplane, had its start in the rail station.

No wonder that even before the start of a journey, the sights of the station fill us with energy. Like piers berthed with ships, the platforms in a station bristle with anticipation. The steps up into a train, the corridors leading to seats or compartments, and the first view out the windows at the clutter of rushing people, porters, and carts, quickens the consciousness. In *Remembrance of Things Past* (1922), Marcel Proust, who notoriously loved no place more than his bedroom, depicts the anxiety that began at the station and accompanied rail travel. "Unhappily those marvelous places, railway stations, from which one sets out for a remote destination, are tragic places also, for if in them the miracle is accomplished whereby scenes which hitherto have had no existence save in our minds are about to become the scenes among which we shall be living, for that very reason we must, as we emerge from the waiting room, abandon any thought of presently finding ourselves once more in the familiar room which but a moment ago still housed us. We must lay aside all hope of going home to sleep in our own bed, once we have decided to penetrate into the pestiferous cavern through which we gain access to the mystery, into one of those glass-roofed sheds, like that of Saint-Lazare into which I went to find the train for Balbec."[6] For Proust, the rail journey signals an end to familiar scenes and the beginning of the strangeness of the world. He realizes that the speed and range of train travel resemble the workings of the imagination, with its sudden turns and long detours. When the traveler is out on the tracks, gazing at farmsteads, forests, and towns, his thought might take on such linear momentum as to threaten the stability of self-consciousness. Indeed, Proust fears that motion and the parade of new sights will unmoor his soul, driving it ever forward, away from familiarity. Returning to a sense of self might be as arduous as retracing the long miles of a voyage. Yet for Proust, writing in the second decade of the twentieth century, train travel also offers the possibility of a new type of self.

6. Marcel Proust, *Remembrance of Things Past*, trans. C.K. Scott Moncrieff and Terence Kilmartin (New York: Random House, 1981), I: 694.

The early moments of the trip, the glance up at glass-roofed, steel-framed sheds, signal that the experiences from the train might be enlightening. They might lead our vision across a moving geography, and even make us wonder whether the center of modern subjectivity lies within motion and the vastness of engineered miles and sights.

If the journey from a rail station is accompanied by anticipation of the landscape to be experienced, it is colored also by the staccato rhythms that connect ticket counters, corridors, and waiting rooms with the sensations of the train pulling out, and then by the almost imperceptible feeling one has of initial movement, the gathering velocity, the disappointment of slowing down or halting. The early moments of a train journey are characterized by motion arrested by congestion and vision assaulted by radical shifts of setting. In cities like New York, where rail tracks are underground, the trip from either Pennsylvania or Grand Central Station begins in the darkness of twisting tunnels, and gradually moves toward the light of sky and city vistas. On trains going north, the experience is always unexpected. Surfacing onto the elevated platform at Park Avenue north of 96th Street, the traveler is startled to see, not far from the prosperity of Midtown, block after block of tenements and public housing, and in the distance bridges and suburbs.

Most rail journeys begin closer to the ground, slowly proceeding from the station, past switchyards and locomotive sheds into industrial areas and working-class districts, past city into suburb, and sometimes out of the urbanized region altogether into farmland or wilderness. On certain trips, such as the route from Buenos Aires to Mendoza that crosses the Argentine Pampas, the outskirts of the capital are soon followed by extensive plains of cultivated grasslands. In contrast, on trips through the American Eastern Seaboard, or the densely populated countries of northwest Europe, or the industrial corridors of Japan, the edges of one city blur into those of the next. Already by the early decades of the twentieth century, the sequence of departure from a large station revealed the expansive scale of the modern city and the time it took to get beyond its limits.

Arrival reverses the sequence. The cessation of the engine's roar and hiss, the last clouds of billowing smoke, the abrupt transition from motion to stasis—with all this the journey ends. But not before the mass of the city

Italian Riviera

begins to crowd the traveler's perception; unlike the break into the open, the release from confinement that characterizes departure, arrival is a return to darkness and enclosure, an accumulation of bridges, tracks, and walls, as witnessed in Ruttmann's *Berlin*. In *Stamboul Train*, Graham Greene describes a rail trip across Europe in the early 1930s, noting how stations present themselves without warning, how suddenly one is confronted by "a flashing glimpse of water between tall gray houses, of lights burning in upper rooms, cut off abruptly by the arch of the station, and then the train slid to rest in a great echoing hall."[7] In "The Artificial Nigger," first published in the 1950s, Flannery O'Connor makes us feel how disconcerting the rail yards of Atlanta could be to a young boy arriving from the countryside of central Georgia. "Nelson saw lines and lines of silver tracks multiplying and criss-crossing. Then before he could start counting them, the face in the window stared out at him, gray but distinct, and he looked the other way. The train was in the station."[8] And for the hero of W.G. Sebald's *Austerlitz*, published in 2001, the last stretch of a train journey to Liverpool Station in London always inspires thoughts of entombment. "The train must wind its way over several sets of points through a narrow defile, and where the brick walls rising above both sides of the track with their round arches, columns, and niches, blackened with soot and diesel oil, put me in mind once again that morning of an underground columbarium."[9] Arrival in a great urban station is perhaps the most architectural of rail experiences, a passage through a long, narrowing and darkening threshold, a movement toward a large space where the dynamism of the train will be abruptly halted, and the static pleasures of architectural space and detail can once again be contemplated.

Theodore Dreiser's *Sister Carrie*, published in 1900, begins with a lengthy scene on a train bound from Wisconsin for Chicago. Dreiser emphasizes the heightening of visual variety and psychic pressure that accompany the transition from the countryside to the metropolis. At first, the young heroine, Carrie, observes a familiar landscape of fields, lakes, and summer resorts. But she notes as well a faint but growing increase in the scale of development as the train proceeds. And soon things emphatically change. "They were nearing Chicago. Signs were everywhere numerous. Trains flashed

7. Graham Greene, *Stamboul Train* (London: William Heinemann, 1932), 191.

8. Flannery O'Connor, "The Artificial Nigger," in *The Complete Stories* (New York: Farrar, Straus & Giroux, 1971), 258.

9. W.G. Sebald, *Austerlitz*, trans. Anthea Bell (New York: Random House, 2001), 36.

by them. Across wide stretches of flat, open prairie they could see lines of
telegraph poles stalking across the fields toward the great city. Far away
were indications of suburban towns, some big smokestacks towering high in
the air. Frequently there were two-story frame houses standing out in the
open fields, without fence or trees, lone outposts of the approaching army of
homes."[10] Dreiser's most dynamic passages remark upon places on the far
periphery of Chicago, fresh farmland seared by real estate forces, a landscape
no longer country but not quite city. This uneven frontier of urban development,
punched out along rail lines, foreshadows the automobile urbanity that will
occur soon afterward.

The entry into Chicago in *Sister Carrie* conveys the visual breadth of

Closer to the city, Carrie's train affords tightly framed views of streets,
telephone poles, and grain elevators. When the train passes over the Chicago
River, she sees little more than a muddy creek whose waters vanish under
the masts of sailing ships and planks of wharves. Dreiser describes less of
the city because rural people like Carrie had never before seen such sights.
The fine points of architectural style and building typology would have gone
unnoticed by them. The rail view, for travelers unfamiliar with cities, consists
of the thick torpor of urban texture. Appropriately, then, the journey comes
to an end "under a great shadowy train shed where the lamps were already
beginning to shine out, with passenger cars all about and the train moving
at a snail's pace."[11]

The entry into Chicago in *Sister Carrie* conveys the visual breadth of
the rail view. From a train, in a brief period, it is possible to see a succession of landscapes, the large plots of rural fields giving way to the finer grids
of cities, treetops and farmhouses to roofscapes and skylines. Along the way,
the meaning of buildings and cities changes. Not only does the rail view sever
distance between places, suturing town and city into a montage of dissimilar
images, but also the speed of the train runs our eyes past architecture in a
wholly new way. From the train, architecture is witnessed as a torrent of
images from which viewers can often discern only the gist of customary
meanings.

10. Theodore Dreiser, *Sister Carrie* (New York:
Doubleday, Page & Co., 1900), 8–9.

11. Dreiser, 10.

Before the iron horse replaced the real horse, before iron tracks were laid over earthen roads, land travel was arduous, slow, and often perilous. Until the past century, road travel was notoriously difficult. Made of compacted dirt or gravel, most roads were scarred, filled with obstacles, and often curved out of control. In spring, they were muddy. In summer, grass and weeds sprouted between the grooves made by wheels, and dirt and dust swirled in the air. In winter, snow and ice made passage treacherous. What weary travelers would have rhapsodized about a sluggish voyage in a horse-drawn carriage, the views of landscape bumping up to the tops of roofs one instant and then plunging down to the earth seconds later? Equine travel was slow, often frustratingly so; but it did offer rich smells and sounds, and long hours in which to observe the details of a fence, the groove in the clapboards of a house, the rotation of a windmill. And before rail travel, the uneven motion of animal locomotion was felt all over the body. A rutted road reverberated in the bones and muscles. One with the road and its borderland of fences and facades, the pre-rail traveler was immersed in her surroundings.

How different is train travel, the slide of steel wheel on steel track that induces out-of-body and out-of-place sensations? From our first minutes on a train, its mechanical force either carries us brilliantly along or sets us blatantly apart. In *The Octopus*, Norris tells how "the long train, now out upon the main line, settled itself to its pace, the prolonged, even gallop that it would hold for the better part of the week, spinning out the miles as a cotton spinner spins thread."[12] The metaphor of the factory worker is apt. Boarding a train, passengers enter a production line of sorts, a machine that spins out movement, mile after mile. Train movement becomes human movement. The railroad's embankments, bridges, and tunnels become the passenger's space. Most of all, the train itself reorients the passenger's understanding of space.

Among modes of land transportation, the elongated compartments of trains most closely approximate architectural space. While not approaching the hierarchy of spaces in an ocean liner, trains possess a variety of discrete rooms—viewing cars, dining cars, club cars, sleeping quarters, the outdoor ledges between cars—and passageways that resemble streets. A single train

12. Norris, 411.

can carry hundreds of people, and social interaction, especially in trains with compartments instead of tiered seating, can be intriguing. Seeing the world from a train is like seeing it from a moving village. This is especially true of express trains and their luxury cars. In *Of Time and the River*, Thomas Wolfe describes a Pullman car crossing the American countryside at night: "[O]utside there was the raw and desolate-looking country, there were the great steel coaches, the terrific locomotives, the shining rails, the sweep of the tracks, the vast indifferent dinginess and rust of colors, the powerful mechanical expertness, and the huge indifference to suave finish. And inside there were the opulent green and luxury of the Pullman cars, the soft glow of the lights, and people fixed there for an instant in incomparably rich and vivid little pictures of their life and destiny, as they were all hurled onward, a thousand atoms, to their journey's end somewhere upon the mighty continent, across the immense and lonely visage of the everlasting earth."[13]

To some early rail travelers, the train felt like a marvelous architectural stand-in, a new building type put into perpetual motion. Writing in the 1850s, Nathaniel Hawthorne, in *The House of the Seven Gables*, raises the possibility of a train-architecture. Looking from the window of a train, the novel's protagonists, Clifford and Hepzibah, watch the world outside hurtling past, as if they were in a moving building. "At one moment, they were rattling through a solitude; the next, a village had grown up around them; a few breaths more, and it had vanished, as if swallowed by an earthquake. The spires of meetinghouses seemed set adrift from their foundations; the broad-based hills glided away. Everything was unfixed from its age-long rest, and moving at whirlwind speed in a direction opposite to their own."[14] Not only do train passengers now occupy a mobile built space, but older architectures acquire mobility as well. Hawthorne's Clifford rhapsodizes that railroads are the greatest of things, that they spiritualize travel. He even predicts that railroads will impose a new nomadism: "Transition being so facile, what can be any man's inducement to tarry in one spot? Why, therefore, should he build a more cumbrous habitation than can readily be carried off with him? Why should he make himself a prisoner for life in brick, and stone, and old worm-eaten timber, when he may just as easily dwell, in one sense, nowhere, in a better sense, wherever the fit and beautiful shall offer him a home?"[15]

13. Thomas Wolfe, *Of Time and the River* (New York: Charles Scribner's Sons, 1935), 410.

14. Nathaniel Hawthorne, *The House of the Seven Gables*, in the *Complete Novels and Selected Tales of Nathaniel Hawthorne* (New York: Modern Library, 1937), 397.

15. Hawthorne, 399.

Barcelona

Already in Hawthorne's time—only the first generation of rail travel—fixed buildings and cities could seem antiquated. To an adventurous spirit, words like "roof" and "hearthstone" had become dull. Railroads offered the possibility of a daring life on the road, sights impossible within the confines of a house or the narrow streets of a town. Railroads not only produced the sensation of modernity in space, they also highlighted the restlessness of the age.

Becoming a modern man or woman, a railroad man or woman, meant seeing the built world in novel ways. From the train, viewers look at buildings and cities anew, as they did in childhood. Almost no one can remember their first steps or their first sights. But many remember their first rail journey. Since these early, skewed train sensations hearken back to the wonder of infancy, the rail view encourages a radical visuality. Like our own initial movements about the world, the mechanical sensations from a train connect at first neither with our body nor our brains. Yet since the train extends our body beyond our impulses and control, it extends our mind beyond our understanding, and our imagination beyond traditional aesthetics. The rail view vaults perception into adventurous sight lines that merge the human eye with mechanical motion.

The rail traveler occupies several types of mechanized viewing platforms. Some offer expansive vistas: the front of the train, in the head car or locomotive; the back, in the caboose; and old Pullman Palace cars or newer panoramic-view railcars with glass-bubble roofs that project sight lines above the body of the train. Such vantage points allow rail travelers to see in a large viewing arc, in excess of 180 degrees; they enable us to see where we have come from and where we are going. Most rail travelers, however, experience such expansive sights only briefly, if at all. The side view from seating compartments offers neither open sight lines nor a good sense of destination. This most common rail perspective works as a kind of blinder, limiting vision to one side.

In either case, at the front or at the sides, one of the principal characteristics of rail perception is its relentless framing of landscape. Up front, rapid momentum down the tracks creates an impression of landscape angling off from a distant, fixed center. The forward railroad vista resembles perspectival counterpoint, the art of combining and relating lines around a single vanishing point, the world seen as receding planes from a central set of tracks. From the locomotive, the engineer sees the landscape sliced in two by the train tracks. This phenomenon has been captured in many photographs, such as those by William Rau and Andreas Feininger.[16] In Rau's "Duncannon Curve" (1906), the camera view from a train centers on tracks that extend toward the horizon line and (along with adjacent tracks on both sides) divide the frame into receding diagonals. Ranges of mountains on both sides of the tracks accentuate the separate lines of force that converge in the distance. Feininger's "Railroad Tracks in Nebraska" (1952) shows a perspectival view of rails disappearing in the distance. In the flat countryside no other trains or objects are visible. Shot from a height directly above those tracks, probably atop a cowcatcher attached to the front of a locomotive, the photograph records the division of land into line and plane. Reinforced by parallel telegraph wires, this view makes the landscape look abstract, almost like a musical score. In her 1956 story, "The Affair at Grover Station," Willa Cather notices something similar. She writes that as the train leaves, "the telegraph poles scored the sky like a musical staff as they flashed by, and the stars, seen between the wires, looked like the notes of some erratic symphony."[17]

From the side windows, especially when a train is stopped or moving slowly, the rail view deemphasizes the vanishing lines of perspective in favor of the horizon line and the parallel lines of the train, tracks, telephone wires, and station platforms. Richard Misrach's 1983 photograph, "The Santa Fe," captures how railroads split landscapes into quadrangles parallel with the horizon. Misrach shot the image not from a train, but from hundreds of feet away in the middle of desert sagebrush. The frame divides cleanly between an expanse of empty desert and open sky. And beneath the horizon line there is an equally powerful line, a line created not by nature but by culture, by railroad tracks and freight train cars. In the expanse of the American West, the lines of tracks and railcars create, in effect, a second horizon line. Almost as much as do earth and sky, the railroad structures the landscape and our view of it.

At outdoor stations along a route, the passenger's sideways view is structured not only by the train and horizon, but also by the lines of architecture—resulting in a series of frames within frames. For passengers, one

16. *The Hand of Man: Railroads in American Prints and Photographs* (Baltimore: Baltimore Museum of Art, 1978).

17. Willa Cather, "The Affair at Grover Station," in *Five Stories* (New York: Vintage Books, 1956), 113.

frame is split between the view out of the train and the space of viewing within the train, a foreground taken up with a cabin's walls and features. Other frames are created by the infrastructure of the railroad station; for instance, by the piers that support roof canopies. Such frames divide what might have been an expansive, uninterrupted view of a place. The compartmentalized view echoes the rooms and corridors of the train. And since buildings and structures close to the tracks disrupt far views, the view from trains favors not the vertical but the horizontal; building scale amplifies laterally, parallel with the tracks. Buildings thus come to resemble a kind of train architecture, the corridor walls of an endless building.

At speeds of more than twenty-five miles per hour, this lateral amplification becomes noticeable. The relentless momentum of the train fragments the visual field into mobile pieces; the forward (or receding) movement propels the elements of an architectural landscape into varying rates of motion. Straight ahead or straight behind, objects remain stationary, yet seem to grow or shrink. To the passenger looking back, the view of a village far from the tracks seems still, something to be stared at, while trees and buildings nearer the train fly backward. On a spectrum to either side of a forward or rearward position, pieces of the landscape move at different speeds. Those closest to straight-ahead vision slide by slowly. Further to the sides, the landscape momentum quickens, to the point at which, at ninety degrees from the train, objects become a watery blur. Travelers tend to fix their attention on the most stable forms in the viewing field. These are usually objects in the distance, which passengers, depending upon the speed of the train, follow for as long as possible. Rail travelers thus experience a muscular rhythm of slides and jerks, as their eyes pan an object till it blurs by, and then jump ahead to connect with the next interesting feature.[18] Around these stable objects, which we follow closely, all else shoots across our viewing field. If one is looking out the right side of the train, the landscape moves in two directions around stable objects, such as houses transmission towers, smokestacks. Above, the landscape shifts to the left and approximates the movement of the train. Below, the landscape moves to the right, away from the train and its destination. Because of the linear progression of the train and simultaneous saccadic eye movements that focus on semistable objects,

18. James J. Gibson, *The Perception of the Visual World* (Boston: Houghton Mifflin, 1950), 124–126.

the rail view of a city pits an observer against building forms that constant-ly seem to be blowing away.

In *The Railway Journey*, published in 1977, the cultural historian Wolfgang Schivelbusch coined a new term for a type of aesthetic experi-ence—panoramic perception. Schivelbusch locates panoramic perception in the passenger's side view from a swift-moving train, and describes it as a condition in which the machine characteristics of the train merge with human perception to create hybridized sight.[19] The velocity of the train intensifies the sense of a separation between rail viewer and outside space. Objects within the train car are seen according to the usual optical patterns of discernment; this is not the case with the landscape rushing by. Close-up views are especially taxing. Not only do objects to the sides of the train win-dow move by more rapidly than those up ahead, but objects in the fore-ground also move by more quickly than those in the background. From a speeding train, passengers must strain to see objects near the tracks. The rail journey weakens any relationship with the blur of landscape within a couple of hundred feet from the train. It is much easier to observe images in the distance. This distant landscape flattens into something like a painterly panorama, a surface appreciated for its planar and linear outlines and not for its three-dimensional forms or palpable textures.

Panoramic views from a train resemble the long-range views of a city from a stationary high point. Isolated between the foreground blur and the sky, large and regular buildings or structures stand out. The rail journey is like a picture show of separate significant forms—a church steeple, a farm-stead, a row of smokestacks. Rail viewers begin to see architecture as group-ings of bold distant shapes. The intricacies of detail and context give way to the certainties of outline and scale. A new way of seeing is thus born, one that will intensify with the great distances of air travel. In a sense, the mod-ern city of bold shapes, blank walls, and slab-like towers already existed in the panoramic perception of the nineteenth-century rail traveler. Early in the twentieth century, the German architect Peter Behrens noted that the speed of trains turned cities into silhouettes.[20] This insight may have inspired him and other modern architects to design buildings whose visual impact derives less from ornament than from volume and outline.

19. Wolfgang Schivelbusch, *The Railway Journey: Trains and Travel in the Nineteenth Century*, trans. Anselm Hollo (New York: Urizen Books, 1979), 57–72.

20. Stanford Anderson, "Modern Architecture and Industry: Peter Behrens and the Cultural Policy of Historical Determinism," *Oppositions* 11 (1977), 76.

Chicago el

Panoramic vision turns the view of the city into a sequence of disembodied and abstracted forms. Schivelbusch realizes that since rail passengers perceive specific objects poorly, they tend not to look closely or carefully. Speed anesthetizes vision. Sight becomes absentminded. Instead of observing a building's form, rail passengers see odd features in the shifting juxtapositions brought about by the train's velocity and their own haphazard concentration. A new type of building is seen. This is not the building carefully designed by the architect, but instead a building interconnected with other buildings, other objects, and other images in the mind. A tower, turret, and tympanum from different buildings become parts of a single streaming image whose substance has nothing to do with the customary meanings of these architectural elements. In many cases, the whole resulting from such panoramic perception is less than the parts; in some cases it is coarse and crude. But in other situations, original architectural assemblages come together momentarily, ungrounded from site as well as aesthetic dictates.

While the long view from the train illuminates various artistic possibilities, the same cannot be said of the foreground. For a population constantly traveling, constantly tuning the level of their attention, the out-of-focus trackside takes on a forlorn quality, which, as urban historian John Stilgoe points out, becomes more acute the faster the train travels. "As a train gathers speed, passengers viewing the landscape at right angles discover that the spatial details nearest the window are the first to blur," writes Stilgoe. "At five miles an hour, an intent observer can discern flowers and other elements of the scene immediately adjacent to the rails, but at ten miles an hour he must look at objects fifteen feet from the side of the car. At thirty miles an hour, everything within the thirty- or forty-foot mark appears blurred, unless the observer is willing to swivel his head as the train passes. Increases in speed force the observer to look ever further from the car, and particularly east of the Mississippi River, such long views are rare. Even in farming country, trees and high bushes growing in the protected right-of-way make vistas few. At ninety miles an hour, the railroad passenger intrigued by the passing scene must fix his attention only on very distant objects; doing otherwise creates eyestrain and headache."[21] Fast speeds turn the track's environs into a forgotten zone. Often, panoramic perception leads to boredom. Viewers learn, during many trips down the same tracks, how not to look; sometimes

21. John Stilgoe, *Metropolitan Corridor* (New Haven: Yale University, 1982), 250.

they notice the architecture outside the window only to forget it the next instant. The often-seen landscape can become a featureless void, akin to that void into which the train hurtles. Urban space can begin to look like video static. Much of the neglect of urban space attributed to the automobile era—to the rise of suburbia—had already begun in the railroad era, with its new forms of perception. Waste space is the product not only of affluence, but also of velocity.

It is panoramic perception that makes the architecture outside the train compartment seem like a motion picture. The viewing field inside the compartment resembles the dark foreground of the auditorium, while that beyond is like the lit, flat background of the screen. The eye of the traveler becomes like the eye of the film projector, and the scene outside the train window can seem fictive and fantastical. In Schivelbusch's description, "panoramic perception, in contrast to traditional perception, no longer belongs to the same space as the perceived objects; the traveler sees the objects, landscapes, etc., through the apparatus which moves him through the world. That machine and the motion it creates become integrated into his visual perception: thus he can only see things in motion... evanescent reality has become the new reality."[22]

Although the rail view does not break spatial or temporal continuity, as does film, the abrupt changes in view caused by a rushing train can seem like a form of editing. From the windows of a fast train, images of buildings multiply, simplify, and compress into montage-like sequences. In Japan, the bullet train between Osaka and Tokyo routinely exceeds 180 miles per hour. Leaving Osaka is hardly distinguishable from entering nearby Kyoto, so fast does the train amalgamate each city's furthest suburbs. As the train passes through Nagoya, or for that matter most cities along the route, the view consists of distant megastructures surrounded by a bleary cityscape. On the fast train, smaller pieces of the landscape fuse together; only the large structures retain distinctness. The Japan of the bullet-train view contains little more than factory complexes, high-rise buildings, and expansive, netted golf driving ranges.

The perceptual velocities of rail perception do not necessarily cease when railroads slow down or stop. Especially during a train's frequent stops and unexplained delays in towns and cities, the deep gaze through a side

22. Schivelbusch, 66.

window encourages an intense scrutiny of architectural details, which can transform our understanding of commonplace things. For although the train has stopped, the visual thrust of the passengers typically has not. The railway's arrested motion transfers to the surroundings; motionless buildings animate with the velocity of the voyage. Rail viewers scan the buildings back and forth, compressing the earlier linear pace of vision into the current, confined frame. For a few minutes, a grain elevator might grow into a visual universe all its own.

A unique pleasure arises from our ability to glimpse so much so ephemerally from trains. Buildings and structures seen from a fast-moving train in the zoomscape fade quickly from memory. They resemble brief social encounters, and can feel all the more delightful for their lack of substance. In "A Passing Glance," Robert Frost evokes this pleasure.

> I often see flowers from a passing car
> That are gone before I can tell what they are.
> I want to get out of the train and go back
> To see what they were beside the track . . .
> Was something brushed across my mind
> That no one on earth will ever find?
> Heaven gives its glimpses only to those
> Not in a position to look too close."[23]

THE CORRIDOR

The linear movement of the train has inspired stupendous proposals for cities. In the 1990s, the Dutch architect Rem Koolhaas predicted the creation of a trans-European city centered at the intersection of high-speed train lines at Lille, a branching metropolis that would encompass northern France, Great Britain, Germany, and the Benelux countries. Koolhaas's megalopolis was made possible by train velocities that would allow people to inhabit a geography shaped by continual movement. "What is important about this place," he writes, "is not where it is but where it leads, and how quickly."[24] Hawthorne's dream of rail nomadism seems closer to fruition today, a century and a half later. Koolhaas's was not the first proposal for a circulatory

23. Robert Frost, "A Passing Glimpse," in *Complete Poems of Robert Frost* (New York: Henry Holt & Co., 1949), 311.

24. O.M.A., Rem Koolhaas, and Bruce Mau, *S,M,L,XL*, ed. Jennifer Sigler (New York: Monacelli, 1995), 1170.

city, a train-based architecture. More than a century earlier, in 1882, the Spanish architect Arturo Soria y Mata had proposed a narrow linear city, just 500 meters wide, that would extend thousands of miles along a rail axis from Cadiz, Spain, to St. Petersburg, Russia—a trans-European linearopolis. In 1910, in *Roadtown*, the American writer Edgar Chambless proposed something similar: a multilevel linear city structured around rail lines. All such futurist visions were motivated by the train's ability to blast away urban boundaries and fuse city and countryside into super-regions.

For more than a century now, largely because of train travel, cities have become a mechanized conglomeration of superhuman scale. In 1890, describing the landscape of northern France, Emile Zola wrote: "It was like an immense body, a mammoth earth-hugging body, the head at Paris, the ribs all down the line, the limbs spreading wide at the junctions, the feet and hands at Havre and other terminal cities. On and on it went, endless, mechanical triumph that it was, hurtling into the future with mechanical directness, deliberately indifferent to the vestiges of the human."[25] Packed with people, and lit up at night like a tall building turned on its side, the train brought with it an all-encompassing systemization, the city and countryside joined together, restructured by the rationality of mechanized transportation.

Not only did the rail corridor connect and extend existing places, it also created a new type of place, a mixed rural-urban topography. The eco-tourist landscape of today, marked by the presence of urbanity, yet appealing for its nonurban qualities, has its origins in the rail era. Especially in sparsely settled lands like the United States, Canada, Argentina, and Australia, railroads opened up large regions not only for settlement but also for tourism. Unlike in Europe, where railroads were largely laid out in accord with settlement patterns, railroads in these newer nations pioneered not only new cities but also tourism on the routes between cities.[26] As railroads were built through wilderness, the view from the train assembled a host of magnificent natural and urban features into the pieces of a new natural/national aesthetic. Early tourist destinations like New York's Catskill Mountains or New Hampshire's White Mountains were accessed by rail, and much of the excitement of the visit consisted in the rail journey and its moving scenes. The photographic legacy of sites such as Yosemite National Park can be

25. Emile Zola, *The Beast in Man*, trans. Alex Brown (London: Elek Books, 1956), 39–40.

26. James E. Vance, *The North American Railroad: Its Origins, Evolution, and Geography* (Baltimore: Johns Hopkins University, 1995), 25.

traced to the development of the railroad. Already during the 1850s in the United States, books were published consisting of stereoscopic and photographic views of dramatic scenes along rail lines. In the 1870s, travel guides commissioned photographers and painters to illustrate choice vistas along the Western lines.[27] The landscapes popularized by railroads encompassed mountain ranges and river gorges, as well as the elements of the rail corridor itself, including bridges, tunnels, stations, and the infinite miles of track and telegraph wire. In addition to their function as transportation, then, railroads are a viewing auditorium with considerable crossover appeal—beginning with the sights from the railroad itself, spreading to rail-accessed tourist destinations, and continuing in books and magazines filled with photographs taken from the journeys.

Like a book of photographs of a place, views from the railroad corridor capture only a slice of its fullness. Trains unfold image-narratives that reorient the perception of architecture away from a multidimensional pedestrian experience and into a linear encounter. For train commuters, the sights along a corridor are usually limited to single-surfaced images of built form, distinct from the multi-angled views of cities possible through explorations on foot (or in cars). Again and again, the fixed rail routes pass the same buildings, cross the same bridges, and overlook the same rivers. They allow no glimpses of the opposite sides of those buildings, or of different angles of the bridges or rivers. Similar to the permanent perspectives captured for a motion picture, the lens of the railroad window affords repeated views of the same places. Consequently, like a movie, railroads draw together disparate sights into image narratives. Seen often enough, these narratives can become the primary source of knowledge about the architecture of a region. In *The Human Beast*, Zola depicts a train trip between Paris and Le Havre. "From Havre to Motteville there were meadows and level fields, intersected by hedges with apple-trees," he writes. "After that, as far as Rouen, it was undulating wasteland. After Rouen, they followed the Seine, crossing it at Sotteville, Oissel, and Pont-de-l'Arche, while it flowed through vast level stretches of country, constantly reappearing, broad and meandering. After Gaillon, they kept to its left bank, and here it was a sluggish stream, bordered by willows. They skirted hilly country, leaving the river at Bonnières,

27. Susan Darby Walther, *The Railroad in the American Landscape: 1850–1950* (Wellesley, Massachusetts: Wellesley College Museum, 1981), 39–40, 49–50.

only to come out on it suddenly again at Rosny, when they emerged from Rolleboise tunnel. It was their friendly guardian all the way. Before reaching Paris, they crossed it three more times. Then came Mantes with its church tower among the trees, Triel with the white patches of its plaster-kilns, Poissy, which they ran through the heart of, next, the two green walls of the St. Germain Forest, at Colombes, feeling of Paris, a glimpse of Asnières Bridge, and the Arc de Triomphe in the distance, towering above leprous industrial sites bristling with their smokestacks. The engine then plunged into the Batignolles tunnel, coming out into the echoing reverberating station."[28] Zola describes buildings in the precise contexts in which one would see them from the train, and no place else. He notices the Gothic cathedral at Mantes not from the town's streets but through the rows of trees that line the tracks. He recognizes Triel for the plaster kilns along the rail corridor, and perhaps nothing more—the town has by chance been baked into a curious image. The wide forest of St. Germain becomes a narrow passage between green walls, an image perhaps suggested to Zola by the constricting walls of building he has just seen from the train at Poissy. The vocabulary we use to distinguish and remember places or buildings is flexible, and always evolving. It can be restructured by repetitive mechanical action, by what we see as we travel in a train. If panoramic perception reduces buildings to silhouettes in sequence, then the fixed viewing angles of the tracks further channel our understanding of architecture into linear successions of images that by now have achieved aesthetic importance.

The linear view along the rail corridor has another critical characteristic: From the train, passengers see the rear views of a place. They view not main roads or city streets, not town walls or central squares or prominent facades, but rather the back sides of factories, warehouses, workers' quarters, and older structures rudely served by the development of the railroad. Rail travelers thus peer at places perhaps never meant to be displayed or observed, and certainly not designed for the train's rolling and rushing manner of perception. In *Stamboul Train*, Graham Greene describes the view from a train journeying through Bruges. "The sunset lit up tall dripping walls, alleys with stagnant water radiant for a moment with liquid light," he writes. "Somewhere within the dingy casing lay the ancient city, like a notorious

28. Zola, 235.

Bridge across the Delaware River, Trenton, New Jersey

jewel, too stared at, talked of, trafficked over. Then a wilderness of allotments opened through the steam, sometimes the monotony broken by tall ugly villas facing every way, decorated with colored tiles, which now absorbed the evening. The sparks from the express became visible, like hordes of scarlet beetles tempted into the air by the night; they fell and smouldered by the track, touched leaves and twigs and cabbage stalks and turned to soot.... Then darkness fell outside, and passengers through the glass could see only the transparent reflection of their own features."[29] Bruges seen from the tracks bears little resemblance to the medieval town that has become the tourist mecca of Flanders. Steaming through the city, the train offers no views of church facades, of canals or market squares, but instead reveals blank walls and nouveau-riche villas, dingy backyards and littered embankments. Those who see Bruges from the train will hardly notice its storied art and architecture.

But the view from the rail corridor is not without its own grandeur. Traveling through Liege, Greene notices how industrial structures now dominate the landscape, supplanting older landmarks like churches and chateaux: "The great blast furnaces of Liege rose along the line like ancient castles burning in a border raid."[30] Large and dramatic in form, like castles and cathedrals, factories and furnaces punctuate the image narrative of the rail corridor. Their manufacturing power, the clouds of smoke and exhaust, the sprawling buildings and machines, all accord with the railroad's new mechanical order. Passing through Detroit or Shanghai or Turin, rail viewers are exposed to a procession of buildings of remarkable scale, shape, and color. Over time, some industrial views have even become objects of nostalgia. Along the Amtrak corridor between New York and Philadelphia, the sign "Trenton Makes, the World Takes," attached in 1935 to a truss bridge over the Delaware River, has become a landmark of the journey. Today, this memento of the city's industrial past is what most train travelers remember best about the capital of New Jersey.

From 1850 to 1950, the first century of railroad travel, the austere and utilitarian sights of the industrial corridor contrasted dramatically with the ornament-laden architecture that dominated most other districts of the city. Throughout the industrial age, architects and their patrons devoted

29. Greene, 13–14.

30. Ibid., 19.

much energy and wealth to erecting imitations of aristocratic palaces—not only for civic institutions and upper-middle-class housing but also for working-class apartments and office buildings as well. Done up in relatively cheap, mass-produced surfaces, much of the modern middle-class city thus denied the facts of its mass production. Not so along the railroad corridor, with its undecorated buildings of brick, concrete, and steel, the vigorous new architecture that expressed its structure and use. Those looking at cities from trains saw not plaster Corinthian pilasters but rather brick chimneys. More than anywhere else in the modern metropolis, the train corridor offered glimpses of the world of machine production—of mountains of sand, salt, and coal, of blast furnaces that tapered into valves and chimneys, of steel-and-glass sheds that sheltered production lines. Guidebooks of the era wrote with admiration of the aesthetics of the industrial zone, the lights and power, the brutish but fantastic steel mills, lumberyards, and oil refineries.[31]

More than any other zone, with the possible exception of the skyscraper business district, the rail corridor introduced the modern public to an architectural landscape shaped by technology, oblivious to aesthetic refinements. For a time, the corridor could be seen as harbinger of the city of the future, a cityscape running on the fiery momentum of the industrial age. The turn toward a modern architectural aesthetic coincides with the growth of rail travel through industrial zones, for here travelers could see immense grain elevators, endlessly long warehouses and factories—architecture that was radical. It is not surprising, then, that the rejection of architectural modernism that began in the 1960s, especially in the United States, coincides with the decline in rail travel and with the increasing deterioration of the industrial architecture of the corridor. As the industries along the rail corridor declined, so too did the public's interest in their utilitarian forms. Buildings that had once stimulated a futuristic imagination had become, by the postwar years, reminders of inevitable obsolescence. Rail corridors all too clearly exhibited evidence of the outmoding of industrial processes, and, by implication, of the myth of technological progress. Bricks crumbled. Paint cracked. Walls collapsed. Buildings were abandoned. Garbage piled up. In no other zone of the city did gleaming modernity turn as quickly to rusting obscurity. Sometimes only flaking signs remind contemporary rail travelers of the corridor's manufacturing heyday.

31. Stilgoe, 96.

Factory near Milan

The urban rail passenger looks out along lines of trains and track threaded tightly into the fabric of the city. Cable cars, trolleys and light-rail vehicles, elevated trains, and subways trek between stops, not stations, pulling in and out every few minutes. Journeys are relatively short, but can extend, especially in the newer metro systems, as far as thirty or forty miles. In all its varieties—at ground level on streets, below grade in tunnels, depressed in concrete channels, or elevated on posts—urban transit cuts into the heart of the city. Its rails squeeze between and behind buildings, snake around, climb over, and jut under urban infrastructure. Unlike intercity trains, with their long vistas, urban railcars move, more often than not, knee-deep through station platforms, alongside walls, past pediments, within inches of windows, in sight of backyards.

Over the decades, cable cars or electric trolleys have shared their paths with pedestrians, horses, carts, drays, automobiles, and trucks. Here passengers observe the city from its most vital and teeming public space, the street. In these circumstances, as the film of the San Francisco cable car shows, rail passengers move slowly, in concert with the urban free-for-all. Via uneven tempos, the view approximates that of pedestrians—stops and starts, extended gazes and quick turns, shifting walls of people and vehicles, and slow pans along street walls with enough time to appreciate cornice lines, statues, and signs. Still, in railcars, passengers move more quickly and smoothly than do pedestrians, and they do not control the stops and starts. They also look from a point within the street, rather than from the sidewalk—a slightly larger space for scrutinizing the enclosing buildings. And they see the city, not within its unbroken sweep of space, but from a glazed compartment. The street rail experience affords commuters some of the pedestrian's leisured intimacy with architecture, as well as the mechanized vehicle's greater range, spatial disconnection, steady movement, and seating comfort. There is less time to look at buildings, but there is more to see.

Because of their lethargic pace, and because their tracks disrupted automobile movement, cable cars and trolleys were the first urban rail systems to be dismantled and replaced by buses, especially in the United

States. Buses afford a similar viewing experience, albeit from a slightly higher position, through generally smaller windows, and on a trajectory that habitually swerves back and forth toward the sidewalk for stops. Recently, though, light-rail vehicles have been making a comeback in American cities, from Baltimore, Maryland, to Long Beach, California. In the search for speed, however, they dart along separate corridors, between or astride the lanes dedicated to the internal combustion engine. These new light-rail systems resemble the interurbans of old—the prewar networks that connected cities like New York and Boston. Trips along these older lines afforded a viewing experience that combined aspects of those of the intercity train and the street trolley. On open stretches, distanced from buildings and unencumbered by other vehicles, the interurbans treated passengers to views of the far-flung buildings, parks, and districts of the city and its suburbs. In denser parts of city, though, inching and twisting along, passengers were immersed in the details of buildings.

Elevated trains, or els, routinely negotiate cities in similar ways, one minute providing distanced, sweeping views and the next taking their passengers into almost tactile encounters with building mass and social life. In a spectacularly flat city like Chicago, the el functions like a hilly ridge offering moving vistas otherwise unavailable. The city's el trains run either in corridors behind backyards or directly atop streets. Starting on the northwest side of Chicago, for instance, the Ravenswood line winds downtown in s-curves that cross back and forth from backyards to streets. Rushing over residential and industrial districts, the el train passes just over roofs and gables, bringing the passenger's eyes terribly close to buildings. From the forward side of the window, walls and trees come at the viewer like asteroids in a video game and then whoosh harmlessly by. Jerking their eyes back and forth, passengers can focus on the details of backyards, back stairs, auto shops, vacant lots. The el's sight lines are often high enough to see over most buildings, across acres of blocks and streets toward the high points of the city. From these mobile heights, the expanse of Chicago is revealed. The city looks like an intricate swath of building fabric rolled out from the lakefront wall of skyscrapers, an immense but regular succession of structures eventually bleeding out toward the horizon.

Downtown, the el follows an oval track around the skyscrapers of the Loop. Buildings pass by at extra-close range—the spatiality and dynamism of the neighborhoods is here replaced by intimate encounter. As the trains slowly snake around the Loop, they afford clear sight lines into mezzanine and second-story offices. Building details difficult to see from ground level sharpen into focus—the el affords a running commentary on brick, terra-cotta, limestone, granite, steel, and glass compositions. Passing by the office towers, one can read the history of Chicago architecture through the diverse materials used to clad the steel frame, from the masonry of the early twentieth century to the plate glass of mid-century to the complex collages of the postmodern era. The el, of course, also brings transportation dynamism into the heart of the business district. Above the clogged streets, the trains run on their own schedules; from some angles, they might also remind us of certain utopian visions for "cities of the future" with multiple circulation levels.

In no other visual experience do viewers come so close to the interior lives of buildings. Describing an elevated train ride in Manhattan, William Dean Howells, in his 1890 novel *A Hazard of New Fortunes*, illustrates this strange sensation of trains skirting too close to buildings. On the old Manhattan elevated lines, trains routinely shifted between public and private views of architecture, city side and domestic side, front cornices and living rooms and back porches and kitchens. Howells's protagonist notes the details and frequent hideousness of certain signs and facades. He remarks on the insolence with which the railway structure grazes buildings, dishonoring their pillars and pediments, crossing a line, so to speak, of architectural respectability. Yet at the same time, we are treated to a wide array of sights one would never see at ground level: "The vistas of shabby cross streets; the survival of an old hip-roofed house here and there at their angles; the Swiss chalet, histrionic decorativeness of the stations in prospect or retrospect; the vagaries of the lines that narrowed together or stretched apart according to the width of the avenue, but always in wanton disregard of the life that dwelt, and bought and sold, and rejoiced or sorrowed, and clattered or crawled, around, fellow, above."[32] Amid the el's indignities, there is the view. The elevated train entertains, a cinema streaming across the city. Along its narrow corridor, twenty to thirty feet above the street, fleeting intimacies

32. William Dean Howells, *A Hazard of New Fortunes* (New York: E.P. Dutton, 1952), 199.

are formed with countless facades and interiors. The el provides a galloping gallery of seats open onto an ever-changing stage whose plot is life, anytime, all over the city. Indeed, some key effects that early cinema strove to achieve appear as a natural course of events on trains: the rocking of the body in a kind of pendulum effect; the frequent changes of scenery; and the domi-nance of vision over all other senses.[33] Yet on the train, the buildings and streets do not move past our eyes. Our eyes move past them.

Our eyes also roam between light and darkness, the visible and invis-ible city, architecture seen on or above the earth's surface, and felt from below. From their beginnings, subways have risen out of the earth and sunk back in, mixing elevated and subterranean passage. The most riveting view on the Boston subway system occurs when Red Line trains rise out of the tunnel from Cambridge to cross over the Longfellow Bridge before descend-ing again under downtown Boston. For a moment, the underground journey opens up to vistas of the Charles River backed by the brick terraces of Beacon Hill and the golden dome of the Massachusetts State House. The routes of several American metro systems, such as those in Atlanta, Washington, and San Francisco, alternate between bright open spaces and the dim lamp-lit obscurity of the tunnel. On the Bay Area Rapid Transit between Berkeley and San Francisco, trains switch several times from zones of illumination to those of enclosure. Heading south from the underground station in downtown Berkeley, soon after the train pulls out, the tight view of a dark concrete wall speckles with light. The train climbs up through con-crete walls that gradually brighten and suddenly yield to views of the neigh-boring streets and houses, just yards away, and then higher, to a level where passengers can see the roofs, skylights, and vents of small buildings as well as the hills in the distance. After the train descends again below grade, the view changes from the tops of buildings to the undersides of roads. As we pass under and through the piers of an adjacent freeway our eyes weave around the thick concrete forms. Later, after subterranean passage through downtown Oakland, the train ascends once more above backyards and small frame houses, and then shows us the towering steel cranes of the port of Oakland. Finally, before the train prospect cascades into the tunnel to San Francisco, stretches of the Bay and San Francisco skyline come briefly into

33. Lynne Kirby, *Parallel Tracks: The Railroad and Silent Cinema* (Durham: Duke University, 1997), 155.

focus. Better than any other mode of observation, the lateral and vertical views from the train expose the multilayered and interwoven infrastructure of the modern city.

To travel still further within the rail zoomscape, we need to go underground and stay there, to ride trains that never see the light of day, trains that give us the sensation of the city as a twisting, flashing tunnel between points on an unseen surface above. On a subway, hurtling through passageways lit only by small lamps, the passenger might be lulled into an extraordinary state of mind. The subway evokes the underworld of myth and religion, the passage from life to the hereafter. For millennia, human cultures have equated tubular channel into the ground with death—"through me the way into the woeful city," says Dante, in *The Inferno*, of the route to Hell. Strangely, sight may seem especially acute underground, as we feel the train's motion as it passes under the foundations of buildings. Subway riders experience cities through a combination of geographical ambiguity and anticipation. Under New York City, for instance, expectations swell as the Manhattan-bound E train heads west from 23rd Street and Ely Avenue in Queens. As the train gathers speed, the long gap between stations indicates that it has crossed the East River. The view, or non-view, out the subway tunnel brings into play a form of extravisual urban perception. Underground, the full-bodied city contracts into major and minor stops, a series of large and small dots on a map; a sense of location emerges from the spatial rhythm of station stops. In this case, the passage under the East River leads not across bridges with their superior views but instead through noisy, jostling darkness. The subway plunges passengers into the deepest of urban recesses, a path along which no liberating vistas intrude. The city seen from the subway is so confining that it becomes almost personal. Disparate districts are connected by the individual traveler's trajectory; the rest of the city is blocked out. Subways recast understanding of urbanity as a journey across gray space, perhaps portending colorful possibilities.

The view of architecture from trains represents the first phase of the zoomscape. But it did not occur alone. During the mid-nineteenth century, photography, too, transformed architecture into surface extracted from place. But unlike the exactness of photographic reproduction, the rail view's synthetic and abstracting insights catapult architecture back at us, transformed. Seated in a train, at rest, the passenger may notice a viewing field split apart, shaded into silhouette, and understood through succession. Or the rail view may fill up with so many buildings close by the window that their forms begin to ricochet around the compartment and our imagination. The rail view's intensification of perception is captured by Vladimir Nabokov in a remembrance from childhood: "When, on such journeys as these, the train changed its pace to a dignified amble and all but grazed house fronts and shop signs, as we passed through some big German town, I used to feel a twofold excitement, which terminal stations could not provide. I saw a city with its toy-like trams, linden trees, and brick walls enter into the compartment, hobnob with the mirrors, and fill to the brim the windows on the corridor side."[34] Sometimes, lying perchance on one's back in the train compartment, watching the reflections of building silhouettes dance along the walls, the train's space merges with buildings outside and perception suffuses in optical shadows.

34. Vladimir Nabokov, "First Love," in *Nabokov's Dozen: A Collection of Thirteen Stories* (Garden City, New York: Doubleday & Co., 1958), 57.

CHAPTER 2

AUTOMOBILE

DURING THE 1880S, ENGINEERING into the internal combustion engine by Gottlieb Daimler and Karl Benz led to a new phenomenon in land loco-motion, the gas-powered automobile. Mass production began in France in the 1890s and by 1902 had spread to the United States, when Ransome Eli Olds came up with the idea of assembly-line production. Between 1909 and 1927, the Ford Motor Company, based in Detroit, built more than fif-teen million Model T cars. By 1925, in the United States alone, approxi-mately seventeen million automobiles operated on hundreds of thousands of miles of roads, more than twenty thousand of them paved. The automobile age had arrived.

Automobiles have shaped the physique and perception of contempo-rary cities. Railroads had already begun to expand the city beyond its tradi-tional limits. But while railroads were fast, they kept to their tracks; now the technological pursuit of velocity began to turn, reverse, and spread at the behest of the automobile and its exponentially branching network of roads. During the past century, car and truck culture has filled in the gaps between the radial routes of the railroads, crowding the outskirts of cities with hap-hazard roadside attractions and turning drivers into sovereign navigators of a metropolis where vehicular circulation infiltrates everywhere. The flexibility of automobile movement has caused urban magnitude to swell into hun-dreds (and even thousands) of square miles. The daunting scope of the automobile landscape is most apparent from an aerial view. Reaching from scattered points on a far periphery to the dense cross-hatchings of old down-towns and the megastructures of malls, the vehicular city resembles an organism that grows, not through replication, but through mutation. In this crazy quilt of development, not only do the patches stand out from each other; but the stitches also widen into fat lines and curlicues, intricate con-figurations of concrete and asphalt that weave personal mobility into metro-politan geography.

As with railroads, speed determines much of the automobile view. Speed turns the city seen through the windshield into a surface of motion, a stream of form that somehow eludes the consciousness of form.[1] The glass, steel, and plastic compartment of the automobile frames a view of the built environment through penetration and dispersion. In cars, drivers wriggle through gaps and shoot down empty roads. As they course through a city or

1. Kris Lackey, *Roadframes: The American Highway Narrative* (Lincoln: University of Nebraska Press, 1997), 77.

suburb, buildings and other structures lurch toward them and then give way. When traffic is light, the effect can be grand and processional. At the same time, like the train, driving encourages a nonchalant way of looking. Most sights are off to the side, constantly slipping away; the view ahead is dictated less by urban form than roadway space. The aesthetics of the automobile view are shaped by the brief encounter, a quick and potent mix of vision with form that almost instantaneously evaporates. Seen quickly, buildings and other urban features metamorphose into supple shapes and receding outlines. The excitement of viewing architecture from an automobile lies in such metamorphoses, which can seem like the transformation of mass into energy.

The fast view from cars reflects the variable qualities of a vehicular metropolis. Combining the freedom of walking or cycling with the velocity of the train, automobiles break free of the dedicated tracks and restricting views of the railroad. Changing direction at the driver's will, cars navigate the city as far as the roadside goes, showing us architecture from multiple angles and individual perspectives.[2] In cars, trucks, or on motorcycles, people construct an expansive sense of place. Whether on highways, arterials, or collector streets, the vehicular experience encompasses the whole of the metropolis. Automobiles encourage an understanding of architecture as landscape instead of landmark; and although they greatly facilitate access to individual landmarks, cars are impatient with stasis and singularity.

With each decade, it gets harder to distinguish the culture of the automobile from the culture of the city. Since roads cross boundaries between city and countryside at many points, the automobile view recasts relationships between rural and urban landscapes and redefines the notion of built sprawl and skyline image. Within cities or suburbs, automobiles institute their own architectural vocabulary—acres of asphalt, systems of lighting and signage, and the familiar yet fungible world of retail design. Beyond cities, expressways provide a hybrid state of mobility, combining the controlled separation and velocity of the rail corridor with the freedom of movement of the car. The automobile crafts knowledge of architecture on the go, prompting a dance-like interplay between observer and building, where buildings continually change and infrastructure usually cuts in.

2. Wolfgang Sachs, *For the Love of the Automobile: Looking Back into the History of our Desires* [1984], trans. Don Reneau (Berkeley: University of California Press, 1992), 155.

The effects of automobile culture and vision are felt worldwide. *A Taste of Cherry*, by Iranian film director Abbas Kiarostami, is a lengthy exploration of the developing periphery of Tehran as seen from an automobile. In this 1997 movie, Tehran is shown via vehicular passages that lead not to monuments of historic architecture but instead back to the raw earth from which civilization is shaped. The film follows the progress of a Range Rover, driven by a Mr. Badii, meandering through a landscape disturbed by cars, buses, and trucks, and yet only understandable through their influence and aesthetics. Kiarostami delights in showing the unlovely sights of the vehicular city—garbage dumps of tires, piles of steel piping and stone tiles, cement factories, frameworks of rising apartment buildings, roads snaking up mountains. This new urban zone is a place of advancing unrest where the natural landscape has been devastated, but where the urban regime has not yet become dominant, a no-man's-land between control and chaos. In some places the land lies raw under the sun; in others, there are newly planted trees and buildings under construction. Everywhere, the land seesaws back and forth between the uneven rhythms of vehicular development and restless movement; and because vehicular culture allows constant intrusions onto undeveloped land, such disturbed zones are now commonplace.

The film begins as Mr. Badii drives along the streets of an older neighborhood, searching for someone or something on the sidewalk. The camera is static and its steady exploration of the streetscape is propelled by the motion of the automobile. In the first shot, the camera stares (from the passenger's front seat) at Mr. Badii driving. Pictured as well is a large boulevard, its buildings, fountains, and benches slightly out of focus. The second shot is from the driver's side and looks out across the passenger seat through the open window at crowds of men standing on the sidewalk. Here the background becomes clearer, architectural details more readable. After a couple of switchbacks between these two vantages, the camera flees the confines of the car and stares at Mr. Badii through the windshield. Through the back windows of the Range Rover, the city is barely discernible, a blur of colored planes. These shots display the differing perspectives of the city seen from the automobile—the quick glance out the back, the steady stare ahead, the diagonal swerve of the eyes across the roadside. Filmgoers see architecture from the automobile's variable viewing angles, its direct and mirrored orientations, and with its mix of casual and purposeful attention.

Kiarostami soon offers the first view of the city unframed by car windows or mirrors. A long view of Tehran encompasses sand-colored skyscrapers and construction cranes; it yields no indication of the city's center. From this point on, frequent long-range shots track the indistinct skyline, the sort of views that do not appear on postcards. Later, as Badii drives to the outskirts of Teheran, the camera breaks fully away from the car and follows its progress from an exterior vantage. Filmgoers see the Range Rover as it moves down a dirt road. Then, from yet another angle, they finally see the road from Mr. Badii's perspective. Out the windshield, the camera twists and turns with the road as a driver would, sweeping the viewer's eyes down the hillsides to the suburban sprawl below. By emphasizing the array of camera angles, Kiarostami reminds us that while the car is moving, a driver's perceptual stance goes through abrupt shifts—from windshield to side-view mirror, windshield again, then rearview mirror, side window, and so forth—that disclose different landscape perspectives. Unlike the steady view out a train or plane window or at a movie or television screen, automotive perception emerges from the kinesthetic movements of the head and upper body, as a driver responds to changing views.

In *A Taste of Cherries*, the tracking of the automobile up and down the barren hills underscores the city as a geological phenomenon, built up from the earth. Mr. Badii, who is planning to commit suicide, is seeking someone to pour dirt onto his grave. In ironic counterpoint, the film charts the activity of digging up the earth to build more city. The film's spiraling journey to the urban edge and its protagonist's journey to the edge of life itself both contradict the liberation promised by the automobile. Roaming over a large terrain, from boulevards to country roads to dirt paths, this automobile journey is certainly expansive, and yet it conveys no sense of romance or freedom. Instead of a stirring score, the grating and shifting gears of the Range Rover dominate the soundtrack. *A Taste of Cherry* suggests that any freedom to be gained from the automobile will be achieved only when the motor is turned off. Here the ultimate urban edge, the earth, frames the edges of both architecture and life. Architecture is made from earth and must return to earth.

Moscow

More than a story about a man's death, *A Taste of Cherry* memorializes urbanity by showing us, through the window of a car, how a city and a man are born and die. This tale of the margins of a city critiques what is often construed as the pragmatic purpose of architecture. Kiarostami's vision of hell emerges from the relentless development of the vehicular city. And so we wonder: Is fleeting automotive perception already a glimpse into a purgatory caused by the automobile? Or is the sprawling vehicular city a new entity whose meaning can emerge only from the automobile and its culture?

An answer to such questions is suggested by another film, *Falling Down* directed by Joel Schumacher and released in 1993. Here the long dominion of automotive movement over foot travel comes to a sweaty halt on a freeway east of downtown Los Angeles. Caught up in the road cacophony of construction signs, gridlock, and heat, the protagonist, who styles himself D-FENS, calls it jammed freeway, climbs up an ivy-covered embankment, and walks west across Los Angeles to the Santa Monica Pier. Once out of the car, he walks through the shadowed, forgotten streets that lie alongside (and sometimes beneath) the freeway. Much of this city is crumbling, seething with danger, and cracking under the stress of massive construction projects. D-FENS, too, is cracking. His crosstown hike disintegrates into a one-man riot. The message is clear: seeing the city from the lanes of the freeway has become the vital option. Leaving your car, you see the urban detritus, the city that the car has made obsolete. And leaving your car, you might lose your life.

More than any other means of transport, automobiles engender fiercely partisan reactions. Early in the twentieth century, many observers praised the car's adventurous mobility.[3] Auto touring and camping became national pastimes, and already before the First World War the sights of many industrialized nations began to be available from the vehicular view.[4] From the 1920s on, urban planners, including Le Corbusier, Ludwig Hilberseimer, and Lucio Costa, designed cities in which the street was given over to the car. Modernist cities were designed with superblocks framed by high-speed expressways. Road construction and its inevitable urban disruptions were everywhere seen as beneficial. The leading historian of architectural modernism, Sigfried Giedion, remarked that the automobile allows us to understand the modern

3. John Stilgoe, *Borderland: Origins of the American Suburb, 1820–1939* (New Haven: Yale University Press, 1988), 272–275.

4. James J. Flink, *The Automobile Age* (Cambridge: MIT Press, 1988), 169–187.

5. Sigfried Giedion, *Space, Time, and Architecture: The Growth of a New Tradition*, fifth edition (Cambridge: Harvard University Press, 1967), 826, 831.

consciousness, which is, in one sense, life in the fast lane. "The meaning and beauty of the parkway cannot be grasped from a single point of observation, as was possible when from a window of the chateau of Versailles the whole expanse of nature could be embraced in one view. It can be revealed only by movement," he wrote. "The space-time feeling of our period can seldom be felt so keenly as when driving, the wheel under one's hands, up and down hills, beneath overpasses, up ramps, and over giant bridges."[5] For Giedion, the automobile culture foretold a new and exciting built environment, the latest stage of modernity, dynamic, complex, and possessed of infinite sights.

These vehicular sights utterly disrupted customary notions of urbanity. Before modern times, as landscape theorist and historian J.B. Jackson describes, cities were experienced as vertical. Visually, they were marked by clusters of towers, walls, and roofs.[6] In the modern age, however, the architectural image of the city gave way to an infrastructural image—the city as a grid, a crisscross of lines, a spaghetti-jumble of expressways. The visual order of the automobile is horizontal and expansive. In "Truck City," Jackson characterizes the changes that automobile usage brings to streetscapes. "The traditional street," he writes, "with its uninterrupted facades and walls of masonry, is being perforated by drive-in facilities, parking lots, underground garages, and service alleys."[7] The traditional city of walled enclosure was turning into the modern city of mobility. The view from the road was becoming a view of the road, a view onto vehicular spaces, a cityscape designed less for pedestrians and more for the physical and visual maneuvers of automobiles.

By the 1960s, there had developed a strident negative critique of the car. Beginning in places like Boston and San Francisco, citizens' groups blocked the constuction of highways that would have run over or through their neighborhoods. Critics began to deplore the ubiquitious commercial strips, lambasting their gaudy, piecemeal development. In *God's Own Junkyard*, published in 1964, Peter Blake decried the entire commerical roadscape of billboards and signage. He describes highways "as hideous scars on the face of the nation—scars that cut across mountains and plains, cities and suburbs, poisoning the landscape and townscape with festering

6. J.B. Jackson, "The Discovery of the Street," in *The Necessity for Ruins* (Amherst: University of Massachusetts Press, 1980), 55.

7. J.B. Jackson, "Truck City," in *The Car and the City: The Automobile, the Built Environment, and Daily Urban Life*, eds. Martin Wachs and Margaret Crawford (Ann Arbor: University of Michigan Press, 1991), 23.

sores along their edges."[8] In Blake's alarmist and well-illustrated tract, the ugly carscape would ultimately push life off the ground and into the unnatural constructed environments of high-rise buildings.

For many critics, the automobile symbolizes much that is wrong with cities and especially suburbs. A host of pejorative terms—strip, sprawl, smog—links urban ills to cars and trucks. Urban problems such as abandonment and ghettoization have been blamed on the car. Much of the attack against the automobile takes aim at its profound transformation of urban form and space. In *Asphalt Nation*, Jane Holtz Kay claims that the automobile literally consumes the space of cities; she notes that a car driving at thirty miles per hour requires 300 times as much space as a pedestrian.[9] The view from the automobile, so this argument goes, is a view onto the world created by the automobile—hence a narcissistic view. For many critics, the automobile isolates its occupants and turns the built environment into a zone of alienating passage through neutral architectural infill. On this note, architectural historian Margaret Crawford warns that "driving from one theme environment to another, the endless, nondescript blocks of the city disappear."[10] In this perspective, the simple act of driving might someday efface the city—at which point, it is possible that no one will mind.[11]

The critics of automobile culture make valid points, and yet the automobile offers so many new ways of seeing cities and of moving through landscapes. If we are to understand and appreciate the visual characteristics of our environments, it is crucial to delve deeper into automobile perception. It is immensely insightful to experience the expanding world from a car. The vehicular landscape, like the rail landscape, encourages an understanding of architecture that is almost cinematic—architecture in motion, buildings assembled through shots, cities understood as scenes. Sitting in a cushioned seat, perhaps alone, the radio tuned to a favorite station, the driver watches as individual buildings or streets become like a moving picture, the frames of an architecture of indeterminate length, direction, and content. Buildings reassemble according to the driver's desires, her arrivals and departures, stops and accelerations. Like the cinema, the automobile facilitates passage into new worlds. [12] And like kinetic cinematography, road vision, with its speed and sight, can be boldly liberating. In an interview of 1966, the sculptor Tony Smith

8. Peter Blake, *God's Own Junkyard: The Planned Deterioration of America's Landscape* (New York: Holt, Rinehart & Winston, 1964), 125.

9. Jane Holtz Kay, *Asphalt Nation: How the Automobile Took Over America and How We Can Take it Back* (New York: Crown, 1997), 67.

10. Margaret Crawford, "The Fifth Ecology: Fantasy, The Automobile, and Los Angeles," in *The Car and the City*, 227.

11. Louis Chevalier, *The Assassination of Paris*, trans. David P. Jordan (Chicago: University of Chicago Press, 1994), 49.

recalled that when he was teaching at Cooper Union during the 1950s, he
took some students to the New Jersey Turnpike, then under construction. "It
was a dark night and there were no lights or shoulder markings, lines, railings, or anything at all except the dark pavement moving through the landscape of the flats, rimmed by hills in the distance, but punctuated by stacks,
towers, fumes, and colored lights," Smith said. "The drive was a revealing
experience. The road and much of the landscape was artificial, and yet it
couldn't be called a work of art. On the other hand, it did something for me
that art had never done. At first, I didn't know what it was but its effect was
to liberate me from many of the ideas I had had about art. It seemed that
there had been a reality there that had not had any expression in art. The
experience on the road was something mapped out but not socially recognized. I thought to myself, it ought to be clear that's the end of art. Most
painting looks pretty pictorial after that. There is no way you can frame it.
You just have to experience it."[13] Smith's reaction to the uncompleted highway is especially interesting, because earlier in the interview he expressed
disdain for most road environments, disparaging, for instance, the drive from
Vermont to New York City. Evidently, Smith saw another aspect of automotive perception than did Giedion; to the sculptor, the artistic wonder lay in
the unforseen encounter with the unfinished and nonfunctional roadscape—
the expressway as a sculpture in motion.

Like art, the automobile allows us to see the urban scene in altered
states of consciousness. In *Lolita*, written in the early 1950s and first published in Europe in 1955, Vladimir Nabokov expresses better than anyone
the erotic nature of driving. "Steering my wife's car with one finger, I con-
tentedly rolled homeward," says the novel's protagonist, Humbert Humbert.
"Smoothly, almost silkily, I turned down into our steep little street. Everything
was somehow so right that day. So blue and green. I knew the sun shone
because my ignition key was reflected in the windshield."[14] Here the forward
momentum of driving suggests hope and possibility. But Nabokov's depiction of driving consciousness extends as well to pathos. To keep his affair
with the twelve-year-old Lolita a secret, Humbert flees his home in New
England and drives west across America. Once on the road, the novel presages
a cultural shift from cities, hotels, and railroads to suburbs, motels, and

12. Giuliana Bruno, "Driven," in *Inside Cars*, ed. J. Abbott Miller (New York: Princeton Architectural Press, 2001), 64.

13. Tony Smith, "Talking with Tony Smith," inter- view by Samuel Wagstaff, *Artforum* 5 (December 1966), 19.

14. Vladimir Nabokov, *Lolita* (New York: Putnam, 1955), 97.

highways. In this postwar landscape of transit and transience, motels, diners, tourist attractions, and gas stations follow one another monotonously, endlessly. Nabokov mentions hardly any cities and no significant buildings; rather he records the car's movement through the anonymous roadside landscape. As he realized, postwar Americans had fallen "under the smooth spell of a nicely graded curve.... Voraciously we consumed those long highways, in rapt silence we glided over their glossy black dance floors."[15] Driving was like a trance and the landscape seen from the automobile was both mesmerizing and forgettable. "I would stare," Humbert says, "at the honest brightness of the gasoline paraphernalia against the splendid green of oaks ... [at] tall trucks studded with colored lights, like dreadful Christmas trees ... hideous bits of tissue paper mimicking pale flowers among the prickles of wind-tortured withered stalks all along the highway ... the whole arrangement opening like a fan."[16]

BORDERLANDS

Upton Sinclair's *Oil*, set in 1912, opens with a chapter called "The Ride." A father and son drive across the coastal ranges of California. Along the way, tilting inward and then outward on the constant curves, the protagonists see the panorama opening and closing, hilltops and ranges rising and falling with the car's shifting orientation.[17] Sinclair describes the new object-life of the road, what the highway reveals about embankments and concrete, guard posts and railroad crossings. The automobile view had become a kind of primer on the new roadside landscape. Another chapter looks at billboards, then the harbingers of automotive visuality. Rural roads were often more powerfully marked by automobile culture than were urban streets, with billboards and other signs plastered on barns and erected alongside fields, advertising tires, fruits and vegetables, motels and restaurants. Some advertisements were civic boosters, and near a town, the roadside could resemble a deck of cards heralding a town's accomplishments, business statistics, and ambitions.

Early in the age of the automobile, however, apart from signs, the roadside had not yet acquired the sprawl of vehicular development. Sharp edges divided urban and rural landscapes. Roads passed through agricultural lands

15. Ibid., 154.

16. Ibid., 155.

17. Upton Sinclair, *Oil* (New York: Grosset & Dunlop, 1927), 6.

until quite near a town's boundary. For a brief period, because of their mobility, automobiles allowed people to experience the contrasts between town and country. On a single drive, one could experience city streets and farm fields, or different towns and cities, expansive and individualized itineraries of business or pleasure. Old-timers, born before vinyl siding and Astroturf, recall orchards almost nuzzling downtowns and residential rows ending in meadows. The highway led straight from woods and fields to houses and streets, a steady gathering of building mass and density around the car.

Driving toward a city could feel like an artistic experience. Because of its speed, and because the driver and passengers might focus their attention at certain places, even stopping at special vistas, the car assembles landscapes in an almost painterly way. In the 1920s, inspired by a trip to Pamplona, Ernest Hemingway describes this sort of driving encounter in *The Sun Also Rises*. "After a while we came out of the mountains," he writes, "and there were trees along both sides of the road, and a stream and ripe fields of grain, and the road went on, very white and straight ahead, and then lifted to a little rise, and off on the left was a hill with an old castle, with buildings close around it and a field of grain going right up to the walls and shifting in the wind. . . . Then we crossed a wide plain, and there was a big river off on the right shining in the sun from between the line of trees, and away off you could see the plateau of Pamplona rising out of the plain, and the walls of the city, and the great brown cathedral, and the broken skyline of the other churches. In back of the plateau were the mountains, and every way you looked there were other mountains, and ahead the road stretched out white across the plain going toward Pamplona."[18] The Spanish countryside Hemingway describes is not wilderness. Buildings and other structures mark the places of civilization; so do the cultivated fields. But each view, including the first sight of Pamplona, consists of such perfectly framed and delineated forms that one might have the impression of walking in a garden and admiring a succession of views. In this case the sights are dispersed over a far larger area, and thus create an unintentional picturesque landscape. Hemingway's passage brings together the elements of the pastoral landscape as the basis for a new automotive visuality: old buildings followed by ruins, then by fields, rows of trees, a lake, all joined by a winding

18. Ernest Hemingway, *The Sun Also Rises* (New York: Charles Scribner's Sons, 1926), 93–94.

road, which is itself part of the scene. In a car, through a sequence of panoramas, viewers create their own versions of landscape tableaux. But of course, the elements have not been arrayed on a planar surface by an artist; in a sense, each driver becomes an artist, as automotive experience of approaching a city creates a fleeting but memorable landscape in the mind of the motorist.

Auto touring typically consists of a leisurely drive along a meandering country road, far from cities and highways. Whether in the heart of France or on the flanks of Vermont's Green Mountains, the road should provide the opportunity for a visual conversation with defined landscape features: a range of mountains, a stream, farmsteads and barns, and most important of all, in the distance, a village or town. In idyllic circumstances, one glimpses the town from far away, its church steeple or castle turrets coming into view from roads that are still rural. Seen this way, the new prospect of a town or city harmonizes with the vehicular passage through the countryside. The elements of nature and of architecture are delightfully interspersed, tree with tower, meadow with masonry. Negotiating between country and city in this manner would not be possible without the speed and comfort of the car. Only the automobile affords us the chance to string together extensive itineraries of urban and rural features, to glimpse a city from afar and minutes later enter its network of streets.

The sequences of the automobile journey recall an argument made by urban theorist Gordon Cullen in his 1960 *Townscape*. Cullen coined the term "serial vision" to describe how a walk through a town can disclose a picturesque cityscape, a shifting interplay of towers and spires at every bend in the road, fresh alignments and groupings of buildings, pleasurable projections and recessions from the street wall.[19] Following the ideas of Camillo Sitte's *City Planning According to Artistic Principles*, Cullen advocated for architectural contrasts in style and scale as well as considerable spatial enclosure for new urban design; conversely, he recommended against construction of long straight roads lacking diverse features, precisely the roads favored in the automotive age. Cullen does not mention cars, but it is clear that the speed of automobiles introduces the drama of juxtaposition into roads that would be monotonous on foot. As William H. Whyte notes in *The Last Landscape*,

19. Gordon Cullen, *Townscape* (London: The Architectural Press, 1961), 11, 19.

our appreciation of a picturesque landscape seen from an automobile depends on the brevity and remoteness of the view. From a distance, seen from a car driving at more than thirty miles per hour, a New England landscape of meadow, church, and town might look beautiful. That same view, witnessed at close range by a pedestrian, might disclose a rancid marsh and a deteriorated main street of nondescript storefronts.[20] Viewed from the automobile, disparate elements can fuse into striking compositions. Velocity can rearrange the parts of an architectural landscape into otherwise imperceptible rhythms and harmonies. The sort of picturesque views that Cullen enjoyed while walking are attainable as well from a fleet car.

Such artistic entrances into a city can also occur where uniformity or emptiness turns abruptly to variety or abundance, and where the change in the landscape precipitates equally unexpected reactions in the viewer. At one time, driving from the Dead Sea along the West Bank of the Jordan River, one could see Jerusalem appear at the top of a mountain pass—a portrait of the city with its domes and stone walls. Almost too much to take in after hours of driving through desert, the city flashed forth for a second and then disappeared behind a curve in the road, only to reappear moments later, looking almost otherworldly. Similar vehicular sightings are possible in many places where roads pierce sudden view corridors through mountains and the flanks of those mountains temporarily hide the spread of urbanity.

The picturesque experience of the vehicular roadside is, however, harder and harder to come by. Automobile culture contributes to the destruction of the natural environment and rural countryside. In bucolic landscapes, automobile tourism stimulates the construction of motels, service stations, vista points, and amusements that elongate and muddy the once tight urban-rural edge. Places like the red canyons of Sedona, Arizona, deteriorate in the wake of development, the views of rock spires cluttered with signs for Happy Meals. Nowadays, the sprawl of Jerusalem's suburbs prepares drivers for the urban spectacle ahead and robs it of its exciting suddenness. Even more insidiously, the subdivisions that surround most North American cities, because of their uniformity, their large planes of color and texture, confront the automobile viewer with an architectural equivalent of wilderness—the absence of any landmarks that might aid geographic comprehension and

20. William H. Whyte, *The Last Landscape*
(Garden City, New York: Doubleday & Co., 1968),
312–313.

artistic contrast. Fields of corn follow fields of gray slate roofs. Hillsides of chaparral alternate with hillsides of red tile roofs. At each bend in the road, with each additional mile, we suffer the monotony of sameness. Driver and passenger glide adrift in the suburban sea.

Once, and not that long ago, Los Angeles, too, slid abruptly into view as one approached the city driving on the mountain passes from the high desert. In *The Air-Conditioned Nightmare*, Henry Miller, after driving from the Grand Canyon through the Mojave Desert, describes the first view of the Inland Empire east of Los Angeles from a canyon between the San Gabriel and San Bernardino Mountains. "Somewhere about a mile up towards God and its winged satellites the whole works comes toppling down on you," Miller writes. "All the ranges converge suddenly—like a publicity stunt. Then comes a burst of green, the wildest, greenest green imaginable, as if to prove beyond the shadow of a doubt that California is indeed the Paradise it boasts of being. Everything but the ocean seems jammed into this mile-high circus at sixty miles an hour."[21] Miller saw such scenes in 1945. Today, such sudden sightings of city lights or of the "greenest green" of citrus groves rarely happen. Too much of the vehicular city has advanced into the desert. Driving through the Mojave these days, one encounters the first signs of Los Angeles almost 150 miles inland. North of Twenty-Nine Palms, in desert washes filled with creosote bushes, isolated structures pop up in the distance. And from Twenty-Nine Palms, on through Yucca Valley, then Banning and San Bernardino and the merging madness of the freeway, the roadside denies the possibility of escape. One urban outburst follows the other—Dryvit-walled subdivisions and shopping centers, tilt-up warehouses, trailer parks, billboards, flying overpasses. The flow of automobile urbanity out to the desert points increasingly erases urban-rural boundaries.

Questions arise. Is it the deterioration of a neat town-country boundary that offends people? Or is it that the development-spattered borderlands lack the sharp visible contours of both older cities and rural countryside? And can this condition be blamed on the automobile? Although the term is recent, sprawl itself has a long history. Sprawl may have been greatly exacerbated by the railroad and automobile, but it predates both technologies.

Early in *Other Voices, Other Rooms*, written in the mid-1940s, Truman Capote remarks on the journey of a teenage boy from New Orleans to rural

21. Henry Miller, *The Air-Conditioned Nightmare*
(New York: New Directions, 1945), 245.

Pyramids at Giza

Mississippi. The novel is set in a Southern landscape created before the age of the automobile, but which augers some of the changes the car will cause. Riding on a bus, the boy regards the old countryside as unwholesome, a nasty landscape with few signs of human life. An old Mississippi town is not a picturesque blend of fields and farmsteads, but a cluster of derelict sheds. "A house. A gray clump of Negro cabins. An unpainted clapboard church with a rain-rod steeple, and three Holy panes of ruby glass. A sign: the Lord Jesus is Coming! Are you ready? A little black child wearing a big straw hat and clutching tight a pail of blackberries. Over all the sun's stinging gaze. Soon there was a short, unpaved and nameless street, lined with similar one-floored houses, some nicer-looking than others; each had a front porch and a yard, and in some yards grew scraggly rose bushes and crepe myrtle and China trees. . . . Then a red-barn livery stable: horses, wagons, buggies, mules, men. An abrupt bend in the road: Noon City."[22] Like Hemingway's Pamplona, Capote's southern town has clear boundaries. But in this case, neither the town nor the surroundings possess any clarity of form. Both landscape and town sprawl within themselves, although not into each other.

In Capote's tale, excessive variety causes visual chaos. But as contemporary suburban subdivisions and industrial districts show, so too does excessive homogeneity or repetition. Automobile viewers sense sprawl whenever a city or suburb appears to lack visual order, whenever a place consists of mostly one thing or of too many unconnected things. Of course, over time, through exposure, most places disclose hierarchies and structures—the urbanized equivalents of head, body, and limbs. Yet because the automobile offers diverse routes, it does not impose anything approaching the railroad's perceptual routines. Cars thus facilitate not only the construction of sprawl but also its perception. Because of their mobility, they offer too many views of too much cityscape—more than most of us can comprehend. In cities overgrown to thousands of square miles, overexposure to the environment of sprawl is logical and inevitable.

Nowadays, driving to New York City, like driving to Los Angeles, offers little to travelers who seek orderly transitions or clear hierarchies of urban form. Too much of the region has been urbanized. We drive through the metropolitan area as if in the embrace of a riotous machine, which blasts energy

22. Truman Capote, *Other Voices, Other Rooms*
(New York: Random House, 1948), 16.

past us and threatens to consume us. In Don DeLillo's *Underworld*, Brian Glassic plans to drive to Manhattan through New Jersey and the Lincoln Tunnel in order to avoid the George Washington Bridge. DeLillo's novel was published in 1998, making it nearly contemporaneous with *The Sopranos*, whose credit sequence shows a similar drive and includes some of the same sights. But unlike the television drama, the novel presents an automotive view of the city bereft of the picturesque, filled with the grotesque. "He drove along turnpikes and skyways, seeing Manhattan come and go in a valium sunset, smoky and golden," writes DeLillo. "He drove past enormous tank farms, squat white cylinders arrayed across the swampland, and the same white dome tanks in smaller groupings and long lines of tank cars rolling down the tracks. He went past power pylons with their spindly arms akimbo. He drove into the spewing smoke of acres of burning truck tires and the planes descended and the transit cranes stood in rows at the marine terminal and he saw billboards for Hertz and Avis and Chevy Blazer, for Marlboro, Continental and Goodyear, and he realized that all the things around him, the planes taking off and landing, the streaking cars, the tires on the cars, the cigarettes that the drivers were dousing in their ashtrays—all these were on the billboards around him, systematically linked in some self-referring relationship that had a kind of neurotic tightness, an inescapability, as if the billboards were generating reality."[23] The drive through the metropolis suggests not only the presence of productive urbanity—gas tanks, airplanes, ports—but also the power of consumption, evident in the billboard advertisements that seem to orchestrate the urban assemblage. There is no mention of the Empire State Building or of other landmarks. The sights flash by, architecture obscured by image. And Brian Glassic misses the exit for the tunnel to Manhattan; he ends up at the garbage dump at Fresh Kills in Staten Island. DeLillo's metropolitan New York seems sometimes as death-filled as Kiarostami's Tehran; sometimes it recalls Tony Smith's exhilarating drive into the future of art. The sprawling city is the place many of us know best—a city whose spatial and formal complexity is visualized most accurately through the clashing sights of the automotive zoomscape.

23. Don DeLillo, *Underworld* (New York: Scribner, 1997), 183.

Automobiles divide cities into two kinds of terrains: the densely built pre-vehicular city, and the wider and generously spaced strip of the automotive suburb. In the streets of older cities, the view from the car is limited to the lower stories of buildings. This phenomenon is exacerbated by the car's windshield, which divides the view into two planes: the upper perspective toward a street, and the lower part that shows the steering wheel and dash-board. On narrow streets, buildings crowd in around us, but the car too—the compressed space bounded by roof, windows, and dashboard—restricts our view. In such circumstances, driving can create a sort of tunnel vision where the sensation of enclosure becomes intense.

The experience of driving in older cities also depends on traffic. Jammed with buses, trucks, and other cars, even wide boulevards afford only fleeting opportunities to view architecture. Sitting in our cars, we often crawl through streetscapes that are pleasing only when the traffic eases, giv-ing us room to maneuver. The best views of architecture in older cities occur when streets are empty, at dawn, late at night, or Sundays and holidays. In Federico Fellini's *La Dolce Vita*, the hero, Marcello, drives his Fiat convert-ible around Rome at such advantageous moments. Alone on the streets, smoothly circling the Coliseum or racing toward one of the basilicas, he enjoys the rare experience of realizing how wonderfully the ancient city's pro-cessional routes accommodate the visual perspectives of the car.

During the twentieth century, as automobiles remade the city, urban activity shifted from downtown to suburb, from Main Street to commercial strip. Vehicular strips extend the scope of retail zones from feet to miles. Blocks get longer. Streets get wider. There are fewer intersections. To accom-modate cars, buildings on strips are pushed back from the road and detached from each other. Cars surround them, not only on the street, but also in access ways, parking lots, garages, and lanes of drive-through busi-nesses. Various new businesses cater to the automobile: motels, gas sta-tions, fast-food restaurants, and convenience stores. As often as not, the design of such places responds to what retailers construe as the short and wandering attention of consumers, as well as to their vague nostalgia for the Main Streets of the pre-vehicular era. Academic architectural languages are

Verrazzano–Narrows Bridge

less common here than on Main Street, however, and are replaced by loud, even extra-loud forms. As catalogued by photographers from Walker Evans to John Margolies, the modern roadside is a gallery of eye-catching shapes, bright colors, and copious merchandizing information. In *The Kandy-Kolored Tangerine-Flake Streamline Baby*, Tom Wolfe recalls "endless scorched boulevards lined with one-story stores, shops, bowling alleys, skating rinks, tacos drive-ins, all of them shaped not like rectangles but like trapezoids, from the way the roofs slant up from the back and the plate-glass fronts slant out as if they're going to pitch forward on the sidewalk and throw up."[24]

One of America's greatest contributions to urbanism is the populist and expressionistic commercial strip. Here as nowhere else, the peculiar national tension between conformity and eccentricity is apparent—franchise against mom-and-pop, cheap boxy buildings with mansard roofs against quirky structures and innovative designs. On the vehicular strip, every business, like every television commercial, works hard to grab our attention. And like television, the commercial strip is constantly reinventing itself, expanding its powers of suggestion and seduction.

The gaming metropolis of Las Vegas might be the ultimate vehicular city, one of the first designed to be seen from the car. The city's center is a strip of casinos, Highway 91, Las Vegas Boulevard. Tom Wolfe, not surprisingly, was quick to recognize the car-customized architectural lingo of the city in the Nevada desert. Other cities have skylines defined by buildings; not Las Vegas. Here the city proclaims itself through signs. "They tower. They revolve, they oscillate, and they soar in shapes before which the existing vocabulary of art history is helpless," writes Wolfe. "I can only attempt to supply names—Boomerang Modern, Palette Curvilinear, Flash Gordon Ming-Alert Spiral, McDonald's Hamburger Parabola, Mint Casino Elliptical, Miami Beach Kidney."[25] By the early 1960s, Las Vegas boasted the world's most dramatic mass-mediated architecture. It was a cityscape pieced together from a marketplace mélange of entertainment, tourism, television, and fantasy—Times Square, Disneyland, *Your Show of Shows*, and *The Wizard of Oz* rolled into one.

Over the years, the casinos of the Strip have become taller and bulkier, and have morphed from sheds decorated by signs into kitschy simulations of

24. Tom Wolfe, *The Kandy-Kolored Tangerine-Flake Streamline Baby* (New York: Farrar, Straus & Giroux, 1963), 82.

25. Ibid., 8.

historic cities and landmarks. Although ten-story neon sunbursts no longer dominate the scene, the architectural fantasies of Vegas still play to the automobile view. At speeds of twenty to thirty miles per hour, drivers have little chance to observe building details. Architectural snapshots substitute for comprehensive investigations. Tourists drive by simulations of ancient Egypt, New York, Paris, and Venice, as if each were a chapter in a travel guide or a promo for a television program. The substance of the architecture is thin— no greater than the neon signs it has replaced and no less commercial. Fantastical architecture itself has become the signage.

Published in 1972, *Learning from Las* Vegas, by Robert Venturi, Denise Scott Brown, and Steven Izenour, first explored the links between building and signage—how buildings themselves had become signs. The book's analyses of driving and architecture have altered our understanding of the built environment. The authors argued against the architectural profession's obsession with traditional urban spaces, such as piazzas and boulevards, as well as with the ideals of functional and structural clarity. Provocatively, they told us that signs had become more important than buildings, and that commercial symbols, not architectural languages, now dominated the urban landscape.[26] As they pointed out, because "the driver has no time to ponder paradoxical subtleties within a dangerous, sinuous maze, he or she relies on signs for guidance—enormous signs in vast spaces at high speeds."[27] While the commercial strip may look chaotic, the authors recognized that it had generated a new symbolic order, one determined by movement, isolation, and consumerism. This thesis remains as vital as ever. No longer does architecture communicate primarily through its traditional and classical languages. Out on the strip, elite and intricate building languages, intended to convey meaning to pedestrians, no longer work. A new architectural mode of expression has evolved—buildings that communicate to drivers and that convey the commercial messages of commodity culture. Buildings have become like signs, another form of media.

Signs, of course, have crowded the roadside since the beginning of the automobile age. In older shopping districts, signs obscure facades and often project above rooflines. In postwar strips, buildings stand back behind parking lots while freestanding signs occupy the choice real estate at the road's

26. Robert Venturi, Denise Scott Brown, Steven Izenour, *Learning from Las Vegas* (Cambridge: MIT Press, 1972), 13.

27. Venturi, Scott Brown, Izenour, 9.

edge. Signs are not always commercial. Complex systems of traffic signs and lights regulate vehicular movement and command much of a driver's attention. One perceptual difference between drivers and passengers is the freedom of the latter to ignore traffic lights and signage.

More than the pedestrian view, the automotive view is structured by electric illumination. In night driving, lights become the principal means of orientation—lights on the car, above the road, even embedded in the road. Out in the country, the nocturnal view, lit by the car's headlights, resembles a channel of low-lying illumination surrounded by darkness. In the city, flickering lights from cars, streets, buildings, and signs structure a driver's sense of space. Like buildings, lights signify varying levels of enclosure and density. And at night the concentration of lights along roads causes the automotive zone of the city to stand out from the darker spaces of buildings or parks. Many photographers have captured the torrent of red and white lines that defines the roads of the nocturnal city. In Jean-Luc Godard's 1965 film *Pierrot le Fou*, nighttime Paris is dominated by vehicular lights. In a long scene, focused on two characters in a moving car, red brake lights and yellowish headlights trail repeating curves on either side of the windshield, under flickering red, yellow, and green traffic lights and long rows of white streetlights. Traffic lights, like signs, remind us that the experience of driving is determined not only by the physical characteristics of a place, but also by larger (metropolitan or national) systems of communication.

Perhaps that is why waiting at traffic lights can feel like a purgatory. We sit in our car at a red light, stymied from participating in the circulatory system those lights regulate and represent. Still, the time spent waiting allows us to inspect our environs. Automotive perception occurs not only while driving at a constant speed, but also while we start or stop, accelerate or decelerate. Automobile viewers often pay more attention to the architecture of major intersections, where there are stop signs or lights, than to that of minor intersections and the middle of blocks. Strumming the steering wheel to a tune on the radio, we may linger on a peculiar building detail or profile, aware that when the light turns green, we will speed away. City driving supplies us with an uneven rhythm of moving and still images, urban compositions that can seem interminable or tantalizingly brief.

Tourist strip, American Southwest

Yet as with railroads, automobile perception unfolds mostly in motion. Driving a city's streets, highways, and bridges affords a rapid succession of building enclosures and openings, approaching and receding objects. And indeed, when driving—when controlling a powerful technology—we can feel as if we have risen above the fray, found a more heroic version of ourselves as we move at will around the world. This spirit is captured in *Babbitt*, Sinclair Lewis's 1922 novel about a prosperous Midwestern businessman, George Babbitt, and his hometown of Zenith, Ohio.

It was in the 1920s that automobiles began to replace railroads as the preferred mode of urban and regional transportation. Unlike mass transit, with its spotty schedules, crowds, and fixed routes, the automobile offered freedom of movement, a personalized way to see things. Sinclair's hero, Babbitt, who is a real estate broker, feels at home in his car as nowhere else; often melancholy, he feels almost cheerful when he gets into his motorcar and rides around the city. Every street, every block and district, from downtown to suburb, interests him. As he drives past rows of residences and businesses, he enjoys the comforting rhythm of the car's mechanical hum and the roadbed's familiar bumps. Lewis describes the views from the car in lyrical terms."[Babbitt] admired each district along his familiar route to the office: The bungalows and shrubs and winding irregular driveways of Floral Heights. The one-story shops on Smith Street, a glare of plate-glass and new yellow brick; groceries and laundries and drug-stores to supply the more immediate needs of East Side housewives. The market gardens in Dutch Hollow, their shanties patched with corrugated iron and stolen doors. Billboards with crimson goddesses nine feet fall advertising cinema films, pipe tobacco, and talcum powder. The old mansions along Ninth Street, S.E., like aged dandies in filthy linen; wooden castles turned into boarding houses, with muddy walks and rusty hedges, jostled by fast-intruding garages, cheap apartment houses, and fruit-stands conducted by bland, sleek Athenians. Across the belt of railroad-tracks, factories with high-perched water-tanks and tall stacks—factories producing condensed milk, paper boxes, lighting fixtures, motorcars. Then the business center, the thickening darting traffic, the crammed trolleys, unloading, and high doorways of marble and polished granite."[28] On Babbitt's daily rounds, houses and gardens,

28. Sinclair Lewis, *Babbitt* (New York: Harcourt, Brace & Co., 1922), 515.

stores and factories, whoosh by. The city begins to seem more like an assort-ment of isolated scenes—a door, a window, twin dormers, a deep porch—than like continuous built space.

Driving around Zenith, Babbitt means business. For the seller of real estate, the exploration of city space, the survey of streets and buildings, promises financial reward. Babbitt knows he must remember patterns of development and of disinvestment. And he knows, too, that if he is to under-stand where money can be made, he must figure out the city's future, where it will grow, and where it will decline. Sinclair Lewis intuited that the mov-ing cityscape, viewed from the privacy and comfort of the car, is a frontier of acquisition.

The automobile's moving cityscape is also a frontier of personal discov-ery. In a car, drivers can concentrate on their zones of special interest. Indeed, they assemble what amounts to their own private version of a place. Instead of being limited to a pedestrian perimeter or rail corridor, they may take unique branching routes to diverse districts, encompassing sites, buildings, or parks of keen interest to them. The automobile view carries with it innumerable editing options, ellipses past dull blocks, or deliberately slow crawls where the archi-tectural action gets thick. The speed, isolation, and autonomy of the automo-bile allow the driver to see the city he or she wants to see.

Published a few years after *Babbitt*, *Orlando*, by Virginia Woolf, assesses automobile culture and its role in shifting the relationship of the individual to society. Like many of her contemporaries, Woolf marveled at how motor-cars enabled people to avoid the repetitious drudgery of walking, and hence to capture the scintillating freshness of new views of places. She observed also how the moving view from a car differed from the sedentary view from a building. Driving allows us to see more, to live more. Woolf compared driv-ers to athletes sprinting across the landscape. Moments after gazing out her London apartment window at the streets and houses below, and realizing her lonely isolation, Woolf's heroine, Orlando, jumps in her motorcar. "Vast blue blocks of building rose into the air; the red cowls of chimneys were spotted irregularly across the sky; the road shone like silver-headed nails; omnibus-es bore down upon her with sculptured white-faced drivers; she noticed sponges, bird-cages, boxes of green American cloth. But she did not allow these sights to sink into her mind even the fraction of an inch as she crossed the narrow plank of the present, lest she should fall into the raging torrent beneath."[29] Driving jolts us out of our thoughts, out of ourselves. Compared with the limited range of sight when we are still, automobile perception presents a marvelous onrush of sensations whose course can (and often does) change at any moment. The automobile driver is confronted by new and sometimes dangerous pictorial compositions. At least for Woolf, writing before gridlock, driving offered the chance to fill one's eyes with the city, to let one's imagination overflow with the potential of what might appear beyond the bend in the road.

Driving is also appealing because in the car we can occupy exterior space and yet be somewhat shielded from it. The car's velocity and steel shell act as buffers between inside and outside, protecting the driver from unpleasant sensations and nasty weather. Passersby and other cars, as Woolf writes, "may buzz and hum around round the plate-glass windows." But they remain at a distance. In contrast, when Orlando gets out of the car, noxious smells and fierce glare envelop her. The visual field opens up too abruptly to the sky and the endless dimensions of the larger environment. No longer framed by the car, the world outside can be disconcerting.

In the car, somewhat removed from the chaos of the city, drivers can explore danger closely, moving through industrial zones or rough neighborhoods, places too daunting to penetrate on foot, vulnerable and unprotected. Through the windshield—made of safety glass—drivers can peer at blocks of dilapidated storefronts, derelict houses, or toxic factories. The automobile enables perceptual immersion amid social distance. Woolf felt that automotive perception was more daring and volatile than pedestrian perception. The city experienced from the car was a new city; the car allowed driver and passengers to transcend their bodies and customary consciousness of space. Watching buildings glide by, absorbed in the gray blur of asphalt or the passing forms of cars and roadside attractions, the driver experiences an architecture expansive and indeterminate, a succession of scenes that never coalesce. The automobile view, in Woolf's mind, could never be realistic like a representational painting or developmental like a novel. It was like abstract art, or even madness. Of a drive, she relates, "Nothing could be seen whole

29. Virginia Woolf, *Orlando: A Biography* [1928] (New York: Harcourt, Brace, Jovanovich, 1956), 299.

or read from start to finish. What was seen begun—like two friends starting to meet each other across the street—was never seen ended. After twenty minutes the body and mind were like scraps of torn paper tumbling from a sack and, indeed, the process of motoring fast out of London so much resembles the chopping up small of body and mind, which precedes unconsciousness and perhaps death."[30]

What was less obvious in the 1920s than today is that the perceptual consciousness of the car would become so ubiquitous, so normative. Not only has the automobile influenced our vision and mentality, it has also affected the design of buildings and cities, their planning, spacing, size, and aesthetics. Much roadside architecture built in the past century has the chopped-up, scrappy, and endlessly looping characteristics of the road journey described by Virginia Woolf. Today, the automobile driver has access to an outsized architectural terrain—to hundreds of thousands of miles of expressways, strips, and back highways, and to countless towns and cities, with their millions of buildings, truck stops, mobile homes, and shopping centers. The potential perceptual experience is individually controllable, but it is not reducible to any narrative or system. The shapes and experiences of the vehicular metropolis resist definition and reduction.

Roland Barthes's "Myth Today," written in 1957, recognizes the insights of Woolf's analysis of the radical character of automotive perceptual aesthetics, and amplifies them. Because the car is a semi-enclosed compartment, the automobile view possesses a strange duality. Are we looking at the car or at the roadside? Are we gazing at the sun's reflection on a far-off building or on the plate of glass inches from our eyes? "If I am in a car and I look at the scenery through the window," Barthes says, "I can at will focus on the scenery or on the window-pane. At one moment I grasp the presence of the glass and the distance of the landscape; at another, on the contrary, the transparence of the glass and the depth of the landscape; but the result of this alternation is constant: the glass is at once present and empty to me, and the landscape unreal and full."[31] This peculiar, distant intimacy with the landscape allows for a range of perceptions within the same glance, from the object in the world to the automotive framing of its view, from the blur of a building wall to the smudge of dirt on the windshield,

30. Woolf, 307.

31. Roland Barthes, "Myth Today," in Mythologies [1957], trans. Annette Lavers (New York: Hill & Wang, 1972), 123–124.

from the larger organization of the world we are navigating to the workings of machines and the passing fancies of mind.

In all modes of the transportation zoomscape, including trains and planes as well as cars, the characteristics of glass—size, angle, reflectivity, level of transparency—influence and inform the journey's vision-track. Paul Virilio, in "Dromoscopy, or the Ecstasy of Enormities," is fascinated by the glazed windshield and its moving picture show. Because of a car's speed and mobility, city driving for Virilio is akin to a complex artistic and psychological experience, an act of creativity empowered by technology. He argues that the violent movement of the car enlivens inanimate objects and that this determines the relationship between driver and landscape. "[T]he object which precipitates itself on the film of the windshield will just as quickly be forgotten as perceived; put back into the prop room, it will disappear out the rear window," writes Virilio. "Let's disabuse ourselves: we are before a veritable 'seventh art,' that of the dashboard."[32]

To a great extent, automobile aesthetics parallel those of the motion pictures. Drivers sit apart in different cars while negotiating and viewing the same city streets; film audiences, too, sit apart in a dark auditorium, engaged in a collective viewing experience. During the early twentieth century, both cars and films began to craft a society of privatized viewing on a mass scale. Yet Virilio's promotion of the new motor art intentionally displaces film from its customary position as the seventh "lively art." Unlike the cinema, where spectators sit still before a picture that moves, automobiles project travelers into the mise-en-scène. Drivers are part spectator, part actor, part artist. They are witness to the gallery of views, and they, too, become an observed object within this gallery. And drivers direct the show, steering, accelerating, and braking to compose the precise sequence, to choose the angle, and to determine the duration of the view. To Virilio, the windshield is more than a window. It is a glass portal through which drivers anticipate the manifold attractions ahead.

"Dromoscopy" combines the Greek words for "road" and "field of view"; to Virilio, it means the study of the automobile's visual aesthetics of penetration. Dromoscopic perception thus differs from panoramic perception. Unlike that steady, lateral vision out the side of an automobile or train, separated from

32. Paul Virilio, "Dromoscopy, or The Ecstasy of Enormities," *Wide Angle* 20.3 (July 1998), 11–12.

the field of view, dromoscopic perception plunges us into the visual field. It is defined less by the languid gaze at passing forms and building outlines than by a headlong immersion into a free space of movement around which buildings recede. If panoramic perception resembles a linear stroll past pictures in a museum, dromoscopic perception is more like an imaginative leap into the perspectival space of one of those pictures. If panoramic perception turns buildings into objects of distanced reflection, dromoscopic perception approaches the built world through possibilities of engagement, tunneling through passages, turning to avoid collisions, always pursuing a distant horizon. Like a forward track or zoom in a film, the experience of looking out the front windshield of a car, especially on hills or curves, can feel delirious.

And as Virilio points out, automotive dromoscopy accomplishes these feats in real time and real space. Drivers do not look through the windshield at scenes that are themselves changing, as the scenes in a film change through editing. In the car the experience is analogous to the long tracking take—the same moving shot without cuts. Cars move through the same glass portal endlessly. Driving sight is pure circulation, vision pumping through the streets of a city. "This metal box flows through the arteries of the city," Francoise Sagan writes of a drive through Paris, "and slips between its banks, emerging into squares, as if circulating in some vast vascular system it has no wish to block."[33]

EXPRESSWAYS

Driving an expressway through a city radically rearranges urban interaction. These limited-access roads, without traffic lights or intersections, thrust through cities in what becomes their separate space. More like railroads than vehicular roads, expressways are disengaged from their surroundings. Their massive infrastructure separates cars from the architecture and neighborhoods they pass through. At ground level, this same infrastructure often cuts neighborhoods apart. Waste spaces proliferate on the roadway's edges and undersides. Gazing at the roadside along many urban expressways reveals a succession of stores and office parks, but also container-storage lots, blank-walled distribution centers, factories, garbage dumps, and flimsy housing.

33. Francoise Sagan, *With Fondest Regards*, trans. Christine Donougher (New York: E.P. Dutton, 1985), 67.

And yet the much-maligned expressway puts motion and momentum into the larger substance of cities.[34] Expressways knit cities together as much as they tear them apart. On a metropolitan scale, these high-speed roads function as a kind of basilica for automobile culture,[35] their multiple lanes veering as do processional naves, their exit ramps allowing cars to turn onto the side aisles of city streets and the altars of individual destination.

Expressways are zones of movement that catalyze new modes of habitation, a transportation infrastructure that now constitutes its own landscape.[36] The ultimate venue for smooth, dromoscopic projection, expressways (or highways, motorways, parkways, turnpikes, thruways, and freeways) offer great insights. Automobile viewers experience buildings deformed by speed, differentiated into images streaming by windows and mirrors—a sensation of floating through space that is itself floating. The landscape becomes a scenic backdrop in motion, and architectural landmarks turn into actors of the wide windshield.[37] Freeways, as John Cornell wrote in 1941, promise an efficient and smooth magical motion tour. "Now I know how a package feels when it gets an unobstructed ride through a chute to the shipping department," he writes. "I've just made a run out to Pasadena on the completed Arroyo Seco Parkway. From the relatively narrow Figueroa tunnels you immediately find yourself launched like a speedboat in a calm, spacious, divided channel. Channel is the word, too, for it's in the arroyo, below the level of traffic-tormented streets. No brazen pedestrians nor kids riding bikes with their arms folded. No cross streets with too-bold or too-timid drivers jutting their radiators into your path. And no wonder I made it from Elysian Park to Broadway and Glenarm Street in Pasadena in ten minutes without edging over a conservative forty-five miles an hour."[38]

The first limited-access road was built in New York. The Bronx River Parkway begins as a thin concrete strip at the northern edge of the Bronx that curves in harmony with the rolling topography of Westchester County, and for much of the way the road camouflages adjacent buildings with lush plantings. Drivers pass under concrete bridges clad in native stone, along a route lined with trees and meadows—hence the term "parkway." Completed in 1925 (and extended south into the Bronx by 1950), the Bronx River Parkway eventually comprised twenty-five miles of graceful curves and

34. Bruce Webb, "Engaging the Highway, *A + U* 94 (October 1994), 99.

35. David Brodsly, *LA Freeway* (Berkeley: University of California Press, 1981), 5, 24.

36. Edward Dimendberg, "The Will to Motorization: Cinema, Highways, & Modernity," *October* 73 (Summer 1995), 95, 114.

37. Phil Patton, *Open Road: A Celebration of the American Highway* (New York: Simon & Schuster, 1986), 129.

forested vistas. A revolutionary city space was thus created, a motorized environment that was akin to the picturesque panoramas favored by nine-teenth-century park designers like Frederick Law Olmsted, and was a descendant of his two Brooklyn parkways, Ocean Parkway and Eastern Parkway. But with the Bronx River Parkway, picturesque ideas of city plan-ning merged with modernist maxims. This parkway created a new function-al environment devoted exclusively to high-speed car travel—trucks and buses are banned. It also treated motorists to an aesthetic experience, a pleasure road where automobiles move fluidly, their journey undisturbed by disagreeable sights. To this day, the view remains serene and the speed of travel faster than that of city streets.

If the Bronx River Parkway is a vision of an automotive Eden, then the Cross-Bronx Expressway, which bisects the parkway's southern stretch, is limited-access hell. Construction of this seven-mile, six-lane route was com-pleted in 1963. It was one of the most difficult highways projects in history, blasting through ridges, crossing valleys, displacing infrastructure, and lead-ing to the demolition of thousands of tenements in some of New York's poor-est neighborhoods. To drive on the Cross-Bronx Expressway is to experience the worst aspects of expressways. The common experience here is not the adrenaline rush of speed, but the mounting frustration of stalled traffic. Nor are the sights bucolic or calming. At its eastern end, the Cross-Bronx is a maze of crisscrossing lanes spewed out by various bridges and highways, a tangle of concrete that calls to mind the work of sculptor Mark di Suvero. To the west, in Manhattan, the Cross-Bronx is submerged under a residential megastructure supported by piles that straddle the roadway—a design solu-tion once heralded as an ideal of urban habitation. At other points, the expressway squeezes under bridges and elevated train tracks. Its longest stretch powers through a gaseous cavern scarred by graffiti, garbage, and the occasional junked car. To cultural critic Marshall Berman, in his 1982 *All That Is Solid Melts Into Air*, the road offered views mostly of aggressive trucks struggling to get out of the Bronx as quickly as possible. "A glance at the cityscape to the north and south—it is hard to get more than quick glances, because much of the road is below ground and bounded by brick walls ten feet high—will suggest why; hundreds of boarded-up abandoned

38. John Cornell, "Riverbed Route, UN-Ltd.," *Westways* (January 1941), n.p.

buildings and charred and burnt-out hulks of buildings; dozens of blocks covered with nothing at all but shattered bricks and waste."[39] For a while during the 1980s and 1990s, some of the window openings on empty buildings were covered by painted wooden panels (provided by the city government) of puffy clouds and blue sky. But nobody was fooled; the Cross-Bronx Expressway was not picturesque, not even for an instant.

On a scale of aesthetics, most urban expressways lie somewhere between the two Bronx roads. Because no other North American city is as dense as New York, the construction of limited-access highways through urban neighborhoods has not been as disruptive in other places—the Central Artery that cuts through downtown Boston, built during the 1950s and now being replaced by a tunnel, is a notable exception. But no other metropolitan area has developed a parkway system comparable to that of New York— Lake Shore Drive in Chicago and Storrow Drive in Boston are singular parkways in those cities. To experience the widest range of highway views, New York is the place to go.

The single greatest construction project in American history was the Interstate Highway System, begun in 1956, and originally called the National System of Interstate and Defense Highways by the Eisenhower administration. Largely completed by the early 1980s, no building endeavor has so significantly transformed the American landscape in so short a time. During the twenty-five years of intense construction, the appearance of American cities changed more than in any comparable period. Unlike in Europe, where highways connect cities and rarely penetrate past their early-twentieth-century perimeters, in America, expressways slice apart the city. Unlike in Japan, where highways are usually elevated, huge tracts of land in America are dedicated to the expressway. The continuous built fabric between downtowns and inner districts was interrupted almost everywhere by the new superhighways. Albany and St. Louis had their riverfronts cut off from their downtowns. Atlanta and Houston found their downtowns ringed by new roadways. Expressways carved their way through old industrial corridors, declining commercial arteries, and, when all other routes failed, as in the Bronx, straight through dense residential neighborhoods. Since the onset of the interstate, it has become difficult to experience most cities through a

39. Marshall Berman, *All That Is Solid Melts Into Air: The Experience of Modernity* (New York: Simon & Schuster, 1982), 291.

Church of the Autostrada, Giovanni Michelucci, architect

long walk between downtown and outlying neighborhoods. What is more, the interstates not only restructured cities; they also shifted metropolitan dynamism to the periphery. The Capitol Beltway, circling the Washington area and completed in 1964, was one of the first circumferential highways around an older city. Today, more of the region's business activity radiates out from its forty interchanges than from the downtown.

Early opposition to the expressways focused less on their reshaping of urban geography and commerce than on their reshaping of vision. One early critic was Lewis Mumford, whose diatribe against the automobile, "The Highway and the City," dramatized the differences between roads like the Bronx River Parkway and the Cross-Bronx Expressway. To Mumford, writing in 1958, the new urban highways were creating a hellish urban environment worse than the industrial railway corridor. The limited-access roads unfolded new viewing environments of interminable concrete roadway, cloverleaf interchanges, complicated multilevel overpasses. They damaged not only the traditional city, but the sensibilities of motorists as well. To Mumford, roads like the Taconic Parkway or Bronx River Parkway represented the rare instances of the highway as a work of art. This was accomplished by "routing the well-separated roads along the ridgeways, following the contours, and thus, by this single stratagem, both avoiding towns and villages and opening up great views across country, enhanced by lavish planting."[40] The highway should concentrate a motorist's attention not on the architecture of the roadway or roadside but instead on carefully planned views of nature.

Even at the time, Mumford's promotion of a parkway picturesque was dated. From a perceptual point of view, many others saw the new highways as exciting and important. One of the first freeway manifestos was Christopher Tunnard and Boris Pushkarev's 1963 *Man-Made America: Chaos or Control?* The authors explore the aesthetics of expressways, and recognize their potential to become compositions of twisting concrete planes. Tunnard and Pushkarev appreciate how the expressway's "slab and its shoulder form an unwinding ribbon of parallel lines, swinging and changing into various horizontal and inclined planes, standing out in stark white or black against the soft, warm colors of the landscape."[41] Like many such tracts written in the 1960s, *Man-Made America* envisions the expressway as something like an

40. Lewis Mumford, *The Highway and the City* (New York: Harcourt, Brace & World, 1963), 236.

41. Christopher Tunnard and Boris Pushkarev, *Man-Made America: Chaos or Control?* (New Haven: Yale University Press, 1963), 177.

outdoor museum of mobile expressionist sculpture. Although designed by highway engineers and not architects, the expressway was not merely functional. It was a work of art. Years later, in 1995, this sentiment was captured in the photographs that make up Catherine Opie's "Freeway" series, which interpret the various forms of ramps and intersections, and create compositions of straight piers and leaping planes.

The View from the Road, published in 1964, treats the expressway in terms less aesthetic than does *Man-Made America*. For the authors, Donald Appleyard, Kevin Lynch, and John R. Myers, the highway experience mingles technological and artistic perception. Like the views available to pedestrians in historic cities, the views of a large modern city from its highways help us to comprehend the form and meaning of a place. But unlike the pedestrian view, the highway view supplies a new type of machine-driven knowledge. In an extended analysis of the approach to Central Boston over the Mystic River Bridge (now Interstate 95), the authors describe a variety of views and panoramas that exhibit the interplay of major and minor architectural experience and of stable landmarks and rushing cityscape.[42] "Would it be possible to use the highway as a means of education, a way of making the driver aware of the function, history, and human values of his world? The highway could be a linear exposition, running by the vital centers, exposing the working parts, picking out the symbols and historical landmarks. Signs might be used for something more than giving directions or pressing a sale. They could point out the meaning of the scene."[43]

Views from the expressway, especially when the roadway is elevated, resemble the edifying vistas from a train. The motorist is within a moving auditorium, experiencing a distanced metropolis; compared to city driving, highway driving, with its constant and uninterrupted speed, facilitates a smooth and cinematic mode of perception. For the forward-facing highway driver, however, unlike the side-glancing train or car passenger, the roadway in front comprises the bulk of the view. The perceptual experience feels more dromoscopic than panoramic, like the passage across a threshold and into a building. But contrary to driving on city streets, on the expressway the threshold extends indefinitely. Motorists navigate an infinite space, a relentlessly linear slab of asphalt or concrete, framed by cars, guardrails, retaining walls,

42. Donald Appleyard, Kevin Lynch, and John R. Myers, *The View from the Road* (Cambridge: MIT Press, 1964), 29.

43. Appleyard, Lynch, and Myers, 17.

signage, and, to the sides, by cityscape—all rushing by. And occasionally, in tunnels or on bridges, roadway elements become substantial and compelling—the riveted piers and trusses of a bridge, the tiled barrel vaults of a tunnel.

Lawrence Halprin's *Freeways* argues that, given the forward trajectory of vehicular movement, the form of the road itself should be the principal object of the automobile view and road designer.[44] Unlike the authors of *The View from the Road*, Halprin emphasizes views *of* the road. To Halprin, a landscape architect, whatever buildings line the freeway are in the way. They interfere with the driver's appreciation of the highway's design, its composition of structural forces. Halprin is no advocate of parkways that cloister the motorist's view in greenery. Instead, following *Man-Made America*, he argues that the freeway should allow the fast-moving motorist sufficient time to concentrate on the elements of the roadway—on the straightaway or curve, on even planes and ascending or descending slopes, on cylindrical or orthogonal piers and supports. Halprin saw freeway design as an art, the infrastructural equivalent of action painting. Inspired by the turbulent brushwork and color pulsations of abstract expressionist painters, Halprin preferred the windshield view of the energetic abstract forms of the freeway to the side view of the old and staid city. Freeways, he says, inscribe the city with running and crisscrossing geometries. Their surfaces, smooth and continuous, curve expertly, avoiding awkward angles. Their supports taper almost to the road's underbelly, dovetailing verticality and horizontality. Climbing to the sky, splitting off in different directions and descending to street level, the freeway delights our eyes in an almost aerial composition of ramps and overpasses. When we drive, writes Halprin, the freeway structure turns into a kinesthetic "calligraphy where the laws of motion generate a geometry which is part engineering, part painting, part sculpture, but mostly an exercise in choreography in the landscape."[45] Newer expressways continue these structural gymnastics. At five-level interchanges—whose heights can reach 150 feet—lanes peel off and bend overhead like the hulls of ships. Torqued overpasses spindle around piers. Cloverleafs, wishbones, and figure eights are geometrical intricacies that express the weaving together of the metropolis better than any other architectural form.

44. Lawrence Halprin, *Freeways* (New York: Reinhold, 1966), 23.

45. Halprin, 37.

Can the freeway's choreography of the landscape be experienced apart from its environment? Can the expressway be seen as a place apart, as if one were traveling in an aboveground tunnel? Would we even want to ignore the cityscape visible from the roadway? So much of the expressway view, like all vehicular views, projects onto the roadside. Sometimes there is not far to look. In older cities, buildings crowd the road and constrict perception between highway walls and building walls. On the Massachusetts Turnpike through Boston, the lanes come so close to buildings that the roadway's boundaries seem to dissolve into brick walls. On the Jackie Robinson Parkway through Brooklyn and Queens, bends in the roadway continually lead one to look out into the vast complex of adjoining cemeteries.

Even in the suburbs, the expressway view can be constricting. Increasingly, banal sound barriers wall off subdivisions, while the backs of many shopping centers present only expanses of windowless boxes and small signs or logos advertising chain stores. Sometimes the suburban prospect affords longer-range views. But these, too, can be homogeneous— acres of rooftops, antennae, and treetops. Especially in areas lacking topographic variety, expressway driving is monotonous. No wonder, then, that more and more of the roadside has been designed to accommodate the dulled or disinterested perception of the expressway driver. Avoiding the places it passes through, the expressway acknowledges them mainly through city and street names.[46] At intersections, tall skinny poles support signs for motels, fast-food joints, and gas stations—usually fluorescent tubes sheathed in plastic that blaze down on the roadway. Buildings along the expressway are seen for only seconds, and bright colors and conspicuous rooflines serve as visual logos for companies eager to engage viewers moving at superhighway speeds.[47] Millions of people see buildings and places only in such brief cameos. An ever-accumulating series of such fragments makes up the new "vision-bite" architecture of the expressway zoomscape.

Highway viewing alternates between the complexity of these roadside views and the relative minimalism of the roadway itself. Drivers must watch the road, but they also seek diversion, and their field of vision includes both the happenstance and the predictable. Certain elements appear consistently in the changing landscape of any roadside. Often such structures—a down-

46. Marc Augé, *Non-Places: Introduction to an Anthropology of Supermodernity*, trans. John Howe (London: Verso, 1995), 98.

47. Patton, 215.

town skyscraper, a hilltop tower—remain in view for long periods, giving some order to the roadside bedlam. Driving west toward St. Louis through Illinois, the sprawling suburbs sidle up to the expressway long before the Gateway Arch comes into sight. One could be anywhere. Then the arch looms into view, part of the picture in the windshield, and the otherwise disparate features of the suburban roadscape become part of a shared metropolitan identity. Consider Jonathan Holden's "An Introduction to New Jersey," which describes a departure from Manhattan:

> the slow, spiraling climb
> out of Lincoln Tunnel—
> how as you rise the whole
> midtown skyline rises with you
> like a wall of lighted new spring
> while columns of headlights
> floating queasily somehow hold
> formation, though every driver's
> drunk—how the viaduct
> finally slings all lanes off
> strict west toward Secaucus,
> Newark, Delaware Water Gap,
> side by side at seventy,
> the Empire State a lighted target
> fastened to your back while
> all about you flakes of light
> fly faster.[48]

Holden captures the transformative sensations of expressway driving, the feelings of solid buildings running swiftly past, almost liquefying, of immaterial lights becoming substantial, almost solid. Vehicular impressions of the city mix up matter and energy, fixed architecture and mobile transportation. The road and the other cars bob up and down like waves, each swell revealing different buildings. Buildings may look flexible and transient, while the road stays steady. A single structure might dominate the vehicular view. In

48. Jonathan Holden, "An Introduction to New Jersey," in *Drive, They Said: Poems About Americans and Their Cars*, ed. Kurt Brown (Minneapolis: Milkweed Press, 1994), 308.

Holden's poem, the Empire State Building remains the fixed, if receding focal point in the viewer's stream of visual consciousness.

Like the train view, the automobile view is inherently unstable; to focus on one object is to make other objects seem ever more volatile. Focusing on anterior or posterior landmarks might serve to immobilize them, but doing so will make other objects seem to swim around them. In *The View from the Road*, the authors describe how details and textures radiate from the center point straight ahead—how a building can hover over the road. As they write, "Landmarks may move against a background or a foreground, be caught in a moving frame, be masked and revealed, or rotate first one way and then another. Two important landmarks may come into conjunction, to give a powerful sense of being 'on line,'"[49] Through the forward motion of the car, such landmarks become larger as we approach them. Staring straight ahead or behind in a car, we stare hard at—almost penetrate—the horizon, as we move toward (or away from) an architectural goal. From an expressway, though, one never reaches the true threshold into the city. Our steady progress toward a landmark or to downtown ends abruptly on an exit ramp—a degrading conclusion to the magisterial views of the expressway.

The view from the car is volatile in other ways, too. Sudden changes in speed transform the driver's visual field. A traffic jam can jerk the car to a halt, and the stalled motorist will observe unexpected views. A drive on Interstate 95 north of Miami through the suburbs of snowbirds, when the traffic is heavy, can become a visual detour into backyards with swimming pools, palm trees, and half-naked sunbathers. Stuck in traffic, we scrutinize the features of places that passed unnoticed when we zipped by at high speed. And this sort of close viewing can seem somehow voyeuristic, as if we are seeing something we are not meant to see. And of course, stopped in traffic, cars, too, lose their sense of inviolability—the expressway can feel uncomfortably like a public forum, as we peer at other drivers, and they peer back.

In California, freeways are a way of life, an infrastructure of urban hardscape softened by natural scenery. In Los Angeles, the speed and access demanded of the freeway system have led to a priority on efficiency,[50] roadways dominated by the anxiety of commuting and the inevitability of traffic delays. Yet the Los Angeles freeways offer more than just transportation and

49. Appleyard, Lynch, and Myers, 11.

50. Christian Zapatka, *The American Landscape* (New York: Princeton Architectural Press, 1995), 127.

frustration. To drive on them is to become powerfully aware of the astounding expanse of the vehicular metropolis: the nodal bursts of skyscrapers and shopping centers; the miles of low-rise industrial, commercial, or residential buildings lorded over by palm trees; and in the distance the mountains. The freeways are an unexpectedly comprehensible place. The architectural historian Reyner Banham called them "Autopia," and saw them as one of the region's key structural features, a realm at once private and public. "Coming off the freeway is coming in from outdoors," he writes. "A domestic or sociable journey in Los Angeles does not end so much at the door of one's destination as at the off-ramp of the freeway, the mile or two of ground-level streets count as no more than the front drive of the house."[51]

The Los Angeles freeways form a gigantic network that can feel oddly like home—a kind of residence in fluid movement. If one is crossing from Orange County to the San Fernando Valley, many potential routes, different stepladders of freeway transitions and progressions present themselves, as the signs for the San Bernardino, the Harbor, the Ventura, and the Pasadena Freeways point to their miles of asphalt. This infinite system for seamless, forking progression is an important setting in Joan Didion's *Play It As It Lays*. The novel's protagonist, Maria, spends her days driving the freeways of Southern California at high speed, the radio at high volume. Maria navigates the freeways expertly, moving diagonally across four lanes of traffic to reach an exit without braking or losing the beat on the radio. But even in Los Angeles, the adventure of the freeway has its limits. "Sometimes the freeway ran out, in a scrap metal yard in San Pedro or on the main street of Palmdale or out somewhere no place at all where the flawless burning concrete just stopped, turned into common road, abandoned construction sheds rusting beside it. When that happened she would keep in careful control, portage skillfully back, feel for the first time the heavy weight of the becalmed car beneath her and try to keep her eyes on the mainstream, the great pilings, the Cyclone fencing, the deadly oleander, the luminous signs, the organism which absorbed all her reflexes, all her attention." [52]

In San Francisco, with its dense development and hilly topography, the freeways draw out new facets of the city's personality. In "You Have to Pay for the Public Life," first published in 1965, the architect Charles Moore remarks on seeing the city from the highway. "Much of the public excitement

51. Reyner Banham, *Los Angeles: The Architecture of Four Ecologies* (New York: Harper & Row, 1971), 213.

52. Joan Didion, *Play It As It Lays* (New York: Farrar, Straus & Giroux, 1970), 16.

about San Francisco's small dramatic skyline is a function of the capacity to see it, a capacity which is greatly enhanced by the bridges (themselves major California monuments), by the freeways that lead to them, and now by the freeway that comes up from the south and breaks through the hills in the nick of time for a magnificent view of San Francisco."[53] Although the most famous gateways to San Francisco are the Golden Gate and Bay Bridges, the entries from the freeways south of town are surprisingly dramatic. Driving north on Interstate 101 or 280, the motorist registers the sharp break with the natural scenery of San Francisco Bay and San Bruno Mountain, as clusters of office buildings and shopping centers come into view. Turning a corner, motorists are flooded with urban views of undulating hillsides, dense with housing, with gleaming white and bright pastel buildings. Only on the freeways, moving at a fast clip and sweeping round a bend, do we see the vernacular city unfold and reveal itself.

From California to New York, expressways enhance a sense of urban place—they are places to be viewed and places to view the city from. Aside from the el train, the most dynamic place from which to see the Chicago skyline is Lake Shore Drive. In Houston, the skyscrapers have been designed to be seen from the expressways, and postcards feature views of major intersections.[54] Expressways unify the increasingly vast metropolis (much as the television news does). Along with the mass media, expressways have helped to generate the contemporary notion of place as a temporary, changing, and restless conglomeration of individuals. As Jean Baudrillard notes, in *America*, "freeways don't de-nature the city or the landscape, they simply pass through it and unravel it."[55] The limited-access highway carries the penetrating automobile view described by Paul Virilio to its inevitable conclusion. On the swift lanes, there is the maddening notion that countless other nomads are seeing the same landscape out ahead, and driving just as fast into its void.

ROAD FEVER

One of the great lures of the automobile is the promise of escape, escape from the confines of buildings and cities, of personal commitments and social obligations. The automobile promises free movement through landscape, out on the open road. Especially after the Second World War,

53. Charles Moore, "You Have to Pay for the Public Life," *Perspecta* 9/10 (1965), 95.

54. Patton, 110, 115.

55. Jean Baudrillard, *America*, trans. Chris Turner (London: Verso, 1988), 53.

Americans got restless and hit the road. With the federal government constructing highways ocean to ocean, the road offered refuge, a new place around the bend or over the hill, a light and easy existence behind the wheel. Since the highways went almost everywhere, they combined destination with journey, offering the myth of freedom and endless opportunity. Because of the scale of the American landscape, only the zoomscape gives us an overall sense of it. In "Driving the American Landscape," the artist Andrew Cross remarks that the history of the United States could be told as the history of the frames through which the landscape is viewed—first railroads, then motion pictures, then the airplane and, of course, the windshield of the automobile. "Today, there is no landscape if it is not seen through the windscreen, only a series of places, postcard snapshots separated by time and space. It is only within the frame of the windscreen that places co-exist, that they become animated along the continuous narratives of the landscape through which you drive."[56]

Across the pages of Jack Kerouac's On the Road, published in 1957, the cities of America loom, recede, and churn together in feverish motion (and at a feverish pace). In the compartments of cars, buses, and trucks, the hero, Sal Paradise, travels thousands of miles. Rarely stopping, he experiences cities as brief interruptions of the car's delirious velocity. Kerouac describes cities in terms of light and smoke, energy and air. "The distant lights of El Paso and Juarez," he says of West Texas, are "sown in a tremendous valley so big that you could see several railroads puffing at the same time in every direction."[57] Chicago is memorable not for its architectural landmarks, but for its smoking, glowing factories. Des Moines is as vaporous as the clouds wafting over the cornfields. Smokestacks, rail yards, and faraway buildings are all we hear of Denver. Los Angeles is decipherable only at night, with its sprawl of mysterious light. For Kerouac's road warriors, cities are reduced to flashes; complex and lengthy descriptions of place are incompatible with the road's onward ethic of detachment.

Kerouac's only sustained descriptions of cities occur at the end of the road, where one can drive no further. Heading toward San Francisco, Sal Paradise exclaims, "I suddenly realized I was in California. Warm, palmy air—air you can kiss—and palms. Along the storied Sacramento River on a

56. Andrew Cross, "Driving the American Landscape," in Autopia: Cars and Culture, eds., Peter Wollen and Joe Kerr (London: Reaktion Books, 2002), 255.

57. Jack Kerouac, On the Road (New York: Viking Press, 1957), 134–35.

superhighway; into the hills again; up, down; and suddenly the vast expanse of bay (it was just before dawn) with the sleepy lights of Frisco festooned across."[58] And later he says, "we began rolling in the foothills before Oakland and suddenly reached a height and saw stretched out ahead of us the fabulous white city of San Francisco on her eleven mystic hills with the blue Pacific and its advancing wall of potato-patch fog beyond, and smoke and goldenness in the late afternoon of time.... And [we] drove into the Oakland Bay Bridge and it carried us in. The downtown office buildings were just sparkling on their lights; it made you think of Sam Spade."[59] From the car, San Francisco's outcropping of tall buildings and bridges, rising up from the bay, surrounded by mountains, look almost like a movie. Perhaps because of their cinematic qualities, their ability to mimic a sequence of establishing shots, the sights of San Francisco captivate Sal Paradise.

The romance of the road has never really died. Many Americans live their landscape dreams on the road, even if some of the dreams are reflected off cinema screens and television sets—buddy flicks that roam about the red canyons of the West, and car commercials that use those same locations to promote a vehicular aesthetic of liberated perception. Millions of people reside in mobile-home parks and millions more cruise the continent in recreational vehicles. Increasingly, RVs, vans, SUVs, and trucks comprise a bulky yet mobile roadway architecture—structures by which to view the landscape in motion. *Fast Lanes*, Jayne Anne Phillips's 1987 novel, is set in the spacious confines of a truck. Phillips understands the roadside cinematically, as a looping reel of features and trailers. In her novel, a trucker's sense of place elongates from the driver's compartment to the endless highway. "[T]here was the windshield as the continual movie past the glass. It was good driving into the movie.... The truck is what there really was: him and me and the radio, the shell of the space, thin carpet over a floor that reverberated with a hollow ping if you stamped down hard. There were rear-view mirrors turning all that receded sideways, holing the light in glints and angles and the pastels in detached, flat pictures so that any reflected object—car, fence, billboard—seemed just a shape, miraculous in motion."[60] To Phillips's protagonist, each place passed through was merely a point on a gigantic connect-the-dots.

58. Ibid., 50.

59. Ibid., 141.

60. Jayne Anne Phillips, *Fast Lanes* (New York: E.P. Dutton, 1987), 49–50.

How many of us live mobile in dashes from Tucson to Tucumcari, Tehachapi to Tonapah, and pass off all the rest? Are motion and its visual aesthetics a national religion? And does this new faith of the road turn landscape into a schizophrenic mix of escape and confinement? In the 1950s, the photographer Robert Frank traveled the roads of America, critiquing the automobile's relationship to landscape. "U.S. 285, New Mexico" shows a straight highway extending to the horizon, surrounded by nothing but dirt and sky, and one oncoming car off in the distance where the road gently dips. Even on the most deserted of roads, there is always someone else coming toward us, entering our private space and ruining our dream of escape. "Public Park, Ann Arbor Michigan" shows a group of people picnicking on a Sunday afternoon. The landscape is dominated, however, by automobiles parked all over the grass. Chrome bumpers and open car doors intrude on two couples lying on blankets on the lawn. And one picnicker even stays in the car.

The automobile promises freedom through mobility, but the dream can become a nightmare.[61] John Updike's *Rabbit Run*, published in 1960, explores this conundrum in excruciating detail. Early in the novel, a young man, Rabbit Angstrom, sets out from his house on foot with an inventory of errands. Suddenly repelled by the buildings and landscape around him, unhappy in his disappointing marriage and scared of approaching middle age, he takes to the road. Heading south from his Pennsylvania hometown, Rabbit finds himself on a roadway where the cars "run along together like sticks on a stream."[62] In this stream, he is no longer lost. He feels part of the great anonymous flow of highway movement. The familiar sights of the road evoke the excitement of youth. "Square high farmhouses nuzzle the road. Soft chalk sides. In one town a tavern blazes and he stops at a hardware store opposite with two gasoline pumps outside."[63]

But soon Rabbit feels threatened, as traffic and signals impede his flow. Nearing Philadelphia, he turns onto a road leading to the countryside. Escaping the city, Rabbit yearns to leave behind the steadiness of place, the weariness of routine. But he is too timid to follow the open road, which begins to unravel "with infuriating slowness, its black wall wearilessly rising in front of his headlights no matter how they twist. . . . The land refuses to change. The more he drives the more the region resembles the country

61. Cynthia Dettelbach, *In the Driver's Seat: The Automobile in American Literature and Popular Culture* (Westport, Connecticut: Greenwood Press, 1976), 120.

62. John Updike, *Rabbit Run* (New York: Alfred A. Knopf, 1960), 24.

63. Ibid., 26.

around Mt. Judge. The same scruff on the embankments, the same weathered billboards for the same products you wondered anybody would ever want to buy. At the upper edge of his headlight beams the naked tree-twigs make the same net. Indeed the net seems thicker now."[64]

In the middle of the night, Rabbit throws his map out the window and turns homeward. The trip becomes easier, the closer he gets to home. "He comes into Brewer from the south, seeing it in the smoky shadow before dawn as a gradual multiplication of houses among the trees beside the road and then as a treeless waste of industry, shoe factories and bottling plants and company parking lots and knitting mills converted to electronics parts and elephantine gas tanks lifting above trash-filled swampland yet lower than the blue edge of the mountain from whose crest Brewer was a warm carpet woven around a single shade of brick."[65] More precise architectural descriptions accompany the return journey. Buildings that had seemed repellant are now welcoming. In rejecting the detachment of the open road, in trading fleeting road views for detailed hometown close-ups, Rabbit flings himself into the embrace of home. The road journey, however, prefigures extraordinary turbulence. The disintegration of details epitomized by the view from the night highway suggests a greater social disintegration of values—the turbulence of automotive mobility can carry into other parts of life.

The journeys in *Rabbit Run*, *On the Road*, and other road novels suggest the dilemmas of a vehicular perception premised on velocity, isolation, and an infinite horizon. The horizon might be the ultimate architecture of the automobile view. Yet the horizon will always remain elusive, and perhaps, in the grip of motion, even destructive of three-dimensional built form. For Robert Smithson, on a road trip in Mexico, the horizon was both threshold and wall. "Driving away from Merida down Highway 261 one becomes aware of the indifferent horizon," he wrote. "Quite apathetically it rests on the ground devouring everything that looks like something. One is always crossing the horizon, yet it always remains distant. In this line where sky meets earth, objects cease to exist. Since the car was at all times on some leftover horizon, one might say that the car was imprisoned in a line."[66] In good weather, on a flat road, the horizon can induce a peculiar feeling of stasis, similar to the stillness of vision experienced at high altitudes.

64. Ibid., 34.

65. Ibid., 39.

66. Robert Smithson, "Incidents of Mirror-Travel in the Yucatan," in *Robert Smithson: The Collected Writings*, ed. Jack Flam (Berkeley: University of California Press, 1996), 119.

In this quest, the road itself can become mesmerizing—its dark pavement, the yellow and white lines, the telephone poles and streetlights, the roadside architecture whipping by. In his 1990 *The Music of Chance*, Paul Auster evokes this sort of road fever. Early in the novel, the hero, James Nashe, inherits a great deal of money from his father, and impulsively leaves his daughter and everything else for life on the road. He drives the back roads of America, coast to coast, paying little attention to the landscape, seeing essentially nothing. "Speed was of the essence, the joy of sitting in the car and hurtling himself through space. That became a good beyond all others, a hunger to be fed at any price. Nothing around him lasted for more than a moment, and as one moment followed another, it was as though he alone continued to exist. He was a fixed point in a whirl of changes, a body poised in utter stillness as the world rushed through him and disappeared."[67] To Nashe, driving becomes the only reality. In a car, at times, the built environment becomes evanescent, as the driver watches a detached world fleeting by.[68] Louise Erdrich, in her 1986 novel *The Beet Queen*, evokes a similar kind of highway vertigo. When driving, she writes, an empty stretch of highway "stayed so much the same, in fact, that at one point I seemed suspended, my wheels spinning in thin air. I hung motionless in speed above the earth like a fixed star."[69] In the grip of pure movement, the physique and perception of architecture can reduce to a dimension of one.

67. Paul Auster, *The Music of Chance* (New York: Viking Press, 1990), 11–12.

68. Kristin Ross, *Fast Cars, Clean Bodies: Decolonialization and the Reordering of French Culture* (Cambridge: MIT Press, 1995), 39

69. Louise Erdrich, *The Beet Queen* (New York: Henry Holt and Company, 1986), 320.

Eastern Washington

CHAPTER 3

AIRPLANE

IN 1903, ON A SPIT OF LAND at Kitty Hawk, North Carolina, Orville Wright's twelve-second flight ten feet in the air made history. The attempt to pilot a flying machine, dating back centuries, had finally succeeded. Commercial air service began in 1914, and airplanes became a spectacular feature of battle in the First World War. By the 1920s, governments had begun to form national airlines, and after Charles Lindbergh's nonstop flight from New York to Paris in 1927, aviation became big business. In 1934, the Boeing 247 was unveiled, accommodating ten passengers and cruising at 155 miles per hour; by 1958, the Boeing 707 jet airliner could carry 184 passengers and travel at 550 miles per hour. Aircraft now offered the fastest transportation available, crossing continents and oceans in half a day.

The airplane provides a fresh way of seeing the world. Above roads and rail corridors, above walls and embankments, passengers watch buildings grow into cities and cities grow into regions. Our sight becomes global. Such large perceptions begin on the runway. Planes take off from the largest open spaces in metropolitan areas, spaces that offer greater viewing expanses than either railroads or highways. At low altitudes, the bird's-eye or oblique view from a small plane or helicopter glides over rooftops, and buildings recede and assemble into city portraits. From jets at greater heights, passengers gaze at the built environment from a perpendicular or vertical position; from this vantage, structures flatten into lines and planes. For frequent flyers, the takeoffs and landings, the portraits and cartographies of the aerial view, lead to a mode of seeing detached from place, stretched out in distance.

In aerial ascent, as the land falls away, the view fills with space. The airplane joins sensations of spatial immensity with those of confinement, epitomized by the contrast between the vast sky and the compact cabin. Similar to trains or cars, the aircraft acts as surrogate architecture, providing tighter constraints but also greater opportunities. Pilots see straight ahead through windows that approximate an automobile windshield; commercial passengers peer through small lozenge-shaped side windows. As do train passengers, air travelers rarely see what is ahead, and instead witness a constantly receding horizon. The sideways air view might include as well a bit of wing, engine, propeller, or helicopter blade, technological reminders of this most uncustomary of human points of view.

Oakland, California

Strangely enough, only minutes into a flight, airborne sight is untouched
by speed. On the ground, the velocity of trains and automobiles catapults
vision from foreground to background, from the blur of passing objects to the
clarity of faraway structures. Because of the contact of wheels to the earth,
the momentum of a train car reverberates through the body; muscles and
bones can feel the movement of the vehicle. But when we are in the sky,
both tactile and optical awareness drift away from objects—from those on
the ground, certainly, but also from the engines and wings of the plane.
Aside from wind turbulence, bodily sensation of speed ceases after takeoff
with loss of ground contact and friction. As the plane gains elevation, the
split frame that characterizes ground-level vehicular perception diminishes.
Objects recede into the background. Everything slows as the traveler experiences the static simultaneity of the airborne position and the landscape
below. Roland Barthes, in "The Jet-Man," notes the difference between pilots
of small planes, flying at low altitudes, who are aware of speed, and what
he terms the "jet-man" of a large plane, who feels "motionlessness (at 2,000
kilometers per hour, in level flight, no impression of speed at all), as if the
extravagance of his vocation precisely consisted in overtaking motion, in
going faster than speed."[1]

Glimpsed from great heights, cities and buildings look like still lifes.
More protracted aerial views appear to be animated, slow-motion landscape
assemblages. Pilots and passengers see buildings, roads, bridges, and open
land as set pieces of large shifting compositions. Air travelers become aware
that stable form is fleeting, that the configurations of cities will peter out or
aggregate into new alignments. To the French writer and pioneer of aviation,
Antoine de Saint-Exupery, "one of the miracles of the airplane is that it
plunges a man directly into the heart of a mystery. You are a biologist study-
ing, through your porthole, the human ant-hill, scrutinizing objectively those
towns seated in their plain at the center of their highways which go off like
the spokes of a wheel and, like arteries, nourish them with the quintessence
of the fields."[2] Aerial perception allows us to see form in formation, as one
composition of landscape gives way to another and then another.

The aesthetics of aerial perception are illustrated in the prelude to
Robert Wise and Jerome Robbins's 1961 *West Side Story*, which pioneered

1. Roland Barthes, "The Jet-man," in *Mythologies*, trans. Annette Lavers (New York: Hill & Wang, 1972), 71.

2. Antoine de Saint-Exupery, "Wind, Sand, and Stars," in *Airman's Odyssey*, trans. Lewis Galantiere (New York: Harcourt, Brace & Co., 1939), 68.

the photography of urban landscape from a helicopter. To the tempo of Leonard Bernstein's overture, the first four-and-a-half minutes of the film unfurl a composition of vertical lines and bars that continually changes colors. Then, against a light blue backdrop, the image moves up the screen. Titles appear at the bottom, and both image and letters change from dark blue to white. The larger image resolves into an extreme long shot of Lower Manhattan seen from the sky above New York Harbor. Bernstein's music is followed by harbor sounds, which in turn are followed by the noise of rumbling traffic. A short city symphony follows, consisting of twenty aerial views. In each, the camera tracks slowly from right to left, mechanically sweeping over the city, tracing its straight and curving lines.

The first shots survey the piers, bridges, and roadways of the New York cityscape. Filmgoers see the powerful framework of twentieth-century urban infrastructure; the carefully framed views make us concentrate on its immense scale and uncompromised structure, on the steel and concrete that contrast so vividly with the harbor and the older nineteenth-century environment. An oblique shot focuses on the concrete roadway of a suspension bridge. A vertical view looms over the Hudson River, disclosing piers, sheds, and ocean liners that jut out into the water, perpendicular to the city. But not all of Manhattan consists of grids and straight lines. An especially textured shot stares down at the George Washington Bridge and its intersection with the Henry Hudson Parkway and Interstate 95—a highway engineer's gesture painting. The helicopter view of the multiple surfaces, levels, ramps, and loops displays not only the anxious contours of the roadway experience but also its logical geometry. This energy-packed urban scene reverberates in a later image, which pictures the contorted ramps that connect the Port Authority Bus Terminal with the Lincoln Tunnel, as well as in the sequence of shots that introduces the movie's protagonists, the street gang called the Jets. As the prelude ends, Robbins's choreography seems to echo the sinuous and interlocking curves of the views we have just watched. From a high camera angle, moviegoers see the gang members tightly coiled alongside a chain-link fence. Once the camera has reached ground level, the Jets begin to dance onto a playground in broad strokes of movement that recall the jabbing and hooking intersections of the bridge.

Several of the aerial shots in the *West Side Story* prelude sweep across Manhattan's business districts. Starting with the winding paths and broad lawns of Battery Park, the camera explores the extraordinary rise of the skyscrapers of Wall Street from a network of streets and blocks that date to the seventeenth and eighteenth centuries. From the air, the tall buildings packed close together make the streets look even more crooked, narrow, and dark than they do at ground level. Skyscraper roofs comprise most of the picture. Echoing the irregular shapes of the blocks and buildings are variously sloping, stepped, and flat roof surfaces. Spires and domes, pyramidal and stepped roofs, do not dominate our impression, as they would in a view from the ground. Flat roofs come into their own in the aerial view, their smooth expanses packed with heating, air-conditioning, and ventilation equipment and with water towers. A thousand feet above the street, the roofscapes of Manhattan make us forget facade and focus instead on building plan and mechanical system. In the film this usually unseen architectural zone looks like a gallery of paintings on canvases shaped by floor plates and framed by inky streets.

Above Midtown, *West Side Story's* aerial prelude changes focus, finding exceptional form within the regularity of the city's immense grid. The first such shots, parallel to the grid, emphasize the clarity of the horizontal and vertical lines. These give way to dramatic views of city landmarks, including the United Nations, Empire State Building, and Yankee Stadium. Large, recognizable buildings grab our attention. In another sequence, the camera moves in a linear path over Columbia University, and we are impressed with McKim, Mead, and White's composition, with the insertion of this Beaux Arts superblock within the city grid. Then, in an intriguing variation, the camera moves downtown, scoping out the picturesque landscaping and building layout of Stuyvesant Town. Viewed from above, this mid-century complex of functional redbrick apartment buildings evokes surprising associations. Arrayed around an oval lawn, the buildings in plan can recall a double-transept church, a Shinto gate, and perhaps to children, a lizard. From the sky, buildings and streetscapes seen hundreds of times on the ground break free of their familiar appearance. Aerial perception can make the routine seem unexpected, extraordinary.

The sky sequence of *West Side Story* concludes with three shots that set up the film's dramatic narrative. Tracking west from the greenery of Central Park, the camera pans above the crowded tenements of Hell's Kitchen. Airshafts and rear alleys carve minuscule spaces between the dumbbell-shaped buildings. Apart from concrete playgrounds, the only open spaces are the streets and rooftops. These brief aerial shots prefigure the main settings of the drama. The final zoom to street level aims at the tenements, then slowly dissolves into a shot of the playground. To the sound of whistles and snapping fingers, the camera closes in on the Jets, standing and kneeling by a fence, and then cuts to a close-up of the gang leader. The expansive and unified portrait of Manhattan in the prologue thus contracts into a tragic drama of claustrophobic romance and murder. Except for the tenements, none of the sights seen in the prelude figure in the film. Compared with the grand forms and spaces, the landmarks and monuments viewed in the prologue, the gang struggle that ensues over a few strips of asphalt seems especially pathetic. More than merely establishing the larger setting of the story, *West Side Story's* aerial prologue stands on its own as an enlargement of urban perception, a disturbing reminder of the limitations of our grounded points of view.

The prelude features three types of aerial vantage points. There is the oblique view of Manhattan, in the tradition of bird's-eye views that date to the Renaissance; here buildings in the foreground display their facades, dominating the cityscape seen in the background. There are the views that peer straight down, making building and cityscape appear two-dimensional; these focus on roofs, street alignments, open spaces, and natural features. And there is the zoom shot, such as that from the sky to the street, which breaks the mood of distanced tranquility, creating the sensation of speed; such zooms are like an aircraft landing, experienced by a pilot. As the prelude to *West Side Story* points out, the aerial view radically reconfigures the perception of building and city. Watching West Side Story, we experience New York as a series of vignettes, carefully orchestrated images that impart an air of detached grandeur to tenement and tower alike. Only when the camera quickly descends to the ground, when the poetic rhythm and spatial distance of the aerial view are gone, does the movie approximate the dynamism of flight, as our sight nearly collides with building.

After *West Side Story*, many films exploited exhilarating aerial perspectives. By the 1980s, high-speed film, requiring less light, allowed cinematographers to create nocturnal simulations of flight. Commenting on a series of gliding shots in Ridley Scott's *Someone to Watch Over Me*, the film historian James Sanders says that "right through the glittering skyline, the Chrysler and Empire State Buildings [execute] a dazzling dance in the night sky around us. Gone is the distant, flattened, pictorial image of the city's towers; this skyline comprises the most sculptural objects imaginable, popping up in front of us as if in a three-dimensional movie. Avenues become long, glowing wells of light, scooped out of the dark mass of the city and shooting northwest like arrows. . . . We get the sense of actually flying through the night sky, weightlessly, as we might otherwise hope to do only in our dreams."[3] Television, especially, has used tracking or zooming shots to plunge viewers into aerial rushes between and toward buildings. On the opening credits for news and sports programs, such shots quickly survey metropolitan landmarks. These visual sprints through the sky take viewers for a collective ride, a shared simulation of flight.

Architecture can seem uncanny from lofty altitudes. Although perception from an aircraft does not break the continuum of space or time, its transcendence of gravity and of the earth's surface can feel similar in effect. The higher the altitude and the longer the flight, the more aerial acuity escapes from customary spatial and temporal structures. As we cross time zones and zip through unbounded space, buildings and cities seem to evade our understanding; architecture, normally rising around and above us, slips from our grasp. From the sky, we forfeit the experience not only of entering a building but also of observing its details or lateral approaches. From the sky's great distances, we are hard-pressed to discern the age or identity of most buildings. From the sky's multiple angles, architecture becomes graphic and geographic.

In *Understanding Media*, Marshall McLuhan emphasizes that any new medium—print, film, airplanes—inevitably changes the scale, pace, and pattern of human affairs. Both the railroad and the automobile accelerated, enlarged, and abstracted the continuity of space and the appearance of built form. So, too, does the airplane. McLuhan also realizes that each new medium disrupts earlier modes of production and perception. Coming after the train

3. James Sanders, *Celluloid Skyline: New York and the Movies* (New York: Alfred A. Knopf, 2001), 90.

Expressway interchange

and the automobile, the airplane has encouraged new types of urban form and urban understanding. It challenges the railroad paradigm of linear corridors linking nodes as well as the automobile paradigm of continuous, sprawling urban development. "The railways require a uniform political and economic space," says McLuhan, while airplanes "permit the utmost discontinuity in spatial organization."[4] The airplane paradigm is one of widely dispersed points connected by flight paths over remote landscapes. While rail and auto travel encourage knowledge of a large yet interconnected urbanity, air travel is ungrounded; aloft, we experience urban space as a sequence of detached views, with occasional moments of immersion, at airports. The aerial view thus combines two contradictory perceptual characteristics. On the one hand, travelers feel removed from the landscape they are viewing and are less likely to understand its nuances; on the other hand, travelers see the network of land transportation around which any single automobile or rail journey might occur and are able to understand the landscape's greater structure.

Given its positional range, the airplane offers an almost infinite array of perspectives. The building observed from the air occupies a point seen from another point within a half-sphere of constantly fluctuating radius and position. The aerial zoomscape, like the poetic view, looks at things from unexpected angles and through unusual juxtapositions. "In the sky," Wallace Stevens writes, "an imagined, wooden chair is the clear-point of an edifice, forced up from nothing, evening's chair, Blue-strutted, curule, true—unreal, the center of transformations that transform for transformation's self."[5] As *West Side Story* shows, and as Stevens observes, the aerial view encourages a detached consciousness. On a plane, we experience a "remote intimacy" with the landscape below. High above developed, developing, and undeveloped spaces, as buildings, roads, and skylines come into view among clouds and the rays of the sun, as new connections between ground realities flood the mind, aerial perception shapes our view through imaginative architectures.

TAKEOFF AND LANDING

Before airfields became airports, most people watched the spectacle of flight from the ground. Before the 1950s, air passengers numbered in the tens of thousands. Unlike the great train terminals near the center of cities, airports

4. Marshall McLuhan, *Understanding Media* (New York: McGraw-Hill Book Company, 1964), 36.

5. Wallace Stevens, "Human Arrangement," in *The Collected Poems* (New York: Vintage, 1990), 363.

were situated by necessity on the outskirts. Sited atop old marshes or fields, early airfields consisted typically of a couple of small buildings and an earthen or grass runway; as such they seemed to belong less to the world at hand than to the territory beyond the horizon. All this has changed, of course; today, and especially in the United States, airports, not train stations, are the main venues of public travel. Within metropolitan regions, airports have become vital centers, and they increasingly compete in importance with downtowns. The highways that snake into airports are clogged with cars, taxis, and all sorts of vans and shuttle buses. Past the gauntlet of construction cranes—for airports are always rebuilding and expanding—we experience enormous, labyrinthine spaces. Airports stretch architecture into infrastructure. They are gripping picture shows in themselves.

The navigation of a large airport spurs radical shifts of sensation. Confusing and extensive circulation systems—the long and tortuous corridors, walkways, escalators, and elevator—amplify the speed and freedom of air travel. Multiple security systems add to the traveler's edginess.[6] After the automatic curbside doors, after the progression of our journey is confirmed or denied by the monitors that list departures, a walk through the airport is an exercise in release and restriction. Travelers are first confronted with check-in lines, then with security checkpoints that slow and constrict passage into metal-detecting thresholds that open onto long terminal corridors or waiting railcars. Walking or standing on the moving walkways, we can see the airport tarmac and the waiting planes. Meanwhile, especially in newer airports, the corridor becomes a concourse lined with eateries, shops, and newsstands. At the gates, views onto the apron outside stimulate our expectations of the journey; then we proceed down the dark and expandable jet bridge and into the airplane. The cabin is more confining than anywhere in the airport. Strapped into our seat, we observe the final preparations going on around the airplane underbelly. One might scrutinize the gray concrete rectangles covered with painted lines of different colors and penetrated by hoses and pipes. Or one might notice the small vehicles that carry luggage and Sky Chef containers. Once in motion on the ground, looking through small triple-pane windows, passengers see the airplane side of the airport, a flat zone of taxiways and runways, grassy medians, painted and lighted lines, and small signs bearing cryptic numbers.

6. David Pascoe, *Airspaces* (London: Reaktion Books, 2001), 15.

After the journey to and through the airport, takeoff comes as a great relief. In a commercial jet, it begins with the final turn from the taxiway to the runway, the flight attendant's recounting of safety procedures, and the vibrations of engines. Takeoff exposes most of us to the fastest land speeds we will ever experience, sometimes approaching 150 miles per hour. In approximately twenty seconds, passengers see the outside landscape recede, and then gently curve according to the flight path. The rush of speed brings with it an even more remarkable event, the liftoff. In his 1997 memoir *Burning the Days*, James Salter, a pilot as well as a writer, recalls his experiences of flying. In a small plane, he says, takeoff leads to a sensation that "the ground was speeding by, the wheels skipping, and suddenly we were rising in the din to see the blue tree line beyond the field boundary and, below, the curved roofs of the hangars falling away. Now fields appeared, swimming out in all directions. The earth became limitless, the horizon, unseen before, rose to fill the world, and we were aloft in unstructured air."[7] After takeoff, the elements of architecture diminish as the larger patterns of the urban environment are revealed. Poignantly, if we are leaving home, many places we know well—neighborhood, place of work, road networks—assemble into a single picture with the movement of departure.

In the first few minutes of air travel, several states of perception follow one another in rapid succession. For pilots, takeoff and the first seconds of flight approximate the dromoscopic penetration of automobile driving. For passengers, the experience from the side windows more closely resembles panoramic perception. Yet in both cases, after a short while, the later stages of aerial perception begin—the bird's-eye view and the vertical view. Outside the plane lies the free space of sky, high above the shrinking and disappearing land. Here the horizon line of ground travel, formed by the earth's curvature, fades far below the traveler's eyes and becomes an insignificant aspect of his or her vision. Any sense of uniform, mathematical perspective also diminishes. Aerial perception is cut off from any sense of accurate measure—gained typically through tactile awareness—of the landscape below. At cruising altitude, most passengers either stop looking out the windows or stop trying to identify particular places. Occasionally the pilot announces a major city on the left side of the plane or a deep canyon on the right. But even with the aid of monitors that track the plane's position, pas-

7. James Salter, *Burning the Days* (New York: Random House, 1997), 11.

sengers usually feel perceptually unanchored. Because of the airplane's velocity and altitude, because of the vastness of space around the plane, passengers who look down usually find their eyes wandering freely over a landscape that looks abstract or even alien.

In the approach to landing, we begin to reconnect to the ground below. In part because of the abstract qualities of the view, the visual markers of destination can start to appear hundreds of miles before arrival, when the plane is still at cruising altitude. Air travel constructs viewing corridors along paths that fundamentally change one's understanding of the physical bounds of cities. If one is traveling home, the air traveler may be able to identify some remote site, a particular place in his or her visual consciousness. Up high, bodies of water stand out for their memorable shape or for how they divide regions of land. Mountain ranges and large cities, too, are prominent in the high aerial view. Individual buildings are almost never distinguishable. Only in the last minutes of a journey does our sense of perception connect again to the ground, as cars become discernible on roads, as buildings become distinct forms in the countryside or city, and as the landscape once again looks three-dimensional.

Airports, the last buildings seen while landing, are among the most vivid and complex of built objects, with their networks of runways, taxiways, observation towers, fingered gates, and hangars. While passengers rarely see much of the airport until the plane is on the runway, pilots must scrutinize the airport from the air—they must know the shapes of the four-, five-, and six-runway arrangements, the array of blue edge lights and green taxiway lights. The plan of Heathrow Airport outside London was originally composed, for instance, of two triangles arranged to suggest a Star of David, an easily recognizable shape.[8]

On an approach to New York, the urban environment contrasts dramatically with its natural setting, with surrounding waters, wetlands, and forests. The edges of the Atlantic Ocean, Long Island Sound, Hudson River, and New York Harbor are sharp; the forests gradually give way to suburbia and then to the hard surfaces of the city itself, punctuated by hundreds of tall buildings. In *Another Country*, written in 1962 during the height of the civil rights struggle, James Baldwin describes a landing in New York; his protagonist

8. Wood Lockhart, "A Pilot's Perspective on Airport Design," in *Building for Air Travel: Architecture and Designs for Commercial Aviation*, ed. John Zukowsky (Munich: Prestel, 1996), 221.

seems fascinated by the abstract aerial view of the city, yet reluctant to rejoin the imperfect human society below. "The sun struck, on steel, on bronze, on stone, on glass, on the gray water far beneath them, on the turret tops and the flashing windshields of crawling cars, on the incredible highways, stretching and snarling and turning for mile upon mile upon mile, on the houses, square and high, low and gabled, and on their howling antennae, on the sparse, weak trees, and on those towers, in the distance, of the city of New York. The plane tilted, dropped and worse, and the whole earth slanted, now leaning against the windows of the plane, now dropping out of sight. The sky was a hot, blank blue, and the static light invested everything with its own lack of motion. Only things could be seen from here, the work of people's hands: but the people did not exist."[9]

Decades earlier, in "Flying over London," Virginia Woolf, too, marvels at the sensation of being surrounded by the sky. High above the city, she notices that the familiar architecture of London has given way to a strange spatiality, the sky enclosing her like a translucent and infinitely thick wall. "Habit has fixed the earth immovably in the center of the imagination like a hard ball; everything is made to the scale of houses and streets," writes Woolf. "And as one rises up into the sky, as the sky pours down over one, this little hard granular knob, with its carvings and frettings, dissolves, crumbles, loses its domes, its pinnacles, its firesides."[10] When we view the earth at a distance, familiar places have a primal quality. Here Woolf describes London: "One could see through the Bank of England; all the business houses were transparent; the River Thames was as the Romans saw it, as Paleolithic man saw it, at dawn from a hill shaggy with wood, with the rhinoceros digging his horn into the roots of rhododendrons. So immortally fresh and virginal London looked."[11] Woolf seems torn between fascination at the primeval appearance of cities seen from this most advanced of transportation technologies, and revulsion at leaving behind familiar humanity and accustomed architectural enclosure. From high up, the ground begins to look like a vision from hell and she nicknames the pilot "Charon." Unlike Baldwin, as the plane descends, she happily discerns domes and towers once more, and grows excited by the movements of people; there is a place for her on the ground.

9. James Baldwin, *Another Country* (New York: The Dial Press, 1962), 432.

10. Virginia Woolf, *Collected Essays*, Volume Four (London: Hogarth Press, 1967), 167.

11. Ibid., 168.

Berlin

Usually, our descent from the sky involves the loss of abstract vision and social detachment. Upon landing, the air traveler reorients to the socio-spatial consciousness of the ground, to the axes, thresholds, and walls of buildings and public spaces. But the aerial experience can carry over to life on the land. Motion pictures, most powerfully, exhibit this odd situation. Like *West Side Story*, Leni Riefenstahl's infamous *Triumph of the Will* shows how architecture, seen from above, can frame future action on the ground. *West Side Story's* aerial photography zoomed from expansive views of the city to cramped crime-ridden streets. Made shortly after Adolf Hitler's ascent to power, *Triumph of the Will* follows the Führer's journey from a plane in the clouds above Nuremberg to a drive through the crowded city streets. After landing, as the film shows, a city and its people will be led by the "divinity" who has just alighted. The totalizing aerial comprehension Hitler commanded when in the plane—in the realm of the gods—will become manifest in his feverish domination of the "religious" rally that rest of the film documents.

Set to Richard Wagner's overtures to *Rienzi* and *Die Meistersinger von Nürnberg*, *Triumph of the Will* begins as a small airplane carries Hitler to Nuremberg for the Reich Party Day in 1934. Filmgoers see that Hitler is in the plane, peering out the windows toward the propeller, then the left wing, and the billowing clouds beyond, sunlit from above and dark below. Riefenstahl introduces Nuremberg through aerial views of its monuments, the towers and domes of churches, the bulky castle, the market square, and the rows of steep-pitched roofs. No modern buildings intrude into the scene. Riefenstahl equates the city's medieval architecture with its creation by the German race, or *Volk*. From the advanced technology of the airplane, Hitler descends into what seems a city returned to its medieval purity, unspoiled by the cosmopolitanism—what Hitler disdained as the "decadence"—of modern architecture.

Before Hitler's plane lands, the filmgoer becomes aware of streets lined with buildings and trees, and crowded with people. The crowds appear to consist not of individual citizens, but of massed linear forms; they look like blocks, like buildings. From the aerial view, filmgoers can see the sharp lines of houses that mirror the straight lines of saluting citizens; Germany is a nation of bricks and blood. The air view affords a means of perception that unifies particulars into larger and singular configurations. Indeed, the last views from the plane show columns of people marching in unison, in anticipation of Hitler's arrival. Once on the ground, Hitler will travel through the city in an automobile, and various images will recall his aerial view. The outstretched arms correspond to roof angles seen earlier in aerial perspective. The steering wheel of the automobile reminds us of the earlier glimpse of the propeller. In *Triumph of the Will*, cinematography employs aeronautical perception to demonstrate the unity of architecture with society. Only from the mechanized view in the air can the masses be read as a geometric extension of architecture, and the historical city as a foretaste to the city of destiny represented by the party rally and its pillars of lights and speeches of hatred. The aerial view, although detached from landscape and society, can produce striking insights into life on the ground.

BIRD'S-EYE VIEWS

The bird's-eye or oblique aerial view looks down from an altitude of a few thousand feet, and in some cases, as in the helicopter pans in *West Side Story* or the aircraft shots in *Triumph of the Will*, of only a few hundred feet. Commonly seen from helicopters and small planes as well as from larger jets during takeoff and landing, the oblique aerial view tilts down, emphasizing the relief of the landscape and the verticality of buildings. The incline from the vertical axis can vary from a high oblique, from which the horizon of the earth is visible, to a low oblique, in which no horizon appears.[12] Because oblique perception encompasses building height and mass, streets and low-lying forms are usually obscured by taller buildings. Structures in the foreground are prominent; buildings toward the background look smaller and smaller. Because of the scale change, comparative measurements of buildings are difficult to calculate. As a result, oblique views occur less frequently in scientific presentations than in popular and artistic illustrations.

What is most significant about the oblique aerial view is its recasting of architecture; in this view, a distanced observer can discern patterns of building and infrastructure—serpentine rows of houses in subdivisions, outcroppings of malls, tall buildings, and condominium complexes, urbanization

12. Frank E. Reynolds, "Oblique Aerial Photography for Comprehensive Urban Planning," in American Planning Association, *Planning Advisory Service Report*, Number 361 (1981), 1.

encroaching on forests or fields. While the dimension of height is compressed in the bird's-eye view, we often see far greater lengths of cityscape
than we do on the ground. Just as important, the bird's-eye view allows us
to observe a greater scale in the depth dimension—to see the things behind
things, features obscured to travelers on the ground because they are blocked
by intervening buildings. In aerial distance there thus emerges a radical
reorientation of the senses and of relationship to the land. Oblique aerial perception positions us in a distanced and sometimes dominating relationship
to what lies below.

Airborne sight is the apotheosis of a long tradition of attempts to gain
lofty perspectives and, with these, a new understanding of architecture.
Already during the Renaissance and the Baroque eras, artists began to render imaginary views from the sky that depicted a comprehensive image of a
place. For the patrons of these drawings or paintings, the bird's-eye view
organized the scattered aspects of a city—its walls, landmarks, outlying
areas—into a unified portrait, one which could represent a unified society.
"Long before the invention of the airplane," the architectural historian Hubert
Damisch remarks, "men of art were able to obtain, largely through graphic
means, 'bird's-eye-views,' the image of the city being confounded with its
maquette, its relief plan."[13] Some of these views were obtained from high
points on land, such as hills, towers, and belvederes. Others were created
not from an actual site, but from an imagined point in the sky. Working from
a city plan, artists used axonometric projection to represent the ideal verticality and three-dimensional forms of city buildings. The Turgot Plan, drafted
by Louis Bretez in 1740, represents Paris in relief, clearly articulating the
city's squares and monuments. During the nineteenth century, often as an
expression of civic pride, many cities pictured themselves in bird's-eye
views.[14] In an 1854 lithograph of Chicago, the city's buildings and grid
extend to the western horizon from an aerial point somewhere east of the city
and hundreds of feet above Lake Michigan. In this dramatic image, Chicago's
dense center unfolds as the inevitable metropolis connecting the trade of the
Great Lakes and the resources of the American continent.

All through the nineteenth century, writers sought out high places in
order to be inspired and to comprehend their relationship to the world below.

13. Hubert Damisch, *Skyline: The Narcissistic City*, trans. John Goodman (Stanford: Stanford University Press, 2001), 12.

14. John W. Reps, *Bird's-eye Views: Historic Lithographs of North American Cities* (New York: Princeton Architectural Press, 1998).

Through bird's-eye views, one understood how diverse buildings contrasted or accorded with a greater urban whole. A chapter of Victor Hugo's 1831 *Notre-Dame de Paris* is devoted to the panorama of the city seen from the cathedral's towers—views that amalgamate disparate buildings and streets into singular images. Hugo presents two portraits of the city: an imaginary view of how it would have appeared to a medieval visitor, and his own contemporary assessment. He first describes the steep climb up to the towers, leading to "two high platforms inundated with light and air, it was in truth a marvelous picture spread out before you on every side; a spectacle *sui generis* of which those of our readers can best form an idea who have the good fortune to see a purely Gothic city, complete and homogeneous." Writing on the cusp of the industrial era, when Paris, like many cities, was experiencing extraordinary growth, Hugo stresses the importance of the older Gothic Paris with its forest of steeples and spires. He describes practically the entire city viewed from his lofty position, from the cathedral island to distant towers. Later in the chapter, observing scenes of his own era, Hugo laments, "the great edifices are becoming fewer and fewer, are being swallowed up before our eyes by the flood of houses." He adds that while certain modern buildings have admirable features, "I do not despair of Paris offering one day to the view, if seen from a balloon, that wealth of outline, that opulence of detail, that diversity of aspect, that indescribable air of grandeur in its simplicity, of the unexpected in its beauty, which characterizes—a draught-board."[15] These newer views from Notre Dame point out to him how the city and its architecture have changed for the worse—sprawling in residential monotony and consisting of monuments that look like academic exercises. They also demonstrate that the aerial view already, before people took to the air, provided a means of comparison between urban beauty and ugliness, and visions of the city as alternatively picturesque or rational.

In his lifetime (he died in 1885), Hugo would have been able to see Paris from a balloon and experience how the proto-aerial view—both imagined and seen—would be reconfigured into actual aerial representations of the city. Beginning with Gaspard-Felix Nadar's 1858 photographs of Paris from a balloon, bird's-eye viewers took to the real sky. In 1860, a generation after Hugo took in the prospect of Paris, James Wallace Black photographed

15. Victor Hugo, *Notre Dame of Paris*, trans.
John Sturrack (London: Penguin Books, 1978),
136, 144, 145.

Boston from a balloon, the city's buildings, streets, and harbor all gathered within an oval frame. In 1863, Oliver Wendell Holmes remarked on the photograph: "Boston, as the eagle and the wild goose see it, is a very different object from the same place as the solid citizen looks up at its eaves and chimney. The Old South and Trinity Church are two landmarks not to be mistaken. Washington Street slants across the picture as a narrow cleft. Milk Street winds as if the cow path which gave it a name had been followed by the builders of its commercial palaces. Windows, chimneys, and skylights attract the eye in the central parts of the view, exquisitely defined, bewildering in numbers."[16] Holmes underscores the signal qualities of the oblique aerial view: the perceived unity of separate city districts; the ability to compare the forms of diverse monuments; the legibility of street and infrastructure patterns; and the prominence of roofscapes.

Toward the end of the nineteenth century, photographs were taken not only from balloons but also from kites, primitive rockets, and even pigeons. In 1909, flying over Centrocelli, Italy, Wilbur Wright took the first photograph from a plane. By the second decade of the twentieth century, postcards, posters, calendars, and other types of illustration depicted cities in aerial photographs. In such images, people saw architecture in ways previously only imagined. The ideal and abstract perspectives that painters, philosophers, and scientists had cultivated for centuries were now available to all. By the First World War, both military and commercial aviation brought increasing numbers of people into the skies. In a major advance from bird's-eye views experienced from high places on the land, the new flying public could gaze at the entirety of cities and landscapes. Aircraft became a sort of hyper-skyscraper, a mobile platform above the city fabric. The sensation of space below is one of the aerial zoomscape's signature features. At low altitudes, the oblique view from an aircraft can come as close to land as an old-fashioned hilltop or steeple vista, yet it is not fixed to the land.[17] In motion, the viewpoint continually changes.

The aero-technological transformation of vision soon influenced the visual arts. The rapidly changing perspectives of buildings seen from the air recall the Cubist painters' construction of figures whose forms express multiple viewpoints and Futurists' depiction of bodies fractured into the

16. Quoted in Beaumont Newhall, *Airborne Camera: The World from the Air and Outer Space* (New York: Hastings House, 1969), 24-26.

17. William Langewiesche, *Inside the Sky: A Meditation on Flight* (New York: Pantheon Books, 1998), 26.

Phoenix, Arizona

dynamism of movement. Recalling the view from a flight, Gertrude Stein compares the patterns of the ground with those of abstract artists: "Quarter sections make a picture and going over America like that made any one know why the post-cubist painting was what it was," she wrote in her autobiography. "The wandering line of Masson was there, the mixed line of Picasso coming and coming again and following itself into a beginning was there, the simple solution of Braque was there."[18] Because flight allows views to shift along any axis, spatial consciousness expands from viewing corridors along the horizontal ground plane to a range of diagonal angles culminating in the perpendicular, vertical stance. During the 1920s, this new sight from all angles liberated the eye from its usual viewing corridors and perspectives.[19] Artists like El Lissitsky, Paul Klee, and Piet Mondrian were inspired to paint abstract views of agricultural fields and urban grids and boulevards, many of which looked like aerial photographs.

As the work of Lissitsky and Mondrian suggests, the aerial view not only encouraged the introduction of more complexity into representation; it also helped create a new language of form and space. The abstract assemblages of lines, bars, and planes in Kazimir Malevich's Suprematist paintings convey the appearance of buildings seen from a bird's-eye view.[20] Similarly, the austere building blocks of Dutch architects J.J.P. Oud or Willem Dudok may have been influenced by oblique aerial angles. An aerial-view rendering of 1931 shows the regular slabs of Oud's Blijdorp housing estate in Rotterdam; at the edge of the image we glimpse the wing of a biplane.[21] By this time, the speed of trains had already shown architects a vision of building form without detail or ornament. The bird's-eye view from an airplane encouraged abstraction, too, the emphasis of mass over facade, of complex forms over simple boxes. In oblique angles from the sky, buildings in even the flattest of cities seem to be arrayed one atop the other. While we might notice the upper parts of facades, the larger impression of such views is of irregular, overlapping masses. The aerial view may have influenced early twentieth-century architecture's shift of articulation from ornament and symmetry to surface, mass, and their varied juxtapositions.

From aerial angles, architecture is apprehended within its greater context. The elements of infrastructure—roadways, bridges, culverts, and factories—

18. Gertrude Stein, *Everybody's Autobiography* (New York: Cooper Square Publishing, 1971), 191.

19. Christoph Asendorf, "Fluctuations of Forms: The Airplane and Spatial Experience," *Daidalos* 37 (September 1990), 32, 35.

20. Robert Wohl, *A Passion for Wings: Aviation and the Western Imagination, 1908–1918* (New Haven: Yale University Press, 1994), 173–77.

21. Richard Koshalek, ed., *At the End of the Century: One Hundred Years of Architecture* (New York: Harry N. Abrams, 1998), 241.

merge with buildings into a cityscape of forms and routes. With air travel, it has become possible to perceive urban conditions previously visible only through drawings or maps. Regarding transportation, the aerial view has helped locate logical sites for new infrastructure. In the field of housing, it has assisted in the identification of overcrowding. And with respect to open space, it has pointed out the areas of a city not served by parks. Emphasizing the entire city more than individual buildings, the bird's-eye (and vertical) view has enabled architects to judge the wisdom or thoughtlessness of urban form. Historically, the aerial view's impact on city design was all the greater because of the discipline's ongoing efforts to reform the industrial metropolis. Since the nineteenth century, architects had bemoaned the problems caused by the rapid growth of cities throughout Europe and North America—the crowding and disease, the lack of light, greenery, and sanitation. During the interwar years, the sky view gave empirical proof of the industrial city's shortcomings.

In "The Chaos of City Planning," written in the early 1920s, German architect Hans Schmidt used the insights of the aerial view to condemn the lack of rhythmic and organic features in the appearance of industrial cities, and to argue that the air view suggests restorative design principles of regularity, unity, and economy.[22] In 1933, the air view—both bird's-eye and vertical-—was used extensively at the fourth congress of the International Congress of Modern Architects (CIAM), which took place aboard a steamship sailing between Marseilles and Athens. The organization most responsible for the worldwide dissemination of modernist urbanism, CIAM relied on comparative city plans based on aerial photography. Later, in *Can Our Cities Survive?*, a quasi-official articulation of CIAM urbanism published in 1942, the Spanish architect José Luis Sert proposed a complete urban makeover on the evidence of aerial views. Writing after the greatest air campaign in the history of warfare, the Battle of Britain, Sert noticed that the German Luftwaffe, in seeking to destroy Britain's cities, had revealed, in their reconnaissance photos, a minimalist environment of building foundations and cadastral (street/block) organization. To Sert, the air view exposed a new urban facade, one that was horizontal and not vertical.[23] From the air, the huge scale and disorder of the industrialized metropolis were apparent. So, too, were huge-scale architectural and planning solutions.

22. Hans Schmidt, *Beiträge zur Architektur, 1924-1964* (Berlin: Verlag für Bauweisen, 1965), 17.

23. José Luis Sert, *Can Our Cities Survive?* (Cambridge: Harvard University Press, 1944), 2.

It was the Swiss-French architect and theorist Le Corbusier—arguably the most influential designer of the twentieth century—who devised some of the most far-reaching solutions. His illustrated text of 1935, *Aircraft*, was written during a period when he was turning his attention from the design of houses to that of cities. With his typical bravado, Le Corbusier claims that the bird's-eye view offered proof of the decline of large cities worldwide. "The airplane instills, above all a new conscience, the modern conscience," he claimed. "Cities, with their misery, must be torn down. They must be largely destroyed and fresh cities built."[24] The oblique view thus became a catalyst for radical urban change. Part of Le Corbusier's critique was based on the trajectory of aerial perception. As urban historian M. Christine Boyer writes, "[T]he airplane allowed for new orthogonal routes that passed over and through all objects, disregarding political boundaries and flowing like primordial rivers back to the sea."[25] The airplane's flight straight over the contours of the earth established for Le Corbusier its relevance to architectural theory, its ability to discern what he saw as the true order that lies beneath the false appearance of things. In "Towards a Synthesis," of 1942, he surmises that "the plane cuts right across the old roads zigzagging through the valleys, it flies over them unrestrained, going direct to its destination at 500 km/h.... Travelers will no longer take the boat or the train; they will be 'vital' passengers, an 'elite,' full of potentialities. Goods, leaving the rail and the road, will fly down from the sky....It is evident that air travel will not repeat the role of the roads with their weekend or paid-holiday tourists and the strings of ramshackle vehicles. The air route is man who has grown wings, a fact of great moment with majestic but dangerous consequences."[26] Just as a plane can fly across the land in a straight line, disregarding natural and cultural conventions, so, too, must buildings and infrastructure be designed to be ruthlessly functional, indifferent to physical and historical contexts.

The photographs in *Aircraft* include images of airplanes as well as aerial shots of natural landscapes and cities. Alone among these categories, according to Le Corbusier, cities fail to live up to the simple principles the air view sets for spacious, functional form. A bird's-eye view of Philadelphia shows the city from the west, with the towers of downtown in the background. But Le Corbusier has little interest in the dense central city. Instead,

24. Le Corbusier, *Aircraft* (London: Studio Publications, 1935), 5.

25. M. Christine Boyer, "Mobility and Modernism in the Postwar City," *CENTER* 5 (1989), 88.

26. Le Corbusier, "Towards a Synthesis," in *The Complete Architectural Works: Volume IV, 1936-46*, ed. W. Boesiger (London: Thames and Hudson, 1946), 70.

he lets the broad path of Market Street dominate the picture. Running straight like the path of the airplane, the boulevard contrasts with the surrounding blocks of tightly packed (and presumably irrational) cityscape—a razor cut into the false visual consciousness of the city. The architect's most strident comments appear alongside photographs of Paris, especially an oblique view of the Madeleine quarter. Here, thick concentrations of buildings, old and new, large and small, surround the church. On these irregular blocks and streets, neither individual buildings nor public spaces are visible. Le Corbusier denounces these zones as old, decayed, frightening, and finished. Because they do not stand out when seen from the sky, the districts of older cities accord poorly with his cartographic rationalism. Architects enamored of the aerial view tend to prefer their buildings to be of great scale and surrounded by open spaces. Dense patterns are hard to read from the air. Likewise, in gathering aerial information for planning purposes, it is harder to classify buildings in old cores than in newer districts. Consequently, many modern architects came to prefer the leviathan forms and large spaces of suburban and modern complexes. Their bold geometries were readily discerned from great aerial distances.[27]

Grand complexes visible from thousands of feet above the earth dominate the work that Le Corbusier published in *Aircraft*. On facing pages, he places his proposal for Algiers and an aerial photograph of Rio de Janeiro, along with two sketches of the city. The photograph of Rio shows the city spreading inland from its bays to the bases of steep mountains. His sketches, made during a flight in 1929, "just when the conception of a vast program of organic town-planning came like a revelation," ignore the older districts and stress the wide sweep of the bay and dramatic rise of the mountains. These extra-large topographic gestures appear in his plan for Algiers, a vision of a city of widely spaced skyscrapers constructed along the gigantic curve of a superhighway. The aerial view, as the images of *Aircraft* show, was by no means a clear picture of either sound or unwholesome urban form. Typically, it illustrated both problems and solutions. It was up to the architect, in reading an aerial photograph or gazing from a plane, to diagnose the urban condition and propose methods of treatment.

Even more than he realized, Le Corbusier was in sync with technological and commercial developments. During the interwar years, many architectural

27. Melville C. Branch, *Aerial Photography in Urban Planning and Research* (Cambridge: Harvard University Press, 1948), 13–14.

landscapes could already be read easily from the air. The new technologies of railroads and automobiles had already encouraged the construction of buildings and urban spaces on a grander scale than ever before seen: skyscraper offices and high-rise residences in rail-serviced downtowns; outlying one-story factory complexes with buildings shaped like spheres, cones, and cylinders, and served by rail spurs and trucking routes; housing subdivisions that reached to the city's edge and were accessed by new highways. The large-scale planning that many architects credited to the insights of the aerial view was already underway before people began to scrutinize architecture from the sky. Aerial journeys and photographs accelerated a process begun earlier in the age of mechanized transportation.

Nor did these tendencies slow down after the Second World War. A low-density, horizontal automotive landscape spread first throughout the United States, and by the 1960s had broadened to Europe and other parts of the world. At the same time, skyscrapers and superblock residential districts expanded not only the traditional downtown but also established high-rise zones throughout most metropolitan areas. Buildings for industry, institutions (such as prisons, hospitals, and military bases), and airports grew to gargantuan scale. Because of such large-scale development, figure/ground distinctions were much more apparent in a city viewed from the air in the mid-twentieth century than they would have been in earlier eras.

Alas, the oblique view down at the postwar metropolis, contrary to the hopes of Le Corbusier and many architects, often displayed an unsatisfying landscape. Megastructures were more dominant than they had been earlier in the century, and they were highly readable from the air, and highways threaded metropolitan regions, their wide lines bolder than those of the rail corridors. But with few exceptions, the big buildings and big infrastructure seemed to lack coordination, at least as far as one could see from the aerial view. Like the roadway strip, cluttered with advertising and merchandising, the aerial view of urbanism revealed unsystematic and confusing patterns. Very rarely did the new large-scale projects seem to be planned with the attention to natural topography and the coordination of architectural design that Le Corbusier had shown in the Algiers plan. Instead, newer developments mixed uncomfortably with older architecture, and appeared from aerial vantage points as if they would consume what remained of the preindustrial city.

Regional mall

In the early 1970s, a helicopter ride over the San Francisco Bay Area led the landscape architect Robert Royston to decry the chaos below.[28] While Royston could have gleaned aspects of the chaos from a journey on the region's roads, the aerial view revealed large-scale complexes not visible from the roadside, obscured by plantings and fences and infringing everywhere on the natural environment. Royston shared Le Corbusier's belief in public planning that sought to exceed commercial considerations. But the landscape architect, like many others, had lost faith in architecture's ability to remake the city in grand strokes and proposals that assumed a tabula rasa. Royston preferred smaller gestures in tune with the natural and historical landscape of creeks, watersheds, older communities, and established agricultural fields. Since the 1970s, most architects and planners have increasingly refrained from using the insights of the aerial view to propose a comprehensive reordering of the city. Aerial planning would henceforth precipitate smaller urban interventions and frequently advocate for the restoration of disturbed natural environments.

Unfortunately, the search for knowledge and inspiration that motivated the aerial view has been accompanied as well by manifold impulses toward destruction. Beginning in the twentieth century, cities have been assaulted as never before by wartime bombing campaigns. Since the First World War, bird's-eye views (and photographs) from planes have been a staple of aerial reconnaissance. The Spanish Civil War was the first conflict in which cities were extensively bombed. In "Prelude to Apocalypse," a poem based on his experiences during that war, André Malraux describes an air battle above the Alcazar of Toledo that links the destructive nature of air power with the aerial view and its perceptual aesthetics. From the air, the entirety of small cities is visible in a single glance. Strong forms stand out from the air, as do the colors and shapes of battle. An entire city can seem to leap into the fight. Malraux describes how his plane seemed to be stationary as the buildings of the town appeared to move menacingly: "The Alcazar swept underneath, with a few ill-timed shells circling it like satellites, spun round and sheered off to the right."[29] In another passage, he describes the distinct appearance of entire cities lit by gunfire: "Seen from the opposite direction now, Talavera had changed in appearance like a man who turns round: the confused light

28. Peter Walker and Melanie Simo, *Invisible Gardens: The Search for Modernism in the American Landscape* (Cambridge: MIT Press, 1994), 119.

thrown upon the streets from the military staff offices had given place to the lighted rectangles of windows. Its far-flung lights had given the town a vague semblance of life, and the sharply defined lights revealed by the plane's return journey had suggested something still more precise; but now that it was in darkness the town really came into being. Like sparks struck from a flint, the short flames of the machine guns appeared and disappeared."[30] The buildings of Talavera, because of their gun emplacements, appear as protagonists in the fight. Momentarily, the roofs of Toledo seem covered not by tiles but by smoke from burning houses. Buildings, as Malraux sees them from the air, emit energy in the heat of battle.

From the perspective of a bomber pilot, the substance of atmosphere and of architecture are often confused with each other. Black or white puffs in the sky are not necessarily clouds, and lights below are not always those illuminating buildings or streets. During war, they might point to burning buildings or firing targets.[31] On radar screens after bombing raids, the fires of cities, not autumnal grain fields, appear golden from high altitudes. In the aerial view of warfare, the appearance of buildings can easily be confused with that of smoke and fire. During the 1991 Gulf War between the United States and Iraq, television viewers were shown nightly bird's-eye views of the skyline of Baghdad illuminated by tracer lines of antiaircraft fire—a macabre display of lights and explosions. In perhaps the most replayed images of the war, television audiences watched radar-guided strikes by American bombers on strategic Iraqi targets; the images were so immediate that the viewers themselves seemed to be the bombardiers. Home audiences could see an Iraqi building through the crosshairs of a laser targeting system, usually depicted in an oblique angle that emphasized its substantial form. A few seconds later, the bunker, bridge, or government office would blow up. Such images, taken at high altitudes from the belly-mounted laser designator of a F-117A Stealth bomber, are especially dehumanized—it is too easy to forget that the buildings are real, and that they shelter people.

STRAIGHT DOWN

Compared to the oblique view, the vertical view positions the eyes or camera perpendicular to the earth's surface. At customary aircraft heights

29. André Malraux, "Prelude to Apocalypse," ed. Selden Rodman, The Poetry of Flight: An Anthology (New York: Duell, Sloan, and Pearce, 1941), 153.

30. Malraux, 156.

31. Leroy Newby, Target Ploesti: View from a Bombsight (Novato, Ca.: Presidio Press, 1983), 61.

between 2,000 and 40,000 feet, buildings read as flat planes. Cities seem to consist largely of streets, block and lot patterns, rooftops, open spaces, and topographic features. There is no sense of architecture's three-dimensionality, of building facades or heights, unless stereoscopic methods are used to calculate heights. Reduced to line and plane, architecture loses its perspectival illusionism. Because of consistent scale, a vertical aerial view or photograph makes buildings look like miniature blueprints, the city like a map. Individual elements may be measured mathematically against each other as well as against the whole building. Horizontal distances can be accurately recorded. The identification of buildings proceeds on the basis of their size, outline, color, and position with respect to one another. The perception of architecture begins to equate with the exactitude of the parallel rule, set square, and circle template.

The lack of information about a building's elevation is compensated for by an abundance of other data—circulation routes, topography, soils, land-use patterns, urban density, available development sites, natural features.[32] For purposes of traffic control, vertical views reveal commuter patterns, vehicle loads, and points of frequent congestion. For law enforcement, perpendicular perception shows the routes of egress—roof exits, scuttle holes, skylights—on a building's roofscape. Taken at intervals, vertical aerial photographs show seasonal cycles as well as changes brought about by building demolition, deterioration, and new development; for instance, comparative vertical photographs measure annual rates of erosion affecting urbanized areas built on ocean cliffs. Archaeologists use vertical photographs to detect historical sites, to discern ancient cultivations patterns, the foundation markings of lost buildings, and the remains of sites like Woodhenge, an ancient gathering place near Stonehenge.[33] For millennia, various cultures have carved immense two-dimensional figurations—or geoglyphs—on the surface of the earth, such as the hundreds of figures and patterns carved by the Nazca peoples in what is now Peru. These patterns went largely unnoticed until the 1920s, when they were discovered from the air, the only vantage from which their full extent can be seen. Since taking to the air, modern societies have begun to read visual scripts created, perhaps, only for divine eyes.[34] In *Inside the Sky*, essayist William Langewiesche, himself a pilot, explores the insights

32. Frank Scarlett, "The Application of Air Photography to Architecture and Town Planning," *RIBA Journal* 53 (June 1946), 321.

33. Leo Deuel, *Flights into Yesterday: The Story of Aerial Archaeology* (New York: St. Martin's Press, 1969), 10.

34. Lucy Lippard, "America Landscape," in *Markings: Aerial Views of Sacred Landscapes*, ed. Marilyn Bridges (Metuchen, New Jersey: The Garden Limited, 1986), 56.

gained from the sky. The aerial perspective, he writes "lets us see that our struggles form patterns on the land, that these patterns repeat to an extent which before we had not known, and that there is a sense to them."[35]

Architecture reduced to two dimensions by the vertical view reveals a new personality—the roof, or the fifth facade.[36] Remarked upon by the German art historian Fritz Wichert in 1909, the aerial view turns the roof into the fifth facade, the new front of the building.[37] In oblique views, building tops crown a city's skyline. Viewed from straight down, however, roofs, whether flat, curved, or pitched, appear planar. On large buildings, air travelers notice mechanical equipment, ductwork, exhausts, storage tanks, bowtie vents, flood-lamp coronets on skylights, and solar panels; on houses, they observe chimneys, skylights, gutters, dormers, and roofing materials—clay tiles, slate or wood shingles, sheet metal, asphalt, gravel, or tar. Sometimes we can make out storage sheds, terraces, gardens, swimming pools, heliports, and giant signs or numbers. And while the fifth facade exposes existing functions, it can also stimulate landscape architects to design gardens readable from tall buildings and aircraft.[38]

In the air view, not only the elements within a roof stand out; the shapes of buildings, as expressed by their roofs, are a primary source of information. At the scale of cities, because grids and straight lines predominate, irregular and round shapes leap to the fore.[39] The polygons, ovals, and circles of sports stadiums, gas tanks, factories, and exceptional buildings like the Pentagon, all help identify places. Unlike ground observations that rarely reveal a building's or city's plan, vertical views disclose the shape of multiwinged castles or hospitals, of intricate highway interchanges, as well as of the buildings that comprise large institutions like universities.

Vertical aerial views offer new visual knowledge, an architectural zone consisting entirely of the tops of things—roofs, streets, infrastructure, and open spaces. Deemphasizing the figure/ground and private/public distinctions of buildings and cities, they encourage us to focus on less noticed parts of the city. Private rooftops and outdoor spaces can be read alongside public spaces like streets and parks. In Grand Design: The Earth from Above and Below from Above, Georg Gerster shoots vertical aerial photographs that provide comparisons of the formal variety of worldwide urban settlement. "Only

148

35. Langewiesche, 4.

36. The Architectural Forum (March 1957), 144.

37. Fritz Wichert, "Luftschiffahrt und Architektur," Frankfurter Zeitung (March 21, 1909), 1.

38. Elizabeth Kassler, Modern Gardens (New York: Museum of Modern Art, 1964), 15–16.

39. Branch, 41.

a perpendicular view exhaustively deals with the potential of elevation," he comments. "This perspective alone both alienates and concentrates, allowing a visually exciting tight-rope walk between information and abstraction."[40] Gerster favors images that reveal how patterns of urban configurations emerge from societal functions, building materials, and relationships to nature. The photographs illustrate relative density and scale, dwelling and lot shape, location and extent of exterior space, building relationship to streets, and distribution of common space. And not only do his vertical aerial views show rooftops, they can also peer down into private spaces—backyards, courtyards, pools, and hot tubs. (With the aid of satellite cameras, features as small as atriums and the rooms beneath skylights are also occasionally visible from space.) The voyeurism encouraged by the train has its aerial counterpart in such al fresco eavesdropping.

Gerster's photograph of the oasis town of El Oued in Algeria show a relentlessly rectilinear city. Consisting of large residential compounds surrounding courtyards, the city's interior spaces are almost entirely covered by a grid of small vaulted roofs. From the air, this grid of roofs reinforces the city's street grid. At ground level, the streets and walls would prevent awareness of the uniformity of El Oued's design, and of how each segment of the city reads as a miniaturized version of the whole. The town's standardized plan suggests a degree of standardization as well in its cultural demographics. An aerial photograph of Labbezanga in Mali similarly reveals patterns indiscernible from the ground. We see that in Labbezanga residential compounds are formed around outdoor courtyards. Circular granaries and dwellings wind, beadlike, through the village, enclosing narrow streets and courtyards in what appears to be mixed public-private space. Labbezanga does not present, however, a uniform urban order. Older circular houses with conical roofs contrast with newer, larger rectangular houses with flat roofs. If Labbezanga's older curved dwellings respond to its location on an island in the Niger River, the rectangular compounds suggest recent social and religious developments and the presence of competing cultural forces.

Aerial views of Japan and the United States allow us to compare two very different ways of planning a single-family residential suburb. Gerster's photograph of Nagasaki shows a housing district with few exterior spaces.

40. Georg Gerster, *Below from Above: Aerial Photography* (New York: Abbeville, 1986), n.p.

Gas tanks, south of Philadelphia

Buildings are crammed along narrow streets that follow the city's hilly topography. The only open spaces are a few small pockets of trees and one long, winding road. Most streets are hardly visible, indicated primarily by the junctures of house roofs. Nor do the houses open onto courtyards or rear yards; instead, they butt up against each other. The aerial view helps us understand why Japanese residential design emphasizes ground-level impressions of open space—the compositions of potted plants in front of houses, the tiny rear gardens meant not to be entered but to enhance the spatiality of a house. In contrast, an aerial photograph of a Seattle suburb shows a subdivision on a gently sloping site, with curving streets and an abundance of open land. From the air, the extent and character of these spaces are expressed in vivid colors—the dark gray roofs of the large houses, the light gray driveways, the beige sidewalks, the green lawns, the trees with reddish autumn leaves, the blue swimming pools. Gerster's use of color film enhances the contrasting zones of the American suburb and accentuates their extremely generous sizes. Looking at this image, we can begin to understand the casual (and sometimes neglectful) relationship to space that characterizes much of American culture.

Gerster's vertical aerial photographs divulge the patterns of architecture and urbanism—outline, size, position, spacing, color, and texture—that help us understand cultural differences. Through such photographs or in the experience of flight we gain new insights into the landscapes we inhabit— urban, suburban, rural, and increasingly exurban. In 1951, writing for the first issue of his journal *Landscape*, J.B. Jackson emphasized the significance of the vertical aerial view in understanding the configurations of the buildings, fields, and infrastructure that make up the cultural landscape. Jackson encouraged readers to look anew at the rapidly developing world and to appreciate the complex relationships of built and unbuilt. "It is from the air that the true relationship between the natural and the human landscape is first clearly revealed," he wrote. "The peaks and canyons lose much of their impressiveness when seen from above; their vertical dimensions are scarcely discernible except for the blue shadows they cast; and the non-human portion of the country becomes an almost featureless tawny brown surface. What catches our eye and arouses our interest is not the sandy wastes and the naked rocks, but the evidence of man: the lonely windmills and tanks with trails converging upon them; the long straight lines of fences, often dividing the overgrazed range from the one properly managed; the broad pattern of contour plowing and tractor cultivating. The farmhouses appear to be surrounded by groves of trees and a complexity of gardens and corrals and yards. The roads meander to the nearest village or railroad, or to the highway and the city. The harmonious and intricate design which man makes in the course of living and working on the face of the earth slowly evolves beneath us; bright green, dark brown, white, or glittering in the sun, silent and empty of movement (so it appears) except for the small shadow of the plane rippling over fields and roofs. It is a picture we are seeing, an image which stirs us not only because of its beauty and vastness but because of its meaning."[41] From an airplane, we can tell—or decipher—the history of a place. Why are some areas agricultural and others urban? Why do the networks of roads take certain directions? How do historical phases of urban development transform rural land differently?

Today only the vertical aerial view can give us a sense of the vast scale of road systems or suburban development, and of the relationship of each to topography and watersheds. On a regional scale, people in aircraft observe the nature of contemporary exurban development—the spacing of ranchettes and mini-mansions located on outsized acreages just beyond suburbia. Aerial viewers see the true scope of engineering endeavors and their creation of interdependent human and natural environments—the routes of high-tension wires supplying power or those of irrigation channels supplying water. In *Taking Measures Across the American Landscape*, landscape historian Denis Cosgrove writes about the Tennessee Valley Authority's landscape of dams and regulated rivers, visible in its complete form only from a high vertical view: "It is measured in the shapes of the lakes formed behind the river dams and follows the natural lines of the land, tracing its contours up the valleys and counter-pointing the serpentine forms and natural colors of terrain and water with the strong geometric lines and concrete tones of the dams."[42]

A flight in a jet plane across the United States discloses in five or six hours an astonishing amount of information on the nation's historical rela-

41. J.B. Jackson, "The Need for Being Versed in Country Things," *Landscape* 1 (Spring 1951), 4.

42. Denis Cosgrove, "The Measures of America," in James Corner and Alex MacLean, *Taking Measures Across the American Landscape* (New Haven: Yale University Press, 1995), 10.

tionship to nature, technology, and urbanism. Immediately after takeoff from an eastern city, travelers notice that the Atlantic seacoast is almost completely built up, a gray swath of development blanketing the land near the ocean beaches and its bays and along the rivers that flow into the ocean. Suburbs can be distinguished from cities by their greater greenery and their serpentine road networks. Further inland, the extensive eastern forest begins to envelop the edges of the megalopolis, and soon the view down is of undulating expanses of green, brown, or white—depending on the season—cut apart here and there by rivers. The chief sign of human presence in the mountainous terrain is a network of roads that wind around hills, cross bridges, and occasionally become the dense cross-hatchings of towns or cities.

When forests give way to farmsteads and roads straighten out, one is over the Midwest. The geometries of agricultural development dominate the flat and fertile Midwest and Great Plains. While large and small cities hug the major rivers and littoral of the Great Lakes, the spaces between them are more generous than on the Eastern Seaboard. And because of the land's flatness, city and countryside alike follow the lines of the mile-square national grid—first measured by the geographer Thomas Hutchins in 1785. The seemingly endless succession of squares is dominated by agricultural fields; older farmhouses are sited at roadsides. Contour plowing and strip farming carve precise paths for tractors and combines, resulting in patterns of remarkable complexity visible only from the air. Reactions to this view, which can last a couple of hours in the transcontinental journey, vary from boredom to fascination to disgust. In *The Franchiser*, his 1976 novel about a traveling salesman in the Midwest, Stanley Elkin sees the business logic of the land: "America appearing like an image in a crystal ball, the straight furrows in the plowed ground like justified print, the hard-edged Euclidian geometry of survey and civilization."[43] In his 1969 *Design with Nature*, which uses aerial photographs to create an argument for ecological design, Ian McHarg finds the geometry abhorrent: "The maps all show the continent to be green wild landscapes save for the sepia cities huddle on lakes and seaboards, but look from a plane as it crosses the continent and makes an idiocy of distance, see the wild green sectioned as rigorously as the city.

43. Stanley Elkin, *The Franchiser* (New York: Farrar Straus & Giroux, 1976), 52.

154 In the great plains nature persists only in the meandering stream and the flood plain forest, a meaningful geometry in the Mondrian patterns of unknowing men."44

Gradually, west of the 100th meridian, farms give way to rangeland, a landscape of paler greens and browns. As the land becomes arid, center-pivot irrigators draw circles within the squares of the mile grid. Hills reappear and the grids distort. Roads jag and splinter. Towns dwindle. The West begins in the front ranges of the Rocky Mountains, and for the next hour and a half the landscape below the plane is largely unpopulated. Mountains and deserts fill the view. Over Utah and Nevada, the few roads that cut through the sand wastes look out of place. Aside from the occasional urbanized area like Salt Lake City or Reno, not until the plane is within 150 miles of the Pacific Ocean do agriculture and urban development again dominate the scene. Over California's Central Valley, the view down shows a complex pattern of roads, farms, cities, and infrastructure. If one is traveling in winter, the fields and meadows below are the traveler's first encounter with green. Finally, crossing the Coast Ranges, if one is heading to San Francisco, steep grass and chaparral slopes give way to the largest metropolis one will have seen since the Midwest, a metropolis circling the bay and edging the Pacific Ocean.

At night, these shapes and colors abstract into light and dark. Visual distinctions boil down to the degree and character of light, which now out-lines cities, buildings, and roads. Illumination defines the nocturnal aerial view, contributing to our understanding of the land through the densities of human presence, or absence. Seen from the air, most architecture fades into dark homogeneity. Small and low buildings, especially, can be reduced to a single light or small array of white lights, hardly distinguishable from one another. Tall buildings and large complexes such as airports, seaports, sta-diums acquire a more magnified visual presence. So do large cities, whose geographical reach can be grasped clearly by the extent of illumination. At night, the metropolis glows, and newer, sprawling cities, developed during the age of electricity, are particularly magnificent. In *America*, published in 1989, Jean Baudrillard critiques the nation's imitative urban environments, castigating buildings and cities alike as third-generation copies of older

44. Ian McHarg, *Design with Nature* (Garden City, New York: Doubleday & Company, 1969), 23.

European forms. But above Los Angeles at night, he momentarily loses his
acerbic and ironic tone. "There is nothing to match flying over Los Angeles
by night. A sort of luminous, geometric, incandescent immensity, stretching
as far as the eye can see, bursting out from the cracks in the clouds. Only
Hieronymus Bosch's hell can match this inferno effect," he writes. "The
muted fluorescence of all the diagonals: Wilshire, Lincoln, Sunset, Santa
Monica. Already, flying over San Fernando Valley, you come upon the horizontal infinite in every direction. But, once you are beyond the mountain, a
city ten times larger hits you. You will never have encountered anything that
stretches as far as this before. Even the sea cannot match it, since it is not
divided up geometrically. The irregular, scattered flickering of European cities
does not produce the same parallel lines, the same vanishing points, the
same aerial perspectives either. They are medieval cities. This one condenses by night the entire future geometry of the networks of human relations,
gleaming in their abstraction, luminous in their extension, astral in their
reproduction to infinity."[45] Lit up at night, Los Angeles creates an immense
urban impression from the sky.

Many other writers have remarked upon the radiant visuality of the
nocturnal city. Buenos Aires, to Saint-Exupery, after flying over half the South
American continent, seemed to dye "the horizon with pink fires, soon to
flaunt its diadem of jewels, like some fairy hoard."[46] In *About This Life*,
essayist Barry Lopez recalls his wanderings from pole to pole. "One clear
evening at 20,000 feet over Manhattan, I could see," Lopez writes, "every
streetlight halfway to the end of Long Island."[47] The nocturnal aerial view
accords perfectly with his quest to find solitary vantage points of immense
grandeur. In *Paradise News*, novelist David Lodge tells the story of a group
of people on a package tour seeking a brief bit of bliss. When they reach
Honolulu after a long flight across the Pacific, the view below seems prom-
ising: "shimmering strands of light defined themselves as tower blocks,
streets, houses, and moving vehicles. How astonishing it was, to discover
this brilliantly illuminated modern city, pulsing like a star in the black
immensity of the ocean."[48] Only in the nocturnal zoomscape does architecture begin to encompass the earth and the starry firmament. The aerial view
of cities becomes ornamental. Black night turns cities into jeweled cobwebs,

45. Jean Baudrillard, *America*, trans. Chris
Turner (London: Verso, 1988), 51–52.

46. de Saint-Exupery, 278.

47. Barry Lopez, *About This Life: Journeys on
the Threshold of Memory* (New York: Alfred A.
Knopf, 1998), 93.

48. David Lodge, *Paradise News* (London:
Penguin Books, 1991), 66.

brocades of emeralds, sapphires, and rubies. Below the airplane, buildings, shops, streetlights, and the headlights of cars glitter in the darkness. Above the airplane, the moon, planets, stars, and comets shine back. On a clear night, flying above the earth, aerial perception builds sky, city, and stars into the greatest architecture of all.

GLOBALISM

Lately we have become accustomed to seeing the globe from space. In 1959, Explorer 6 took the first photograph of Earth from space. In 1972, Apollo astronauts on route to the moon took one of the most famous photographs of the planet. Centered on Africa with Antarctica visible below, this image provided the first visual document of the Earth as a singular entity. Oceans and continents, desert and rain forest, swirling cloud formations—all are pictured. The Apollo photograph encapsulates the global implications of the aerial view: the higher the altitude, the larger the viewing field.[49] Commenting on the historical path of mechanized vision that led from photography to space travel, Paul Virilio describes what it must be like to view earth from space: "The earth, that phantom limb, no longer extends as far as the eye can see; it presents all aspects of itself for inspection in the strange little window."[50]

Powers of Ten, a 1977 film by Charles and Ray Eames, explores this phenomenon. The film illustrates the changing texture and scale of the aerial view as it ascends from ground level in a Chicago lakefront park to outer space, moving ten times further away every ten seconds. From a helicopter 100 meters above the earth, boats, cars, and the traffic on Lake Shore Drive are visible; so is a sunbather lying on a blanket on the grass. At 1,000 meters, the typical cruising altitude of small planes, the blanket disappears, and the park shrivels between buildings, roads, and other open spaces. The bulk of the view is taken up by the harbor, the Field Museum and the Adler Planetarium, and Soldier's Field and its parking lots. From 10,000 meters, the cruising altitude of jets, the frame divides evenly between the gray of Chicago and the blue of Lake Michigan. The street grid, parks, expressways, and lakefront are visible, mostly as color and outline. At 100,000 meters, the whole metropolitan region comes into view. From these satellite heights, contrasts between the city, suburbs, and surrounding farmland diminish,

49. Margret Dreikausen, *Aerial Perception: The Earth as Seen from Aircraft and Spacecraft and Its Influence on Contemporary Art* (Philadelphia: Art Alliance Press, 1985), 54.

50. Paul Virilio, *The Information Bomb*, trans. Chris Turner (London: Verso, 2000), 18.

although the lake and its harbors are apparent. At one million meters, all of Lake Michigan visible, urban development is no longer readable. The ten-million-meter mark encompasses almost the entire earth, and at 100 million meters, earth becomes a white-and-blue orb against a dark starry background. At one trillion kilometers, the earth is finally subsumed by the sun. Shape is reduced to point, and color replaced by black and white.

As the Eameses' film shows, with each rise in distance from the earth, the objects and their contexts grow larger: from park to building arrangement to city to region, and so on. In aerial viewing at lower altitudes, such as that experienced by ordinary aircraft, the increase in scope brought about by distance likewise leads to a reduction in specificity. The farther the point from which people look at buildings or cities, the less detail they see. Aerial viewers looking down at architecture tend to compare what they are seeing with what came before, what will follow, and what surrounds; people relate a particular object or place to its context within a journey. Aerial globalism has led to a shift in the scale of geographic consciousness.

In a sense, globalism has existed for as long as people have journeyed beyond their home regions. Sea voyages are a form of globalism, giving sailors an expansive understanding of place and geography. But aerial globalism brings about a more thoroughgoing manner of visual reach and cross-cultural comparison. In the latter part of the twentieth century, for the first time in history, the general public began to see aerial impressions of architecture in the course of everyday life. Especially since the 1960s, modern air travel has become less of a spectacular voyage, taken infrequently, and more a means of regular business or pleasure trips. Alongside other aspects of the zoomscape—especially photography, film, and television, but also fast trains—the experience of architecture from the air embeds global perceptions within ordinary sight. Our visual consciousness regularly handles impressions of faraway as well as local places.

There is something expansive, and at the same time disorienting (and even shallow), about seeing whole countries during a day's flight. As Pico Iyer mulls over his crazy life in *The Global Soul*, he writes, "the average person today sees as many images in a day as a Victorian might have in a lifetime.... We wake up, orphaned in West Hollywood and go to sleep, surrounded by our parents in medieval Katmandu; we zigzag across centuries as if they were just settlements in a village."[51] Still, a global idea of place, gleaned from aerial views, does not imply any greater understanding of what one sees. Those persons exposed to a wide array of aerial views and images see more of the wider world; they do not necessarily know more of the world. Aerial globalism extends our vision from that which is near to that which is far, and usually, from that which is seen slowly to that which is merely glimpsed. Instead of viewing local places closely or directly, aerial viewers see many places far removed from each other and themselves. The modern condition of visual surfeit, begun in the age of railroads and photographs and the subject of Iyer's book, has become acute in our era of commonplace air travel. While close-range static viewing can be casual and distracted, it offers the possibility of looking closely and carefully if we choose to do so. Distant viewing from a moving aircraft does not offer this possibility. The understanding of objects is gleaned from the connections we make between far-flung sights.

During the past century, the trails of airborne sight have often led toward the famous and the fantastic. They began, however, less in actual aerial experiences than through photographic representation. During the 1920s, when most people had not yet flown, aerial photographers began to record visual narratives of global architecture. For the first time, people saw images of the great buildings of the world from the air. These suggestive and highly selective images were an early form of global visual consciousness.

In 1928, *National Geographic Magazine* published several aerial photographic narratives. Donald Keyhoe took an ambitious trip, a 20,000-mile aviation journey across the United States with Charles Lindbergh.[52] Most of Keyhoe's photographs focus on a prominent feature of a place, such as a building, work of infrastructure, or topographic condition. St. Louis is shown from the vantage point of the Mississippi River and its two great bridges. Denver is encapsulated by a shot of the Colorado State Capital (although the caption describes a journey to the Rocky Mountains). Long Beach, California, is depicted as a forest of oil derricks. Keyhoe, like most aerial photographers, aimed his camera at forms capable of making an impact from great distances; he thus favored notable landmarks or eccentric structures over the everyday city.

51. Pico Iyer, *The Global Soul: Jet Lag, Shopping Malls, and the Search for Home* (New York: Alfred A. Knopf, 2000), 60.

52. Donald E. Keyhoe, "Seeing America with Lindbergh: The Record of a Tour of More Than 20,000 Miles by Airplane Through 48 States on Schedule Time," *The National Geographic Magazine* 53 (January 1928).

In another essay, Alan Cobham surveys monuments from the Mediterranean Sea to East Asia, often reducing them to visual one-liners. The prominent buildings he shot include ancient Egyptian temples, the Athenian Acropolis, the Taj Mahal, and the Shwe Dagon Pagoda in Burma. Cobham argues that the air view gives travelers a better understanding of the physical relations of different places than does ground travel; he even claims that his memories and impressions of places are more vivid than those of travelers in steamships, trains, or cars.[53] And indeed, his photographs condense historical cultures into single, extraordinary images. While all photographs isolate architecture and landscape, aerial photography is more extreme. Because of its succinct views, because of its ability in a single shot to encapsulate a whole region or architectural style, aerial photography can seem to substitute for an immersion in actual places. Maynard Owen Williams, in "Seeing 3,000 Years of History in Four Hours," brags about the air traveler's ability to experience the great architectural achievements of the Aegean basin—from Istanbul to Athens—between breakfast and lunch.[54] Once, in fact, a nation sought to represent itself through a single monument visible from the air. The International Columbus Lighthouse Competition in Santo Domingo (1929-1930) proposed a massive cruciform earthwork from which vertical shafts of lights would illuminate the sky.[55] Air travelers would not have needed to descend to the Dominican Republic to appreciate the nation's historic significance. They could have remained aloft.

In recent decades, film, video, and air travel have greatly expanded aerial photography's representation of global architecture. As in earlier eras, architectural monuments and engineering marvels continue to comprise the bulk of aerial tourism—Cessna flights around the sights of world cities, helicopter rides over ancient ruins. Film and video taken from aircraft similarly expose viewers to extraordinary places for brief periods. Through editing, they further condense the aerial experience into a succession of awe-inspiring moments in which it is hard to glean any context for what is being seen. In an Imax or Omnimax theater, spectators swoop about the *Blue Planet*, in and out of the *Grand Canyon*, just above the *Fires of Kuwait*, and almost smack into the *Mysteries of Egypt*. On screen, these aerial views are visually arresting. Yet they tell us little about the places we are viewing. The experience

53. Alan Cobham, "Seeing the World from the Air," *The National Geographic Magazine* 53 (March 1928), 375.

54. Maynard Owen Williams, "Seeing 3,000 Years of History in Four Hours," *The National Geographic Magazine* 54 (December 1928), 725.

55. Charles Waldheim, "Aerial Representation and the Recovery of Landscape," in *Recovering Landscape*, 122.

New cars and trucks, American Midwest

of architecture or landscape, either in an aircraft or on the screen, becomes something like an amusement park ride, exciting more for the rush of movement alongside a building than for any understanding of the building's cultural dimension. Aerial tourism and extra-wide-screen videos alike whet the visual appetite for ever more daring and surprising vistas, for narratives that construct something new from something formulaic.

Those persons looking for high adventure often favor aerial sights of wilderness—the regions unreached by commercial air traffic. Much of the globe still lacks appreciable urban development. Away from cities and farmland, off the beaten track, lies a terrain of mystery and foreboding. In "The Path, the Road, the Highway," Philip L. Wagner looks down at Mexico from a small plane, noticing roads, towns, and village clearings almost swallowed by forest and brush. "On flights at lower altitude, the traveler in the south of Mexico looks out on thousands of square miles of mountainous dark green, with a highway occasionally creeping through, and once in a while a recognizable town showing," he writes. "More commonly, he sees amidst the wilds only patchy clearings and thatched huts, alone or in small clusters, far from anywhere."[56] Off common flight paths, the aerial view can become unfamiliar, unsettling. Aside from large bodies of water—such as bays, lakes and rivers—or significant ecological transitions—such as between mountains and plain—urban development is the surest means of orientation from the air. Without buildings, roads, or fields, it is hard to get one's bearings. Most natural landscapes are too intricate to be read from the air. Aside from experts, few can fathom the lands below that veer between extreme uniformity or extreme complexity—wildernesses such as deserts, forests, tundra, ice, water, and sky. Indeed, when flight moves from the clear atmosphere into the blindness of thick clouds or the turbulence of a storm, the sky becomes its own wilderness. Viewed from the troposphere, the world can seem desolate, like a photograph of the surface of Mars or the Moon. The glimpse of a familiar place can elicit elation, like the sighting of land by a sailor. Of an isolated hamlet in Patagonia, Saint-Exupery writes: "Sometimes, after a hundred miles of steppes as desolate as the sea, he encountered a lonely farm-house that seemed to be sailing backwards from him in a great prairie sea, with its freight of human lives; and he saluted with his wings this passing ship."[57]

56. Philip L. Wagner, "The Path, the Road, the Highway," Landscape 10.1 (Fall 1960), 36.

57. Saint-Exupery, 213.

Wagner's and Saint-Exupery's passages point out that while air travel and aerial imagery might take us to the ends of the planet, much remains beyond our grasp. A colossal region of the unknown and unfamiliar surrounds the dramatic and selective images associated with aerial globalism. Most of this wilderness is nature. But some of it is architectural. Aerial views of architecture, too, can provoke feelings of alienation and bewilderment. In the 1930s, in *Round the World Again in Eighty Days*, Jean Cocteau traveled on ocean liners, trains, and airplanes to retrace the fictional journey Jules Verne's character Phileas Fogg took in the nineteenth century. Amid this global voyage, flying to the Grand Canyon from Los Angeles, he views the landscape. "And once more that feeling of 'dehumanization' and utter loneliness, that curious impression that no worlds exist inhabited by man," Cocteau wrote. "All trace of humanity was vanishing from the earth. People were the first to go, then animals, then cars. Of the poor old world that cannot do without us nothing remained but roofs and houses emptied of life, it seemed, by some mysterious cataclysm. Nothing but straight lines, triangles, squares, and rhombs; a world of bleak geometry, of patterned fields and crazy pavements—the work of man; of veins and arteries, volutes, curves and corrugations, shirrs and spirals, dents and dimples—the work of wind and rain."[58] Contrary to many of his close-at-hand experiences on the global trip, Cocteau feels no connection to the city or its natural surroundings when he glimpses them from the air. Houses and industry resolve into stultifying rectangles and grids; the contours of ridges and canyons reveal geometries too intricate to comprehend. To Cocteau, none of these sights feels palpable or cultural. From the air, his view of architecture is of wilderness, visually unfamiliar and estranging.

Aerial globalism spreads the perceptual field of architecture and landscape over remote, immense geographies. In so doing, it resituates the aesthetic field of judgment. Nowadays, some people are more fluent in the skylines and monuments of world cities or in the topographic features of continents than in the facades of their own street. Elemental lines and smooth shapes have increasingly replaced fine-grained textures within the aerial view, and perhaps within our mental maps as well. Some people respond negatively to this massive displacement of sight, while others rejoice in its

58. Jean Cocteau, "Starscapes: The Grand Canyon," in *Open the Sky: An Anthology of the Literature of Flight*, ed. E.M. Quittenden (Oxford: Pergamon Press, 1965), 111.

revelations of the physical world. Even more strikingly than the rail or auto-motive view, the aerial view embodies extremes of artistic subjectivity and scientific objectivity. Through it we see architecture configured toward both mind and universe.

CHAPTER 4

PHOTOGRAPHY

IN ITS BEGINNINGS, photography represented architecture. In 1826,
Joseph Nicéphore Niépce fixed an image, called a heliograph, to a polished
pewter plate; the exposure required eight hours. The scene depicts the buildings and landscape seen from the window of his workshop in Le Gras,
France. In 1835, William Henry Fox Talbot took the earliest surviving photograph—an image of a window in Lacock Abbey, his home in England. For
both experiments, as well as for daguerreotypes—a process of fixing images
to copper plates invented by Louis Daguerre in the late 1830s—the ubiquity, size, and stillness of architecture suited early photography's long exposure times.[1] In the century and a half since these beginnings—as paper
prints became available in the 1850s, as halftones allowed easy magazine
and book reproductions in the 1880s, and as high-speed film permitted
street photography in the mid-twentieth century—photography has caused
images of architecture to be fruitful, to multiply, and to have afterlives.

Photographs are key components of modern mass communication.
Along with video, photography personifies visual culture, that storm of imagery
that ceaselessly confronts us. As Susan Sontag argues in *On Photography*,
photography isolates things from their contexts, turning them into images
within systems of information, classification, and storage. These systems
"range from the crudely chronological order of snapshot sequences pasted in
family albums to the dogged accumulations and meticulous filing needed for
photography's uses in weather forecasting, astronomy, microbiology, geology,
police work, medical training and diagnosis, military reconnaissance, and art
history."[2] Sontag's 1977 book underscores the invasive nature of photography, its tendency to appropriate worldly reality and draw viewers into a
sphere of second-generation imagery. Her thought-provoking critique dis-
counts, however, the fact that photographs are themselves traces of reality—
photochemical imprints of real objects. The photographic appropriation of
reality amounts to a restructuring of reality into something different, added,
or lost. In art, photography uses traces of the real to fabricate new realities,
which can be beautiful, critical, or bewildering. Cindy Sherman's 1978 print
"Untitled Film Still #21" uses a backdrop of Manhattan skyscrapers to render a woman-about-town of the 1950s. In less rarefied contexts, photography propels commerce, through its use in magazines, on posters, billboards,
and the Internet, on product packaging and in advertising. Flip the pages of

1. Beaumont Newhall, *A History of Photography from 1839 to the Present* (Boston: Little, Brown & Company, 1982), 27.

2. Susan Sontag, *On Photography* (New York: Farrar, Straus & Giroux, 1977), 156.

most magazines and you will find striking images—a building or bridge, a range of mountains—in the advertisements for late-model automobiles or brands of vodka.

Photographs expand the representation and scope of the building art. They are a kind of alter ego of building form and identity, facilitating the reputation of a work of architecture and yet diminishing the importance of the actual building. Through photographs, people come to associate architecture with the richness of history and geography. Photographs display the newest creations, the oldest ruins, the most exotic places. They bring us images of cities devastated by war or transformed by urban renewal. They can make stars or scoundrels out of buildings. Yet fame and notoriety have a price: what is photographed does not need to be visited; in fact, what is photogenic might not appear compelling in person. Photography displaces architecture from the context of its physical site to the context of its media presentation—for example, to a book or gallery. Most buildings are perceived not in their real space, but amid other spaces. The cultural reach of photography is remarkable. Circulating images around the world, photography globalizes vision. Somewhat like the aerial view, the photographic perception of architecture ranges far and wide beyond any particular place or building, branching into diverse networks.

In the past 150 years, the photography of architecture has encompassed various approaches, from the celebratory to the critical, from the documentary to the artistic. Architectural photography often strives to record objective information about buildings; but in many cases, photography creates new works of art in its own right.[3] Some photographers, especially in professional magazines, promote new works of architecture; others, more artistically ambitious, dramatize the cultural situations of the building art. The photographic zoomscape has become one of the main means of communication among architects. In school, architectural students are exposed to the breadth of architecture through slide lectures and illustrated texts. In the sphere of practice, architectural photography contributes to the formation of canons and the creation of trends. The modern understanding of architecture would be impossible without the information conveyed rapidly and over great distances by photography. And photographs are the chief way

3. Eric de Maré, *Photography and Architecture*
(New York: Frederick Praeger, 1961), 25–26.

of introducing architecture to the general public and of stimulating a desire for architecture. In tourist guides, large-format books, and shelter and travel magazines, they transform architecture into consumer objects for a mass audience. Photographs of buildings, more than actual buildings, are the catalysts for expenditures on trips and home renovations.

Before photography, architecture was illustrated in paintings, drawings, engravings, lithographs, and etchings.[4] Yet none of these media can achieve the verisimilitude of photography. Even the most painstakingly rendered paintings— Pieter Saenredam's views of seventeenth-century Dutch church interiors, for instance, or Canaletto's eighteenth-century Venetian cityscapes—cannot match the precision of a photograph. By capturing the light reflected from surfaces, and by fixing that light on chemically sensitive paper to develop an image of the building, photographs preserve works of architecture and, as often as not, convince us that we are seeing the real thing. Of course, photography has its own conventions. Photographs capture architecture in miniaturized views. These views are also flat, a two-dimensional layer that must somehow suggest thickness of form and depth of space. In no other art or technology are buildings and cities at once realistically portrayed, and, at the same time, transformed into strictly visual entities. As small, two-dimensional images on paper, they provide a frame through which to view the world. The camera simulates the act of looking within architectural space, through doors, windows, streets, or archways.

In the 1970s, the English artist Gordon Matta-Clark produced a series of photographs illustrating how he cut openings into the walls, floors, and roofs of abandoned buildings. Matta-Clark wanted to offer unusual and unexpected views through the deconstructed buildings, and to demonstrate how the conventions of architecture—door and windows—literally "frame" our experience of the world. The photographs play a documentary role in his project, showing buildings sliced apart, their insides bared. But the photographs also play an artistic role. Their frames further cut and delimit the field of view; we see precise angles on Matta-Clark's operation. Depending upon the site where viewing takes place, the photographs cut open the wall of a building or page of a book, offering windows into the transformation of built space.

4. Ibid., 17.

We might investigate the aesthetics of architectural photography by comparing two photographs: one a famous image of a renowned building, the other an image of an anonymous, even ambiguous construction site. In the first photograph, a house on a river rises up from great flat rocks; large concrete balconies seem to float above a waterfall; building slabs, clad in stone, poke up into the sky. The season is late autumn; the trees around the house are mostly bare. The photograph is of Fallingwater, by Frank Lloyd Wright, arguably the most famous American house by the most famous American architect.

Given its fame, few people have visited the house Wright designed in 1937 for the Pittsburgh businessman Edgar J. Kaufmann. Located in rural Pennsylvania about sixty miles southeast of Pittsburgh, and not served by public transportation, Fallingwater is somewhat remote. The address most frequently given is Bear Run, a place not indicated on most maps. Because of its out-of-the-way location, most people know the house only from photographs.

The photograph was taken in 1937, the year the house was completed, by architectural photographer Bill Hedrich. Hedrich's black-and-white photograph shows the house from a dramatic vantage, encompassing the building, the rocks, and the Bear Run River. Viewed from this angle, the waterfall appears to flow from the house. No windows are visible. The photograph presents the house as a composition of horizontal and vertical masses that echo the rocks and trees. This framing of building and site contributed enormously to the building's fame—and the photograph's fame. Hedrich (a partner in Hedrich Blessing, a premier architectural photography firm) usually attempted to portray the essence of a building without much regard for context. Here his achievement was to construct essence from context. While a visit would offer multiple views of the house, the photograph shows us a single view. By condensing lived experience into fixed image, photography can thus encourage forceful and singular readings of a building. Frank Lloyd Wright considered this the definitive photograph, and it has become the standard view of Fallingwater, the image that most sustains the building's fame.

To many people, Hedrich's photograph is, in a sense, Fallingwater—their only experience of the building. Or is it? Hedrich's photograph and its image are not the same thing. Over the years, similar shots have been taken by many photographers and printed in scores of books, magazines, and pamphlets. Most people have seen imitations of Hedrich's photograph, making it, in this sense, the meta-photograph of Fallingwater. Like most reproductive acts, this process has profound implications for the original building, involving not only the appropriation of architecture by photography, but also the turning of a photographic image into an icon.

Fallingwater's fame thus derives not only from the quality of the building, but also from its status as an iconic image. Indeed, the iconic image has transcended not only Wright's building but also Hedrich's photograph. It now influences, even dominates, the reception of the building, even on visits to the site. The experience of a visit will not reproduce that of the photograph, of course; the sky, trees, ground and details will vary depending on the season and the weather. And most visitors will not wade across the river to find the exact place from which Hedrich took his photograph. In fact, an on-site experience, failing to capture the exactness of the image, might actually fortify the perfection of the iconic image. The point is that the experience of viewing architecture is fundamentally changed by photography—by buildings being prefigured for us endlessly by photographs.

Andreas Gursky's "Hong Kong Island" is a color photograph of a place that is hardly iconic. Gursky focuses his lens on a huge construction site in the heart of the Chinese city. An extreme wide-angle shot encompasses much activity and building form. The principal object of this 1994 photograph is not a building but rather an expanse of yellow and red construction cranes, piles of rocks and reinforcing rods, turquoise tarpaulin; there are only a few people, and they appear dwarfed by the site. The construction site occupies the bottom third of the photograph. Above the site we see part of the skyline of Hong Kong—a few dozen slender skyscrapers ranging fifteen to thirty stories, looking a bit like books on a shelf. Gursky often frames urban environments into giant rectangles packed with detail. Whether of packages of candy on supermarket shelves, of modular windows on high-rise buildings, or of construction equipment on a city block, his images show us both the contemporary city's extraordinary scale and its particulars.

"Hong Kong Island" is particularly enigmatic. It offers us little sense of what is happening or going to happen on the site. While at first, it appears to show a construction site, on closer inspection, it makes us question our initial impression. The space depicted is so large that any high-rise constructed on the site would dwarf its surroundings; the absence of a deep foundation pit provokes further doubt. Perhaps the pit is being dug? Maybe the site is a staging zone for nearby projects? Whatever is occurring will surely be massive and disruptive. But then, in this photograph Hong Kong itself looks massive and disruptive. That Gursky chose to title the image "Hong Kong Island" deepens the mystery, suggesting that the photographer saw the site as peculiarly separate from its environment.

The uncertainties of Gursky's photograph owe to its specific, yet oddly ambiguous depiction of an event in time. Peering into the empty space between crowded buildings, filled with all sorts of construction equipment, the photograph seems to be about the process of building. By photographing an active building site and yet revealing nothing about the object under construction, Gursky stimulates us to think about construction in Hong Kong. He counterposes the instantaneity of the photograph against the duration of a city. We see a moment, a moment that can never happen again, a moment long past; and yet, because we remain uncertain about what this moment is about, our gaze drifts back and forward through time. We are not likely to visit the site and resolve our confusion. Even were Gursky to help us find the same spot where the photograph was taken—probably from a nearby skyscraper, high up in some window—that spot itself would doubtless be different. The alignment of cranes, the piles of construction materials that we see in the image—none of this will recur. The photograph leads neither back to a building's construction nor forward to its ongoing life. "Hong Kong Island" has a past and future both within and outside the life of the city.

If "Hong Kong Island" cannot, despite its date, be fixed in time, Hedrich's photograph of Fallingwater appears timeless, an image of a finished, perfect building. Still, the two photographs have something in common. Both the iconic image of Fallingwater and the ambiguous image of "Hong Kong Island" occupy, in different ways, an eternal present. Gursky's here-and-now is confined to a particular image, not to any site or to any photographic reinterpretation of that site. "Hong Kong Island" encourages us to see an event, not an object; it underscores the difficulty of reconciling an unformed, complex process with either the past or future. Hedrich's photograph of Fallingwater is suspended in time—and hence beyond time. It captures a formed object so perfectly that the moment the photograph was taken, the moment of artistic inspiration, is forever preserved.

The photography of architecture puts buildings into complex temporal situations. To experience a photograph is to experience an image appropriated not only from a building or a site, but also from the passage of time. Time is stopped. The image is static. In photographs, we always view a moment in the past. Much architectural photography, especially commercial photography like Hedrich's, shows us buildings new and pristine, before occupation and use. Such photographs encourage the perception of architecture as everlasting. And by preserving images of buildings that have been destroyed or altered, photography fosters nostalgia, too. Looking at photographs of old buildings can be like looking at the family album and feeling the loss of youth and inevitability of aging.[5] With buildings, of course, aging can be arrested. The discipline of historic preservation depends critically upon photographs. For preservationists, photographs constitute an essential archive; photographs of a building shortly after construction become the datum by which to understand its permutations, the deviations from its original and idealized appearance.

In a book chronicling photography's first century, the architectural photographer and historian Richard Pare notes that the perception of photographs is bound up with the complexities of time. "The photographer," Pare writes, "seeks to reveal aspects of space through his understanding of the effects of time. Time past, in the cumulative age of the building, time present in the photographer's moment, and time future in our present, all are interwoven, becoming an inseparable unity in the perception of each image."[6] Whether these time frames are inseparable or not, the consciousness of time structures the experience of architecture. Because it is two-dimensional, photography can convey extension and duration only by making viewers perceive space and time. Caught up in an image, we let our imaginations wander; we connect the image with the intentions of the photographer, or

5. Neal Leach, "Walter Benjamin, Mimesis, and the Dreamworld of Photography," in *Reconstructing Space: Architecture in Recent German Photography*, ed. Michael Mack (London: Architectural Association Publications, 1999), 15.

6. Richard Pare, *Photography and Architecture, 1839–1939* (Montreal: Canadian Centre for Architecture, 1982), 12.

with the aims of the book author or museum curator who have used or displayed the photograph. Photographs require us to imagine the life of a building in a greater cultural dimension. Far from limiting our understanding to the precise objects that have been captured on film, the fixity of the art stimulates us to find meanings beyond the frame. In "The Photographic Message," published in 1977, Roland Barthes argues that although photographs appear to capture reality naturally, the meanings we glean from them are socially constructed. "Thanks to its codes of connotation, the reading of the photograph is thus always historical; it depends on the reader's knowledge just as though it were a matter of real language, intelligible only if one has learned the signs."[7] Photographic literacy is learned.[8]

These temporal dynamics fundamentally alter the act of viewing architecture. Through diverse means—frontal flatness, different angles and contexts, a focus on details, or in city views—photography transforms architecture in ways that suggest architecture's own transformative powers. The construction of a work of architecture remakes a part of the world, moving around matter, converting it from a mineral or living state to a fabricated state, and creating a new sense of place. Photography, in turn, removes the architectural work from its site, removes as well the dimensions of time and depth, reproduces its image, and introduces that image into new sites. Architecture constructs place; photography transforms place into media.

FRONT AND CENTER

Even more than trains, automobiles, and airplanes, photographs distance us from the architecture we view. Photographs are mediated experience. They can be construed as representations of things in the world, or understood as things of the real world. In either case, photographs are things apart. The photographic perception of architecture usually occurs off site, far from the architecture being viewed. A photograph of a building transcends not only time and place, but also weight, texture, scale, and sometimes even gravity.[9] Photography removes us from architecture. And yet, despite this remove, photography also draws us toward buildings and helps us to see aspects of architecture usually impossible to see.

Of all photographic positions, the frontal stance is the most artificial. In *Architecture Transformed: A History of the Photography of Buildings from*

7. Roland Barthes, "The Photographic Message," in *Image-Music-Text*, trans. Stephen Heath (New York: Noonday Press, 1977), 28.

8. Alan Sekula, "On the Invention of Photographic Meaning," *Artforum* 13 (January 1975), 37.

9. Daniel Naegele, "Photography and Architecture," *History of Photography* 22 (Summer 1998), 98.

1839 to the Present, photographer Cervin Robinson and historian Joel Herschman survey the history of architectural photography. The authors note that frontal photography evolved from the strictness and precision of elevation drawings, from "the clarity unencumbered by context, the flatness, linearity, and above all accurate rendering of proportions of the elevation as against the perspective, which reproduces the experience of actually seeing the monument as a three-dimensional structure in a real setting."[10] Frontal photographs can most easily displace architecture from setting. They show the facade of a building head-on. The lines, textures, material, and shadows of the building are clear. Not much else intrudes—there might be a bit of sky; a piece of ground; a car, even some people. But these are beside the point and they read as inessential. They do not distract us from the facade. Distilled into surface, a building seems larger, its presence enhanced. Its isolation kindles insights. The building is rendered flat, and so we can focus on relationships between the parts, between the composition of ornament and the play of light and shadow. The visual autonomy of the frontal view encourages close encounters with ornament and composition, a focus on textures not tectonics. This is certainly the case with, say, Edouard-Denis Baldus's 1857 photograph of the Pavillon Sully at the Louvre. Baldus was one of the principal photographers of architecture and landscape in nineteenth-century France, famed for his images of railroad stations and bridges. His largest commission, begun in 1855, was the documentation of the Louvre Museum. Frontal photographs such as Baldus's combined the idealization of drawings with the reality of buildings. Photography could thus lift the completed building out of the here-and-now and situate it within the realm of high art.

In the image of the Pavillon Sully, Baldus shows the facade and little else, just a row of bare trees, which enhances our sense of the building as massive and permanent. Instead of showing the pavilion in the context of the Louvre, the image focuses relentlessly on surface, on details. Viewers are encouraged to study the windows, columns, entablatures, and statues, to appreciate the material intricacy of the parts. The image epitomizes the compositional values of French neoclassicism, the desire to create a pleasing equilibrium from a rich vocabulary of architectural elements. Baldus's photograph enlists the viewer in what we might call an inspection of the

10. Cervin Robinson and Joel Herschman,
*Architecture Transformed: A History of the
Photography of Buildings from 1839 to the Present*
(Cambridge: MIT Press, 1987), 6.

dress uniform of the Pavillon Sully. Since all parts of its facade are equally in focus, any awkward proportion would be apparent. But here we find no unruliness. Nor do we find any in the other photographs; Baldus idealized buildings so intently that he often eliminated potential distractions, sometimes erasing neighboring structures from his photographs.[11]

This practice of altering images to enhance the view suggests the extent to which photography is obsessed with surface. It is not surprising, then, that many photographers explore the gradations of light and dark, and how light and dark construct surfaces. Hugo Schmölz's photograph of the model factory complex at the 1914 Werkbund Exhibition in Cologne, designed by Walter Gropius, displays the effects of lighting on brick, glass, and steel surfaces. A wall of glass and steel dominates the image; the eye is drawn to the contrast between the darker, almost toneless brick surfaces at ground level and the shimmering glass above. Just as glass reflects the variations of light intensity and movement, the frontal photograph accentuates the play of light. By concentrating a viewer's attention on light and glass, Schmölz promoted Gropius's pioneering work on the curtain wall. Not only does the frontal photograph concentrate on ornamental detail; it can also help advance new architectural paradigms.

To be sure, photography accords well with a key aesthetic of modern architecture: the replacement of surfaces decorated by historicist ornament with surfaces articulated by the play of light and shadow. In modernist buildings, structural frames of steel or reinforced concrete allow for variably sized and located windows and skylights, and for entire walls of glass. By capturing the effects of light on solid and transparent surfaces, in different seasons and times of day, photographers explored the achievements of architectural modernism. Varying the degree of light or shadow in a photograph can heighten or obscure the forms of a building. Architectural photography can thus enhance our understanding of a building. Black-and-white photography especially delineates shape and form through the gradations of light. The experience of seeing the world reduced to the intensities of light and dark affected the perception—and the history—of architecture, encouraging the modernist aesthetic of expansive glazing and flat white walls.

Frontal photography also emphasizes the shape and composition of facades. We see this clearly in *Industrial Facades*, a book of photographs by

---

11. Barry Bergdoll, "A Matter of Time: Architects, Photographers in Second Empire France," in *The Photographs of Edouard Baldus*, Malcolm Daniel (New York: Metropolitan Museum of Art, 1994), 111.

Bernd and Hilla Becher. As in their other collections, the Bechers do not seek out works of high architecture; they are not interested in revealing the intentions of architects or the trajectories of architectural movements. Instead, they take pictures of vernacular industrial structures: blast furnaces, water towers, cooling towers, gas tanks, and grain elevators. Usually, the Bechers photograph and display multiple examples of such buildings; they show the buildings as types. The photographs are not intended to enlighten us on the workings of these utilitarian buildings. The Bechers do not display the various parts of a factory complex; rather, they show typologically similar features from different complexes. By arraying such images in series, they shift our focus from function to a comparison of form. Viewing multiple images, we can contrast the features of one gas tank, for instance, with those of another, and thus perceive the intricate variety within the type. Or looking at warehouses, we can see how plain brick facades, capped by pediments, are divided into three parts in a great many ways. Aligned one after the other in a book, or in grids on a gallery wall, the photographs make the building look abstracted and neutralized. The frontal images of industrial building seem to become pure form.

The Bechers' series not only depict industrial artifacts; they also begin to constitute taxonomies of such structures. Because of their size, flatness, and portability, photographs can be assembled and reassembled into diverse categorical groupings. Instead of viewing buildings in the context of real space, we see them in the context of abstract visual space. Indeed, early on, photographs significantly advanced the exploration of architectural taxonomies begun earlier, in drawings by architects such as J.N.L. Durand. Unlike drawings, photographs contributed to the modern preoccupation with origins and historical succession. People tend to associate drawings with the era in which they were made; photographs are sometimes associated with the time of their production, but more often with the origins of the buildings they represent. Arraying different photographs alongside one another could be like putting different buildings into a common space; the practice revealed routes of cross-cultural influence and historical change. Thus the development of photography during the second half of the nineteenth century may have contributed to the emerging field of architectural history, helping advance its arguments on both connoisseurship and stylistic succession. The rise of architectural history as a discipline was aided immensely by the ability to place photographs side by side and thus compare buildings from different places and periods.[12]

Through the use of multiples, the Bechers draw attention to both the exceptional nature of each picture and its relationship to the other images. Like artifacts arrayed in a vitrine, the photographs record the singular and the similar. The Bechers' approach not only advances the practice of historical comparison, but also argues for the photograph as an instantiation of historical validity. Photographs become a kind of empirical proof. Not coincidentally, some of the Bechers' early pictures were in the 1975 exhibition, "New Topographics," which argued that photographs should frame existing scenes and convey neutral information, rather than artfully compose new scenes and advance notions of beauty.[13] The New Topographers rejected certain prevailing trends in artistic photography, especially those exemplified by the work of Minor White, Ansel Adams, and Edward Weston. They promised to capture a building and its context in the real light of day, amid actual social circumstances. Still, in these "landscape happenings," architecture is positioned within social or environmental contexts as carefully constructed as those of any romantic photograph. Moreover, many critics are dubious about the possibility of such objectivity, given the art world venues where such photographs are inevitably shown. As photographer and critic Deborah Bright remarks, in the work of the New Topographics, "mats and frames, neutral walls, discreet labels, high rents, and the gallery hush provoke a palpable reverence before the images, even before we've inspected them closely."[14] Are documentary photographs all that different from artistic ones?

The work of Lewis Baltz shows how the subjective or artistic point of view can inform work that strives to be documentary. His entries into the New Topographics exhibition recall the early years of photography, when any built object seemed worth photographing, and before photographers had developed techniques of altering prints. And yet Baltz's photographs are not innocent. He shoots cheap buildings, and he heightens the sense of their cheapness. In so doing, he suggests an anti-aesthetic both critical and beautiful. In *The New Industrial Parks Near Irvine, California*,[15] published in

12. James Ackerman, "On the Origins of Architectural Photography," in *This Is not Architecture: Media Constructions*, ed. Kester Rattenbury (London: Routledge, 2002), 34.

13. *New Topographics: Photographs of a Man-altered Landscape*, ed. William Jenkins (Rochester, New York: International Museum of Photography, 1975), 5.

1975, Baltz examines architectural surfaces by photographing industrial sheds. His approach is more political than objective. Instead of shooting whole buildings, he focuses on modular panels of metal or concrete. Baltz might argue that the individual modules imply the rest of the building, but the focus on the segment emphasizes that the structures are prefabricated and repetitious. The photographs suggest a sense of mystery, too; the fragments of building seem ominous. The one-story sheds, apparently without windows, appear to be inhabited by machines and other inanimate objects. The large openings are scaled for vehicles, not people. The more one looks, the more the invisible interiors become menacing. Such attention to detail recalls early photography; yet it also subverts the sentimental aesthetics of the tradition, showing blank doors, utility boxes, drainpipes, stains on the walls, cheap signage, fluorescent lights. Baltz downplays context. The photos show little ground or sky. But he is careful to show how the sheds have disrupted their settings; here and there we see the cracked surfaces of parking lots, piles of rubble near the buildings, and plants that look almost dead. These images emphasize the destructive nature of industrialized building.

Baltz expressed his political sentiments in a 1982 essay. "The new suburban areas of America pose an array of novel problems for society," he wrote "Conceived in expedience for the sole purpose of maximum profit, pathetically dependent on the automobile, these new cities have disposed themselves formlessly along the frontage roads of every interstate highway. Posing an ecological threat which we are only now beginning to grasp, this new human sprawl is ultimately as alien to urbanism as it is to the land it consumes."[16] And yet we might wonder: Is the new landscape so alien? Baltz's photographs suggest that "this new human sprawl," while ugly and wasteful, is hardly uncommon. As he knows well, it is proliferating worldwide.

Baltz challenges the tradition of frontal photography. From Baldus to the Bechers, this genre of photography strives for the idealism of drawing, the balanced composition of beautiful elements, no matter their function or structure. In most frontal photography, the facade is harmoniously self-contained. But Baltz equates facade not with artistic rules, as does Baldus, or industrial inventions, as do the Bechers, but with large, anonymous, commercial forces. His frontal photographs, following each other on the pages of

14. Deborah Bright, "Of Mother Nature and the Marlboro Man: An Inquiry into the Cultural Meaning of Landscape Photography," in The Contest of Meaning: Critical Histories of Photography, ed. Richard Bolton (Cambridge: MIT Press, 1989), 134.

15. Lewis Baltz, The New Industrial Parks Near Irvine, California (New York: Castelli Graphics, 1975).

16. Lewis Baltz, "Review of The New West," in Reading into Photography: Selected Essays, 1959–1980, eds. Thomas F. Barrow, Shelley Armitage and William E. Tydeman (Albuquerque: University of New Mexico Press, 1982), 58.

the book, seem less isolated from context and less reducible to form. Their flat details suggest the world around them, prosaic roads and parking lots, stores and subdivisions—the everyday world where art and engineering merge. Perhaps most of all, their flatness alludes to the unseen spaces within buildings, the dimension of depth concealed by facade.

ANGLES OF CONTEXT

Photography always situates architecture in new contexts. Sometimes a photograph positions buildings onto the walls of other buildings, as when an image is shown in a gallery. Sometimes it moves buildings onto the printed page, as when an image appears in a book or magazine. New contexts can be generated also within the photographic frame. In the angled view, photographers abandon the tight embrace of the frontal view and show a building in its three dimensions and its environment. In this way, they can show asymmetrical or sculptural buildings, building masses of dramatic depth. On the diagonal, the camera can record the front and side of a building; it can pick up cylindrical, triangular, multifaceted, irregular forms. Angled shots of Roman architecture emphasize the curvature of vaults. Angled shots of Gothic or Victorian buildings reveal picturesque groupings of towers, finials, chimneys, gables, and porches. Angled shots of Brutalist buildings show off powerful concrete piers, walls, and balconies.

Site relationships are important in angled photography—distinctions between foreground and background, between circulation routes and points of access. In angled images, viewers see that buildings are surrounded by streets, driveways, paths, terraces, and plantings, and often other buildings, and maybe even forests or deserts. In an angled photograph, our impression of a building is influenced by environmental features and social forces that change over time. Buildings photographed in this way look more casual, realistic, and less posed. Yet the casualness is usually studied, artful in its own way.

Many angled photographs pose buildings in their urban context. By shooting a cathedral or concert hall surrounded by smaller structures, photographers emphasize the building's height, bulk, and status. In tourist literature, such images symbolize entire cities: Piazza San Marco becomes

"Venice," the Opera House "Sydney." Art historian Alan Trachtenberg, in Reading American Photographs, notes that photographs helped to create the identity of many American cities. Trachtenberg argues that at the beginning of the twentieth century, no single building could encapsulate the metropolis. But photographs could, especially those of Alfred Stieglitz. "Stieglitz's pictures define [New York] by icons, the outside look of places and things . . . repeated motifs of tropes . . . images which evoke the city as a distinct place and time: the horsecar, the ferry, the plaza, the tall building."[17]

Often, the relationships of building to city are established through complex counterpoint. Two photographs of the Flatiron Building in New York, one by Stieglitz, the other by Edward Steichen, taken in 1903 and 1905 respectively, illustrate such contrapuntal variations. Through his images of New York, many illustrated in his influential journal Camera Work, Steiglitz advanced the idea that photography could ennoble the emerging industrial and immigrant metropolis. Steichen, following Stieglitz's lead, crafted even more dreamlike portraits of the great American metropolis. Each photographer views the famous skyscraper from the ground in Madison Square Park. Each shows the building's full 285-foot height (designed by Daniel Burnham, the Flatiron was one of the city's first tall buildings). Such images were new and exhilarating. Skyscrapers had rarely been photographed from such a vantage—usually they had been shown as towers on a skyline. But that approach could not have worked for a building like the Flatiron. Because of the city's density, the Flatiron would not have stood out, even if photographed from a great height. The open space of Madison Square Park allowed the photographers to show the Flatiron's vertical rise. Just as important, the park allowed them to soften the building with landscape, with tree trunks and branches. In each photograph, then, we view a new kind of dialogue between building and nature, a new way of envisioning the city.

These photographs of the Flatiron Building illustrate some of the ideas of romantic painting and early photography. Published in 1860, Villas on the Hudson, by A.A. Turner, features photographs of wealthy residences in upstate New York. In these images, bucolic landscapes accentuate the romantic irregularity of architecture.[18] The complicated shapes of the Victorian buildings are heightened by sloping lawns, mounds of bushes, and

17. Alan Trachtenberg, Reading American Photographs: Images as History, Matthew Brady to Walker Evans (New York: Hill & Wang, 1989), 211.

18. A.A. Turner, Villas on the Hudson (New York: D. Appleton, 1860).

Flatiron Building, as photographed by Edward Steichen

trees whose canopies are like unruly rooftops. At the Flatiron Building, of course, such contrasts were not possible. The challenge for both Stieglitz and Steichen was to translate this picturesque aesthetic to the city, to express the relationship of building to nature so that the skyscraper (and the city) would seem a benign, even natural, presence.

Stieglitz and Steichen responded to the challenge in different ways. Stieglitz angles his camera to picture a wintry scene with no other buildings visible. Shot during the day, the photograph shows the building's intricate design, the pattern of its fenestration, its prominent cornice. But it limits the views of greenery to a clump of snow-covered trees and, in the foreground, the thick trunk of a single tree. Stieglitz focuses attention on the relationship between the shaft of the triangular building and the trunk, with its triangular branching. The form of the tree and the plan of the building mirror each other. Steichen's sepia shot links building and nature through the use of subtle hues. The picture has four distinctly toned areas: a dark ground plane; the slightly lighter silhouettes of the Flatiron and neighboring structures; the light brown sky; and the dark branches of trees. Steichen took the photograph at dusk, when the building, park, and sky would be similar in tone. Earlier in the day, the sun would have made the building's lines too crisp; at night, the lines of the building would appear diminished. In early evening, though, one can see the building's form but none of its details. The indistinct silhouettes of the Flatiron and other buildings blend into the dark patches of sky. The high thin branches of trees, in front of the building, soften its looming edges and smooth its severe geometry.

Rather than representing a high-rise as a conquest of sky and banishment of nature, both Steichen and Stieglitz discovered compelling ways of relating a tall building to a natural setting. The skyscraper could thus symbolize both the triumph of technology and the unexpected harmonies of the urban and the natural. In this way photographs could make us see formal geometries or illuminated textures, and could offer gentler views of the industrial city than those we gain when in its midst.

More than frontal photography, angled photography encourages diverse artistic statements about buildings and their settings. From the 1920s to the 1960s, architectural photographers such as Bill Hedrich, Ezra

Stoller, Julius Shulman, and Margaret Bourke-White explored the aesthetic boundaries of the medium—art for architecture's sake. Often published in mass-market magazines, their photos could make a building or work of infrastructure famous. Architectural critic Robert Campbell remarks on the reach of twentieth-century photography. "It was the age of the magazine—not only architectural and home fashion magazines but also general-interest publications such as *Life* and *Look*. *Life's* first cover, Nov. 23, 1936, was an architectural photograph, an image of Fort Peck Dam by Margaret Bourke-White."[19] (In publications such as *Life*, architectural photographs not only made certain buildings famous; they also worked to encourage associations between consumer goods and the art and architecture displayed in their pages. Readers flipped through magazines filled with striking images of a new world taking shape. The artistic photographs of architecture supported the magazines' overarching visual narratives, which included the display of goods that could be purchased. Features about spectacular new dams and buildings were framed by advertisements—with photographs—for the latest appliances and automobiles. Photographic images of architecture, indirectly, told and sold a larger story about material progress and lifestyle. During the past century, the photographic zoomscape has been a realm of fantasies, some of which remain purely visual, but many of which have become consumable.)

Photographers—both artistic and commercial—have developed many techniques to achieve maximum visual impact. "By highlighting a detail, or deliberately framing an entrance or a plaza," writes design critic Akiko Busch, "photographs single out the significant facts in an unimposing and accessible way."[20] Camera vantage points and framings can accentuate a building's powerful lines and harmonies with its context. Diagonal shots can lead the eye along edges toward foreboding precipices. Through artful cropping, a photograph can make a building appear mysterious. Depth of focus can suggest space flowing through portals, doors, windows, and terraces, the connections between interior and exterior. Elements of mise-en-scène, such as lighting, décor, and fashion, can be manipulated to suggest a compelling narrative. Few mid-century photographers produced more iconic images of architecture than did Ezra Stoller. About the artistic mission, he

19. Robert Campbell, "Modern Exposure," *Preservation* (May/June 2001), 49.

20. Akiko Busch, *The Photography of Architecture: Twelve Views* (New York: Van Nostrand Reinhold, 1987), 7.

writes, "it is the obligation of the photographer to communicate the idea of the building."[21] Reducing a building to an idea, a singular statement, has become a particularly photographic way of apprehending architecture. Today we might well ask: Can the idea of a building be expressed without photography?

The use of architecture to create art photography is exemplified in Julius Shulman's black-and-white portrait of Pierre Koenig's Case Study House #22, high in the Hollywood Hills. This photograph, taken in 1960, has made the house famous; the photograph has become even more famous. Taken at night from the poolside terrace, the image shows a brightly lit living room where two women in evening dresses sit on couches. Wraparound glass walls reveal the lights of Los Angeles below. Shulman's staging dramatizes an already dramatic place. Expertly, he connects the energy of the spectacular house and the glowing nighttime city, showing the kinetic link between the daring architectural lines of the cantilevered house and the apparently limitless reach of the city. Outside, in darkness, the photographer focuses on the beams of living room ceiling and the shimmering Los Angeles grid, the lines of the roof paralleling those of the illuminated streets below. Photographing Case Study House #22 at a perfect angle and in a perfect moment, Shulman created an enduring image of a modernist dwelling. Perhaps most of all, he created an image that captures the particular delights of the modernist lifestyle.

Earlier, in 1947, Shulman photographed Richard Neutra's Kaufmann house in Palm Springs; this image, too, has contributed to the enduring romance of modern living. Here, too, the view and setting are dreamlike. And here, too, the photographer creates potent relationships between the house and its surroundings, and between artificial and natural light. One sees the house at a slight angle, from a garden by a pool, with the San Jacinto mountains in the distance. Preoccupied with the romantic possibilities of light and atmosphere, Shulman took the photograph in twilight.[22] His interpretation of the largely transparent house achieves its power by subduing the immediate material context and emphasizing the illuminated horizon. The black-and-white photograph does not show the wood, stone, glass, or steel surfaces of the house, or the rectilinear building's tenuous relationship to the boulder-filled landscape. Instead, Shulman renders a range of gray textures and

21. Ezra Stoller, "Photography and the Language of Architecture," *Perspecta* 8 (1963), 43.

22. Julius Shulman, *Architecture and Its Photography* (Cologne: Taschen, 1998), 97.

Case Study House #22, as photographed by Julius Shulman

tones—the darkening sky and the jagged line of fading sunlight on the mountain peaks, echoed in the interior lights of the residence, which in turn are reflected on the floor and in the pool. In the foreground, two sinuous lawn chairs and a table play off against the overlapping planes of the mountains.

Shulman's photographs of Case Study #22 and the Kaufmann house epitomize how effectively and ideally angled photography can pair architecture and context. By assembling the elements of building, city, nature, and light in cool consonance, architectural photography can create an idealized moment, reducing vision from the plenitude of direct experience to the perfection of image. "Architectural photography prepares you only for the optimum condition, the best time of day, best position, the standard view, the authorized take, the truth against which all other views will seem irredeemably poor approximations,"[23] writes architectural critic Janet Abrams. Writing about Le Corbusier's carefully staged photographs, architectural historian Thomas Schumacher points out that the wide-angled lenses and set-up shots of architectural photography inevitably make buildings larger and more imposing than they actually are. "With mirrors the space is distended and altered; with props a painterly composition is effected. And with the judicious placement of furniture, tableaux are created. In some cases the placement of furniture for the photo would result in the room being rendered unusable in everyday life."[24] Photographs can make architecture seem rarefied. Picture books of architectural photography impart an image of high design that seems impervious to everyday reality. Visitors to Le Corbusier's Villa Savoye, at Poissy, are often shocked to see that the modernist landmark is surrounded not by expansive green fields, as it seems to be in photographs, but by suburbia.

If photographers of modern architecture suppress unsightly appearances and contexts, other photographers, following a different tradition, have sought out the banal, sullied, and bizarre. In the 1930s and 1940s, the photojournalist Arthur Fellig, known as Weegee, popularized images of lurid scenes, sites of crime, accident, celebrity, play, and outright madness, all set against the backdrop of New York City. During the same years, Helen Levitt took photographs in the streets of New York, telling stories of daily life: children drawing on a sidewalk, a family sitting in a window of their apartment

23. Janet Abrams, "Available for Viewing," in *Site Work: Architecture in Photography Since Early Modernism*, eds. Martin Caiger-Smith and David Chandler (London: The Photographic Gallery, 1991), 77–78.

24. Thomas Schumacher, "Over-Exposure," *Harvard Design Magazine* 9 (Fall 1998), 6–7.

building, an old woman leaning against a spindly tree in a barren courtyard. Later, from the 1950s to the 1970s, Garry Winogrand defined the genre of "street photography," making New York seem like a city of wild human life, filled with free-ranging men, women, and children. While fascinated by the range of human gesture, he concentrates, too, on urban elements such as sidewalks, shop windows, and fire escapes. Sometimes he took his Leica to the suburbs. In his 1958 "Albuquerque, New Mexico," Winogrand shows a child standing just inside an open garage, looking down the steep driveway at a tricycle; he is cut off from his toy, much as the newly minted house looks cut off from its context, from the vast New Mexico desert that reaches to the mountains in the distance.

These urban photographers rarely focused on architecture alone, but they nonetheless revealed much about city and suburb that was usually ignored by high art or commercial photographers. In so doing, urban photographers suggested a new, critical role for architectural photography. Beyond advocating for the intentions of architects or the lifestyles of exceptional buildings, photographers could amplify our knowledge of cultural and visual conditions.[25] Instead of positioning viewers outside the scene, ogling at costly treasures, photographers could locate viewers within realistic and often unsettling contexts.

In a series of 1987 images of One Atlantic Center, an Atlanta skyscraper, Joel Meyerowitz creates an interesting tension between foreground and background, which deflates the building's pretensions.[26] Designed by Philip Johnson and John Burgee, the fifty-story tower is a postmodern landmark, a piece of development that signaled the rise of Atlanta as a major metropolis. Meyerowitz's images suggest that the city's new commercial culture is shallow, skin-deep. Here One Atlantic Center seems to teeter on a razor-thin strip of high-end development in midtown, not far from the city's low-rent district. The angled shots question how a large new building like One Atlantic Center, a commercial landmark, affects the life of a city; they implicitly challenge its autonomy.

In each photograph, One Atlantic Center appears in the distance, against a clear, cloudless sky. Meyerowitz does not idealize the skyscraper; in fact, from whatever angle, it looks the same. We always see the upper

25. Robert A. Benson, "The Image and the Reality," *Inland Architect* 35 (March/April 1991), 66–67.

26. Joel Meyerowitz, *Creating a Sense of Place: Photographs by Joel Meyerowitz* (Washington, D.C.: Smithsonian Institution Press, 1990).

shaft of the building and its pyramidal top; what varies, critically, are the foreground images, which include a baseball diamond surrounded by a chain-link batting cage; uprooted tree stumps and an abandoned building; a vacant lot in the center of which lies a toppled-over stone marker; a gas station; and a parking lot edged by a wall with a mural of a colonial building. Through compositions that deploy repeating geometries, Meyerowitz links the rich and poor Atlanta. For example, in one photograph, we see disturbed earth and the stumps of several trees; these carry the eye up toward the tower. Presenting One Atlantic Center in the context of these poor, decaying neighborhoods, Meyerowitz makes the building a symbol of divided Atlanta, a city of high-rise haves and vacant-lot have-nots.

The photographer Robert Adams, another New Topographics artist, is skilled in revealing the grimness of landscapes. *California: Views by Robert Adams of the Los Angeles Basin, 1978–1983* contains images of places on the periphery of Los Angeles, places untouched by the city's glamour.[27] Shot in cities like Redlands, Riverside, and Long Beach, Adams's photographs show large swaths of disturbed land around buildings or around extensive tracts of houses. In many images, the boundary between the human and natural environments seems to have disappeared. We see tire tracks dug into the earth and garbage scattered on the ground. In one image, ailing trees overlook a large housing subdivision. In another, the drooping branches of a dying eucalyptus frame an empty lot with a small realty sign at its edge; across the street is a small store, some houses, a palm tree, and an entrance ramp of the San Bernardino Freeway. What unifies these black-and-white images is the sky. White, thick with smog, the sky is as disturbed, as polluted as everything else. Its hazy light suffuses architecture and landscape, making atmosphere seem as solid as buildings.

The night sky can be as striking as the day sky. In the work of San Francisco photographer Todd Hido, it has an almost otherworldly glow. Hido's *House Hunting* is another photographic critique of contemporary California; the focus here is on developer houses in the suburbs of San Francisco. Like the houses in Adam's series, these small stucco homes were built right after the Second World War. At the time they represented the American dream; by 2001, when Hido photographed the houses, the dream

27. *California: Views by Robert Adams of the Los Angeles Basin, 1978–1983*, essay by Robert Hass (San Francisco: Fraenkel Gallery, 2000).

had lost much of its allure Taken in the early evening, the photographs show one house at a time. There are no people or cars. There are yuccas and cypresses atop lawns, and wood or stucco walls topped by shallow gabled roofs and television antennae. The accompanying text informs us that the houses are empty, repossessed by banks. Through his use of ambient illumination, Hido creates a sense of eeriness. Often a single light source—car headlights, streetlamps—makes one side of a house appear bright, while the other sides remain dark. One or two windows might radiate blue, white, or yellow light. Faintly greenish or bluish skies reflect the ambient radiance of the metropolis. These diverse types of light seem to cast a spell on the lonely houses, making them appear strange and spooky.

In the photographs of Stieglitz, Steichen, and Shulman, architecture gains expressive power from the artful juxtaposition of building and context. A choice time of day and point of view transform the building into an image that looms larger than life. Yet if photography can elevate architecture through interplay with context, it can also lay bare a building, making it seem disconnected from its surroundings and from the larger culture. Meyerowitz, Adams, and Hido show buildings within dominating and degrading surroundings, environs made ugly and alienating by mass urbanization. In these images, everyday buildings dissolve within fields of capital abandonment and industrial pollution, or within the grids of electric power. In Hido's suburban houses, especially, the quality of light structures our experience of the building. Architecture, in Le Corbusier's famous description in *Towards a New Architecture*, is "the masterly, correct and magnificent play of masses brought together in light." Architecture, in Hido's photos, is the ominous play of ambient light within and around the shell of building mass.

DETAIL

A photograph can concentrate the experience of a building into a single image or series of images. Whether it isolates the building as facade or frames it within a larger setting, the inevitable effect is to transform object into image. In "The Ontology of the Photographic Image" French film theorist André Bazin argues that photography's aesthetic power lies in its ability to expose unseen realities of an object. Bazin understood the link between

From *House Hunting*, Todd Hido

photography and surrealism, arguing that in photography "the logical distinction between what is imaginary and what is real tends to disappear. Every image is to be seen as an object and every object as an image. Hence photography ranks high in the order of surrealist creativity because it produces an image that is a reality of nature, namely, a hallucination that is also a fact."[28] When focusing on the details of buildings, photographers ponder the parts and pieces that produce the illusion of a whole, the patterns, geometries, forms and shapes often overlooked in larger views. At close range, all sorts of "architectures" emerge. "You can discover architecture in strange places, perhaps through a microscope, perhaps in a strata of rock, a jumble of box lids, a rotting doorway, or piled cranks in a pottery works,"[29] observes historian Eric de Maré. The close-up of a leaf can reveal a pattern of veins that looks remarkably like the plan of a medieval city. Detail photography encourages us to see such uncanny likenesses, and to contemplate the connections between large and small, whole and part, real and imagined.

Early architectural photographers attempted to capture the visual universe that can exist within the details of a building. Hired by the Commission des Monuments Historiques to photograph the monuments of France, especially the Gothic cathedrals, Henri Le Secq produced the 1852 *Fragments d'Architecture et Sculpture de la Cathedrale de Chartres*. Of the thirty photographs in the volume, only one, a long view of the cathedral's west towers and transept rising above the city, encompasses anything close to the entirety of the building. All the rest are close-ups of the cathedral's stone statues, the saints and pilgrims carved into the lower walls (in the days before zoom lenses, Le Secq could photograph only what he could reach, hence there are no close-ups of the high buttresses or of the famous clerestory windows). We see the same statuary people visiting the building would witness. These focused, intimate views reinforce the spiritual experience of the building; Le Secq's Chartres emphasizes not the structural but the sculptural, the achievements of the Gothic artisans. His photographs encourage viewers to study and venerate the figures of the Christian story. Le Secq's decision not to depict architectural elements in detail is puzzling, given the contemporaneous project of Baldus. Perhaps to Le Secq, religious piety and sculptural craftsmanship meant more than architectural ornament or structure.

28. André Bazin, "The Ontology of the Photographic Image," in *Classic Essays on Photography*, ed. Alan Trachtenberg (New Haven: Leete's Island Books, 1980), 243.

29. Eric de Maré, *Architectural Photography* (London: Batsford Limited, 1975), 8.

"A Sea of Steps," Frederick Evans's 1903 photograph of Wells Cathedral, shows the details of a great church from a less literal, and hence more modern perspective. Evans focuses on the stairs that lead up to the chapter house. The choice of the stairwell as the subject by which to represent a cathedral was unusual; compared with Le Secq's stone martyrs, the stone stairs seem mundane, even profane. Evans's other notable photographs depict medieval cathedrals, like Gloucester's, through the elaborate tracery of their stone vaults and screens. But as presented here, in isolation, the steps of Wells Cathedral are unexpectedly moving, evocative of procession and ascent, of significant events in the Christian experience and liturgy. With his tight framing, Evans exaggerates the complex angles of the stairs, making them look like the stone blocks of a monument. The stairs are further enhanced by lighting. The source of light is somewhere in the chapter house, unseen; as such it evokes divinity. The careful illumination also lets us see that many of the steps are worn. In another context, this might suggest disrepair or even abandonment; here it speaks to frequent use, and thus to the piety of a church-going society. Through enlargement, lighting, and framing, Evans translates a seemingly minor feature of a building into a poignant expression of human devotion.[30]

Close-up photography of a building is a peculiar endeavor. Rarely are we able, in photographs of architecture, to infer the whole from the part. Buildings have vastly different shapes, sizes, elements, ornaments, and technologies of construction. The close-up of a doorjamb or staircase, for instance, does not yield much understanding of the larger building. Looking at details of buildings encourages us, instead, to reflect on material and form. And in close-up, material and form become abstract; architecture can look like painting or sculpture. A close-up of the cross vaults of an old stone passageway, for instance, discourages awareness of their circulatory or structural functions. The vaults become pictorial.

The photograph's ability to transform a part of a building into an illusion of something else can make viewers feel they are journeying into uncharted lands. At the same time, this photographic facility can also change their impression of familiar or recognizable places. Photographs of details invite close scrutiny. Photographers understand this; writing about

30. Frederick Evans, "Pictorial Pointers for Architectural Photographers," *The Practical Photographers* I, 8 (1904), 47–50.

A Sea of Steps, Frederick Evans

Charles Sheeler, Thomas Stebbins argues that Sheeler sought "to find unsus- pected form and abstraction in architecture."[31] Sheeler photographs build- ings from unusual angles and points of view. He views them straight up and straight down, from extremely acute angles and at extremely close range. In his photographs, buildings and their parts are free not only from urban or natural context, but also from function, structure, and even gravity. A set of stairs in a farmhouse in Doylestown, Pennsylvania, where Sheeler lived for a few years, indicates nothing about the family that lived there. In fact, it looks less like a utilitarian object than like a study in backlighting, shadows, and bold shapes. Whereas Frederick Evans used aesthetic devices to link a stair to the spiritual process of ascension, Sheeler loved shadows for their aesthetic potential, for the sense of distance and abstraction they impart to objects.

In Sheeler's work, built objects are always detached from their con- text. Even in the most complex places, where functional and structural forms create confounding contours, Sheeler has formal resolution in mind. "Criss- Crossed Conveyors," of 1932, photographed at the Ford Motor Company's River Rouge Plant in Dearborn, Michigan, is a case in point. At first, we see what appears to be a random view into the heart of the factory complex. The photograph shows smokestacks, buildings, and water towers; in the fore- ground are large conveyors carrying coke and coal. As shot by Sheeler, how- ever, the scene appears serene; he points his lens at the diagonals of the crossing conveyors, making the busy factory seem oddly stable; the emphasis on a logical geometric center implies that the peripheral parts of the photo- graph, the perplexing variety of factory forms, are also ordered. The great insight of Leo Marx's 1964 study, *The Machine in the Garden*, is that despite America's overwhelming industrial character, its writers and artists have repeatedly constructed myths based on rural ideals. As Marx observes, Sheeler's quest is quintessentially American, a combination of empirical observation and romantic illusionism. Marx notices how successfully Sheeler idealizes the technological landscape. Within vistas that could be construed as bleak or overwhelming, "we observe that Sheeler has eliminated all evi- dence of the frenzied movement and clamor we associate with the industrial scene. The silence is awesome."[32]

---

31. Theodore E. Stebbins and Norman Keyes, *Charles Sheeler: The Photographs* (Boston: Museum of Fine Arts, 1988), 27.

32. Leo Marx, *The Machine in the Garden* (Oxford: Oxford University Press, 1964), 356.

As in his photographs of River Rouge, Sheeler's photographs of Chartres Cathedral concentrate on pure shape. "Flying Buttresses at the Crossing," of 1929, shows a complex intersection of vertical and horizontal buttresses. And here, too, as at Ford, Sheeler finds a still center, one of the cathedral's massive piers. His camera surveys the buttresses springing from the pier, but the image emphasizes not the dynamism of the flying buttresses but the stability of the pier. Since the photograph does not show the larger system of structural supports, it draws attention not to structural actions but to formal patterns. The photograph, which finds a calm center within the maelstrom of structural actions, epitomizes Sheeler's goal—the creation of images that encapsulate and immortalize the awesome world swirling around them.

By isolating pieces of buildings, detail photographs make us familiar with the unfamiliar parts of buildings. The photograph of a roof truss tells us about the truss's structural actions. Close-up photographs allow us to inspect the ornament on the upper reaches of a building: patterns of fretwork, moldings on the architrave of a Greek temple, the wave-like flow of poetry painted on the underside of a mosque's dome, gargoyles projecting from the upper floors of a skyscraper. Many modern photographers—notably Norman McGrath— have sought the views of a building from uncustomary vantage points. McGrath might take his camera into the sky to capture the pattern of skylights on a roof, or underneath on a crane to view the skylights on a high ceiling. He frequently employs a worm's-eye view, looking up at a segment of wall to show its texture.

The photographer Judith Turner shows buildings at such close range that they look like neither buildings nor any recognizable objects. In her 1980 *Photographs Five Architects*, which contains images of works by John Hejduk, Peter Eisenman, Charles Gwathmey and Robert Siegal, Michael Graves, and Richard Meier, the photographs provide no sense of orientation to the architecture. Using no establishing shots, Turner focuses relentlessly on details—light effects, formal juxtapositions, accidental spaces, parts of stairways, windows, ducts, walls, and floors. Only the layout of the book—page breaks between buildings—tells us where one building ends and another begins. The logic of the narrative—why one image follows another—is

Criss-Crossed Conveyors, Charles Sheeler

196 never explained. Each image presents different building elements in complex juxtapositions: columns alongside a stairway, a glass-block wall alongside a dark space that might be a window. Turner forces us to concentrate on the qualities of diverse materials, of glass, steel, and concrete, and on the relationships among windows, walls, and stairs.

The abstraction of Turner's photography underscores the theoretical and artistic goals of the five architects, who in the 1970s were advocating a highly formalist—as opposed to social or political—approach to design. Their work and positions had been presented earlier, in the 1975 book *Five Architects*, which described how this "New York School" was reinterpreting the high modernism of the 1920s. Given the architects' immersion in Cubism, De Stijl, and Purism, Turner's photographs continued their neomodernist project. Turner's details express how the elementary constructions of 1920s high modernism were reconfigured into the structuralist assemblages of 1970s neomodernism. In his introduction to the book, John Hejduk writes that Turner "understands that it is impossible to see architecture in its full complexity at once. Architecture is made up of details, fragments, fabrications. And the very idea behind it can be captured in a fragment, in a detail. And architecture is made up of two dimensions. Turner does believe that the very essence of the spirit of an architecture can be captured in a single still photograph."[33] Hejduk refers not to the essence of a single building, but rather to the essence of architecture understood as a form of communication. Photographic details from one building, then, are part of a larger formal vocabulary and grammar of architecture. The detail, like a linguistic utterance, might not tell us much about a particular building or context, but it might convey a great deal of architectural information.

In this larger sense, the experience of photographs of details can resemble that of the aerial view. Because of the transformations of scale in each case, because of the stillness of each picture, the usual cultural contexts and constraints of architectural perception no longer hold. We notice form in the texture of poured concrete and in the patterns of expressways— forms that would be impossible to see without technological interventions. In both the micro and the macro scale, the parts of buildings and the parts of cities become part of a zoomscape, a manner of architectural perception and information that exceeds the limits of a building or a place.

33. John Hejduk, Introduction to *Judith Turner: Photographs Five Architects* (New York: Rizzoli International Publications, 1980), 11.

The city itself is the subject of much architectural photography. City views group buildings, streets, parks, and infrastructure into wholes that express a neighborhood, town, or metropolis. But cities pose a special challenge for photographers. Buildings are hard enough to depict in a photograph's small format. Cities are trickier. Unless taken from a great distance, usually beyond the city, individual photographs cannot capture the full scale and complexity of a city. And of course, individual photographs that depict the city at human scale are inevitably partial in view, limited in scope. Photographers have solved the problem with the use of multiples, with series of images devoted to conveying the expansive range of the city. These urban portraits can proceed linearly, taking a viewer through a continuous sequence of urban or suburban spaces—mimicking automotive or railroad perception. Or they can array individual urban sites and landmarks thematically, clustering images according to architectural type, style, or designer.

San Francisco was one of the earliest cities to be photographed in serial fashion. Already in 1852, only a few years after the beginning of the Gold Rush, a series of daguerreotypes showed scenes of the waterfront and ships in the bay. San Francisco attracted photographers because it seemed to be an instant city, rapidly growing, transforming every year. The hilly topography made it possible to take photographs that encompassed large areas of the city. Eadweard Muybridge's "Panorama of San Francisco," from 1878, is the best urban portrait of its era. Muybridge represents the city in thirteen continuous images. Unlike earlier painted panoramas, which enclose viewers in the hollow center of a cylinder, Muybridge's panorama unfolds linearly. But similar to those earlier efforts, it, too, was scanned from left to right like a line of text or a painting moving on rollers.[34] In the panorama, San Francisco unfolds as a complete entity in two-dimensional space, a continuous built fabric where the last frame shows a bit of the first frame.

Muybridge took the panorama from a spot atop Nob Hill, above the city's business district. The 360-degree pan is divided between the city's urbanized areas, seen at middle and long distance, and the surrounding mountains and waters, viewed at long range. The foreground city always occupies the bottom of the photographs, while nature takes up the top. Closest in, we see a few unbuilt lots, several mansions, and then, further

34. Martha Sandweiss, "Undecisive Moments: The Narrative Tradition in Western Photography," in *Photography in Nineteenth-Century America*, ed. Martha Sandweiss (New York: Harry N. Abrams, 1991), 113.

away, several churches and a hotel. The downtown is not discernible. Most frames of the panorama are filled with a dense thicket of small buildings that seem to slide down valleys or clutch hillsides.

Muybridge's images emphasize the relationship between city and nature, between the city and its hills, the surrounding mountains, the bay, the harbor, the islands. This relationship emerges in the edge between the developed city and undeveloped outskirts. The edge, which can be followed through each successive photograph, tracks the developing urban frontier, and creates a second photographic skyline of the city, one of geographic limits, not heights. Unlike a typical urban skyline of silhouettes of buildings against the sky, the photographic skyline is made up of the shapes of wharves and masts of ships and, most of all, of the natural surroundings. In this visual epic, San Francisco is flattened into an urban core surrounded by wilderness. When we view the city contained within such a dominant landscape, we become aware that we, too, are contained within the landscape. The photograph thus harkens back to the tradition of bird's-eye city views that encourage the spectator to visualize the city and its environs as an extension of themselves—a kind of photographic skin replacing old urban enclosures, like walls.

In the panorama, San Francisco looks different than it would in person. We get some sense of the hilly topography. Yet strangely, wherever there is urban development, the photograph reduces both the steepness and ubiquity of the hills. The city grid is not prominent; viewers are left unaware of the constant battle between plan and terrain. The images also soften the newness of the city. The long shots make the boomtown look long settled, almost historical. In its day, of course, the panorama was a record of extraordinary conquest. The surrounding landscape is empty, unsettled. Contemporary spectators would have known that a generation earlier, the urban scenes depicted did not exist; almost all of San Francisco was then new. Muybridge's panorama was, among other things, proof of the thriving American civilization. In *Silver Cities*, historian Peter Hales charts the role of photography in documenting and celebrating American progress and settlement. Hales realizes that nineteenth-century photography promoted the myth that the city was the product of intentional human endeavor, not only that of its architects, engineers, and photographers, but also of its leading citizens. "Muybridge's was a culturally crucial fiction," Hales writes. "The streets of his city not only declare his preeminence as the center of his created world but, for his entrepreneurial sponsors, place the heart of the city in the residential neighborhood of the richest and most powerful of San Francisco's citizens. For Muybridge, the city might be his; for Hopkins, Stanford, Crocker, and the other merchant princes, it was *theirs*."[35]

Besides continuous panoramas, cities have been portrayed in images collected in books. Erich Mendelsohn's *America: An Architect's Picturebook*, from 1926, focuses on the precise appearance of individual structures.[36] A leading German architect of the interwar period, Mendelsohn was less interested in covering the totality of the modern city than in disseminating captivating visual information. In a review of the book, El Lissitsky writes, "a first leafing through its pages thrills us like a dramatic film. Before our eyes move pictures that are absolutely unique. In order to understand some of the photographs you must lift the book over your head and rotate it. The architect shows us America not from a distance but from within, as he leads us into the canyon of its streets."[37] Collections like *America* offer large, albeit fragmented views of places. Within a city, of course, the choices of where and what to photograph are innumerable. Should the emphasis be on historical landmarks or emerging architectures, on prominent public buildings and spaces or the larger everyday city, on new districts or declining neighborhoods? For many urban photographers, the choice of what to focus on is, inevitably, personal. In Paris, at the turn of the last century, Eugène Atget shot thousands of photographs of the city, of its squares, streets and alleys, favoring small shops and modest buildings over the capital's famous monuments and ritzy arrondissements. Usually no people are present. Unlike Mendelsohn's deliberately up-to-date American scenes, Atget's Parisian scenes look dated, mundane, and melancholy. Walter Benjamin, in "A Short History of Photography," finds it strange that Atget would photograph the everyday city without its people. Yet to the German cultural critic, the courtyards, terraces, and steps are "not lonely but voiceless; the city in these pictures is swept clean like a house which has not yet found its new tenant."[38] Atget, Benjamin tells us, sought to depict the city uncannily in order to alien-

35. Peter Bacon Hales, *Silver Cities: The Photography of American Urbanization, 1839–1915* (Philadelphia: Temple University Press, 1984), 82.

36. Erich Mendelsohn, *Bilderbuch eines Architekten* (New York: Da Capo, 1976).

37. El Lissitsky, "The Architect's Eye," in *Photography in the Modern Era: European Documents and Critical Writings, 1923–1940*, ed. Christopher Phillips (New York: Metropolitan Museum of Art, 1989), 221–222.

38. Walter Benjamin, "A Short History of Photography," in *Classic Essays on Photography*, 210.

ate viewers. Only by showing ordinary places divested of their familiarity could the photographer begin to understand the city more deeply.

Influenced by Atget, other photographers have sought to evoke the elusive presence of the city. Berenice Abbott's *Changing New York,* published in 1939, includes images ranging from the humble to the monumental: storefronts advertising Italian bread, ten-cent haircuts, and ten-dollar suits; lines of laundry in the backyards of tenements; acute-angled views of skyscrapers; and panoramas of Rockefeller Center and the George Washington Bridge.[39] Certain shots approach the strangeness of Atget's photographs; for instance, "El at Columbus Avenue and Broadway" shows people walking across a street juxtaposed with a carousel horse.

The New American Village, by the Chicago photographer Bob Thall, explores the uniform peculiarity of the new urban periphery. The subject of Thall's 1995 book is Schaumberg and the vicinity of O'Hare International Airport—one of the so-called edge cities, northwest of Chicago. This Cook County edge city is a land of office campuses, parking structures, tract homes, and shopping centers, none more than a generation old. The landscape—lawns and paths, roads and parking lots—appears well maintained and the buildings look clean, if not sparkling. The buildings are larger than those of the city, scaled to the automobile; but none exceed twenty-five stories in height. And without exception, none are exceptional, or architecturally interesting. In this new American city, there is neither artistic inspiration nor nostalgic diversion. Thall sweeps our eyes across suburban vistas dull even by suburban standards, devoid of whimsy, spectacle, or daring. The architectural styles range from late corporate modernism to early corporate postmodernism, the difference being slight variations in fenestration patterns. It is the sort of place one can find almost anywhere in the country—which is precisely the point.

Still, the world Thall shows us is as mysterious and labyrinthine as Atget's Paris. Despite the views of office cubicles and collector roads, of standardized environs, it is hard to get a handle on this place. Thall has portrayed a non-place. The landscape is so relentlessly consistent—most notable for the eerie lack of anything old or anything looking like a landmark—that it is hard to discern any hierarchy or visual narrative. Mendelsohn's

---

39. Berenice Abbott and Bonnie Yochelson,
Berenice Abbot: Changing New York, 1935–1938
(New York: The New Press, 1999).

From *The New American Village*, Bob Thall

America emphasizes achievement. Abbott's New York is a place of old and new, large and small, tenements and skyscrapers. Thall's American village is an environment of bizarre non-presence. Despite its large buildings and spacious roads, and the lack of people or cars, it feels claustrophobic. As Thall writes, "I soon realized that rarely is there a clearly marked public space in these suburbs. Where do the backyards end and the public parks begin? Is a small, residential street public property, or is it the restricted driveway of a private development company? Ponds, parking lots, and sidewalks within shopping malls can look public, but they are usually private properties. There are virtually no places in the edge cities where a stranger has the right to walk around with a camera on his or her shoulder or set up a tripod."[40] Perhaps this is why his photographs have a fugitive quality. We often look from the places along irregular paths that a teenager might ramble; this makes sense, given the lack of clear boundaries between pedestrian and car space and between private and public space. One shot is taken from the small bluff above an arterial that overlooks a large parking lot; another surveys the middle of a residential street framed by houses with three-car garages and distant glass office towers. His odd angles and unusual camera placements expose the unwholesome beauty and unexpected formal alignments of the empty buildings and endless parking lots, of the big-box stores and developer houses. Here, trees and streetlights resemble each other, and the buildings, no matter their function, repeat each other's outlines. Ultimately, viewers glance at an alienated portrait of themselves, at buildings and roadsides both familiar and foreboding. Looking at images of a great city, we are perhaps moved to identify with the cultural achievements of our society; looking at this new American village, we seem to be witnessing our suburban alter ego, the disaffected landscape we have created and must now inhabit.

Like vehicles, photographs reorient perception of the city. The photography of Ed Ruscha can resemble that of Muybridge, in its use of multiples to examine a large contiguous area; or it can be like that of Abbott or Thall, creating portraits of a place from disconnected pieces. But Ruscha has a method all his own; his books of photographs uncover new readings of a place—usually Los Angeles—by focusing on specific building (or urban)

40. Bob Thall, *The New American Village*
(Baltimore: Johns Hopkins University Press, 1999),
15.

types—streets, apartment buildings, pools, parking lots— in a comprehensive and sometimes continuous manner. He is especially fascinated by how transportation technologies such as automobiles and helicopters have structured everyday perception and inspired new artistic impressions.

Los Angeles is so enormous and indefinite that it defies any singular representational gesture. The region is about movement more than place, with freeways that wind around mountains, roads that connect housing, commerce, and industry. In a series of photographs taken from a helicopter, *Thirty-four Parking Lots in Los Angeles*, of 1967, Ruscha studies the commercial parking lot as both formal composition and transportation infrastructure. Each lot has its own personality and surroundings, as well as dimensions and outlines. Some are rectangular, others triangular; some are shaped like fans, others like doughnuts. The parking lots show us the first rung of the wider vehicular world around a building; they are a space connecting building and street. In shooting the lots, Ruscha is not interested in serendipitous moments, the flux of people and vehicles; he is after deeper structures. He photographed the lots early in the morning, mostly on Sundays, when they would be empty. Bereft of cars, the lots reveal interesting patterns. One first notices their internal divisions—the entry and exit sequences, the lines that mark out individual spaces and that create either right-angled or herringbone patterns. We also notice the irregularities of the lots. Oil stains on the asphalt suggest the history of the site. Just as aerial archaeologists notice patterns discernable only from the air, Ruscha shows the splotches of oil and grime that usually go unnoticed. The larger the stain, the more a spot was used. In each lot, the stains indicate the used and unused sections; the former are near buildings or sidewalks.

In another book, Ruscha takes us from the parking lot to the street. *Every Building on the Sunset Strip*, of 1966, is just that: a photograph of every building along a two-mile stretch of Sunset Boulevard from Laurel Canyon to Carol Street, just west of Hollywood and reaching to Beverly Hills. This is the strip of nightclubs that began migrating during the 1930s from the heart of Hollywood to a looser and longer vehicular realm, where Hollywood types could get soused after working late in the studios, on the way home to Beverly Hills or Bel Air. Ruscha places the photographs side by side, recording continuously both sides of the Strip. The tour begins at Schwab's Pharmacy and moves west. When we reach the end, we can turn the book upside down and retrace our journey.

Along this stretch, Ruscha captures the formal variety of the street's (mostly) one-story buildings, the changes in width, massing, historical style, type, and setback. There are Modern, Tudor, Art Deco, Spanish Colonial, French Colonial, and Googie designs. There are hotels, banks, offices, liquor stores, gas stations, apartment buildings, and single-family houses. There is the Burlesque Body Shop. Within the regular rhythm of the shots, all variations are observable—where the buildings seem especially close to one another, where they are unusually wide or tall, where there are shopping areas, and where there are parking lots. We observe as well the trees, signs, poles, parked cars, billboards, for-sale signs, bus stop benches with advertising, and the few pedestrians. Palm trees, their canopies cropped out of the picture, look like telephone poles. Streetlights dangle in the air.

Here, too, Ruscha photographed on Sunday mornings, when the Strip was least itself—when the hippies, hookers, and peddlers were gone, and when the neon lights were turned off. In sunlight with few people or cars, the Sunset Strip looks as sedate as a suburban main street. In daytime, we notice less its isolation from the city than its nearby contexts. To the north are the Hollywood Hills, a scattering of houses and vegetation. To the south, the city is flat, dense, and commercial. On the book's opposing tracks of photographs, Los Angeles has two distinct personalities: the featureless extras of the plains, and the dramatic stars of the canyons.

Ruscha does not photograph buildings as they would be seen from a car, straight ahead through the windshield or at a diagonal from the side. Although he sets up his shots—presumably from a convertible—in the lanes of moving traffic, he places the camera directly in front of the buildings, photographing them head-on. His frontal view can thus study the buildings as they might be studied in an architectural history course—or at a realtor's office. The compositional characteristics that would not be prominent in day-to-day circumstances, either walking or driving, take on greater weight. The Strip turns into a presentation for artistic scrutiny or commodity purchase.

Ruscha's photographs exemplify the disjunction between direct, unreflective perception and the careful, measured observation of photography.

Spectators gaze at parking lots and the Strip the way an architect or historian (or museum visitor) would, somewhat at a distance, and in a framework that favors comparison. Spectators also look at a formal and temporal microcosm of the city. Ruscha's books of the mid-1960s preserve the city in a moment of its history and are themselves part of that history. Indeed, the city pictured this way is an image-narrative of place, an array of views that transcend photography's moment of closure, when the shutter clicks and a scene is fixed forever as an image. Through multiples, these fixed moments coalesce into a larger entity whose perusal requires time, a kind of viewing that approaches the experience of watching a film. And in the city itself, the proliferation of photographic images, on billboards, on buildings, on buses, constructs a spatial viewing environment that when seen in motion is in its own way like a movie.

CHAPTER 5

FILM

AT THE END of the nineteenth century, various terms were coined to describe the invention that put filmed images into motion—Zoetrope, Praxinoscope, Zoopraxiscope, Phanatoscope, Miroscope, Vitascope. The first motion picture show for a paying audience took place in 1895 at the Grand Café in Paris, where Auguste and Louis Lumière premiered ten short films, lasting twenty minutes in all. They called the invention the Cinematographe: the writing or sketching of motion. Cinema caught on and soon motion pictures were being shown in theaters and converted storefronts worldwide. In 1910, the first film theater opened in Paris, seating 5,000 people, ushering in the era of movie palaces. The cinema offered a spectacle that went far beyond the capacities and technologies of theater and photography. In a motion picture, twenty-four photographs per second run through an illuminated frame projected on a large screen in a darkened auditorium, bringing to life new visual worlds.

The earliest filmmakers used stationary cameras. Soon they placed these cameras on moving vehicles, and film audiences experienced (via tracking shots) mechanized locomotion through space and place. Over the years, filmmakers would develop various techniques, like panning or tilting shots that pivot from a fixed point to survey space, mimicking direct or vehicular perception. Other ways of shooting—cuts between close-ups and long-range views, parallel-edited scenes that swivel back and forth between two locations, montage sequences that merge disparate images—expose filmgoers to incomparable sights. Because film has become so popular and important an art form, its visuality has transformed architectural perception. The film theorist Giuliana Bruno does not exaggerate when she writes that "the streetscape is as much a filmic construction as it is an architectural one."[1] By now, after more than a century at the movies, our understanding of the built environment derives not only from dwelling within it but also from watching it on the screen.

Film depends upon architectural imagery to make its depictions of place resonant. Architecture, along with actors, set design, and lighting, contributes to a film's mise-en-scène, its projection of a three-dimensional setting on a flat screen. Mise-en-scène means "that which is put in the scene."[2] In *On the History of Film Style*, film theorist David Bordwell lays out a history of writing and theorizing on film, focusing on stylistic techniques such as framing, editing, focus, sound, color, and mise-en-scène. According to Bordwell, mise-

1. Giuliana Bruno, "Site-Seeing: Architecture and the Moving Image," *Wide Angle* 19 (October 1997), 12.

2. Lutz Bacher, *The Mobile Mise-en-scène: A Critical Analysis of the Theory and Practice of Long-Take Camera Movement in the Narrative Film* (New York: Arno, 1978), 2.

en-scène is "a demonstration of pacing and poise, a sustained choreography of vivid foregrounds, apposite and neatly timed background action, the whole leading the viewer gracefully and unobtrusively from one point of interest to another."[3] Often those points of interest are architectural. Through depictions of real buildings and streets, mise-en-scène creates memorable environments; consider the marvelous images of postwar Vienna in Carol Reed's *The Third Man*, of San Francisco in the 1950s in Alfred Hitchcock's *Vertigo*, of Rome in the 1960s in Federico Fellini's *La Dolce Vita*, of Philadelphia in the 1970s in Sylvester Stallone's *Rocky*, of Rio de Janeiro in the 1980s in Hector Babenco's *Pixote*, of Ho Chi Minh City in the 1990s in Tran Anh Hung's *Cyclo*, and of Sydney in the early 2000s in Ray Lawrence's *Lantana*.

Architecture contributes to cinematic mise-en-scène by supplying boundaries, surfaces, and forms, which help develop plot. Just as important, architectural mise-en-scène becomes an alternative world, worthy of study and appreciation in its own right. Of all the elements of mise-en-scène, architectural landscapes remain most independent of a film. When cinematographers shoot on location, moviegoers see actual buildings and cities; a critical contribution of cinema to cultural history is the documentation of architecture in particular eras. The cinema has compiled a vast archive of the built world. "In the same way that buildings and cities create and preserve images of culture and a particular way of life," writes the architectural historian Juhani Pallasma, "cinema illuminates the cultural archaeology of both the time of its making and the era it depicts."[4]

Most of the time, the buildings and cities of the silver screen only loosely resemble those we perceive directly. Editing changes the flow of time and space. Watching a movie, we engage the era during which the film was made and those it depicts through flow, ellipses, and flashbacks. Editing similarly ruptures the continuum of space, reassembling it beyond the bounds of direct experience. In *Cinema 1*, Gilles Deleuze discusses film as a composite of preverbal signs put together by movement. The assembly of hundreds of different shots, Deleuze writes, "means that different views can be fitted together in an infinite number of ways and, because they are not oriented in relation to each other, constitute a set of singularities."[5] Outlooks on a building or city can be recorded, combined, and animated into cinematic sequences. The

3. David Bordwell, *On the History of Film Style* (Cambridge: Harvard University Press, 1997), 235.

4. Juhani Pallasma, *The Architecture of Image: Existential Space in Cinema* (Helsinki: Rakennustieto Oy, 2001), 13.

5. Gilles Deleuze, *Cinema 1: The Movement-Image* [1983], trans. Hugh Tomlinson and Barbara Habberjam (Minneapolis: University of Minnesota Press, 1986), 111.

built environment thus becomes a kind of vocabulary within the language of film. And it is, of course, the film director who must use this language, who must unite and assemble these "separate elements, that have been recorded by him at differing points of real actual space, into one filmic space," notes Vladimir Pudovkin.[6] Along with Sergei Eisenstein, Pudovkin was one of the theorists of the Russian school of montage, which argued that rapid editing should be the central component of cinematic progression and narrative. Montage, the assembly of unrelated shots, creates new meaning through sequences of images. Most films use montage to some extent, often for practical reasons. For *The Conformist*, released in 1970, director Bernardo Bertolucci shot on location in the late 1960s and, through careful editing, made his movie evoke France and Italy in the Fascist era. For *The Deerhunter*, released in 1978, director Michael Cimino used a steel town in western Pennsylvania for the scenes in a western Pennsylvania steel town; but when the steel workers drive to the mountains to hunt deer, the landscape we are seeing is not in the Alleghenies but in the Rockies.

Because of such discontinuities in time and space, motion pictures transform our understanding of place. Diverse buildings, cities, and landscapes are assembled into hybrid locales that exist only on celluloid. Images of Los Angeles, because it is home to Hollywood, and Toronto or Vancouver, because of cheap production costs, often substitute for other locales—the financial district of London, say, or a fishing village in Maine. Sometimes, it is difficult to distinguish constructed sets from existing buildings. Few filmgoers realize that the opening scene of F.W. Murnau's *Sunrise* takes place on a set—in the 1927 film, we see a train pulling out of a large terminal, through whose transparent walls are visible modern buildings and a moving elevated train. In *Film as Art*, film historian Rudolf Arnheim notes that it is hard for moviegoers to gauge the size of objects on the screen. Movie sets are easily mistaken for the real thing: "A newsreel of an architectural exhibition showed several shots of houses that had been erected on the grounds, and immediately afterward, shots of a little plaster model of the city of Rome. To the spectator both sets of buildings appeared of equal size, although in one they were of ordinary height and taken at the necessary distance, and in the other the models were only a few inches high and photographed close to."[7] Such com-

6. V.I. Pudovkin, *Film Technique and Film Acting* [1924], trans. Ivor Montagu (London: Vision/Mayflower, 1954), 87.

binations of constructed sets and real landscapes encourage a cinematic understanding of place that heightens our awareness of real places. Many of us have been in severe modernist buildings, but no one has experienced the techno-baroque environments—the Korova milk bar, the music arcade—created by Stanley Kubrick for his 1971 *A Clockwork Orange*.

Over the years, architects themselves have designed sets. Hans Poelzig crafted the contorted city of Paul Wegener's 1920 *The Golem*; Robert Mallet-Stevens created the expressionist sets for *L'Inhumaine*, directed in 1923 by Marcel L'Herbier. Some of the most striking cinescapes—those in Fritz Lang's 1927 *Metropolis* or Ridley Scott's 1982 *Blade Runner*—rely heavily on sets. The same holds for some of the cinema's memorable building interiors, which existed only on soundstages, such as Edward Carrere's designs for King Vidor's 1949 *The Fountainhead*, or the monstrous mastic walls in Roman Polanski's 1965 *Repulsion*, in which the boundary between a woman's psyche and her apartment slips away.[8]

But just as no handcrafted (or even digital) re-creation can represent the emotional range of the human face, no fabricated architectural mise-en-scène can re-create the visual depth of real places. The representation and transformation of real architectural landscapes on screen date to the origins of motion pictures. In the 1890s, Thomas Alva Edison and the Lumière brothers shot footage in real settings. Early movies devoted more time to exploring the visual world than to telling dramatic narratives. Film historian Tom Gunning calls these early movies a "cinema of attractions," in which technological, naturalistic, and urban wonders were the main event.[9] These early films showed the potential of movies to transport viewers to lands that few had visited. One of the most popular attractions of the early cinema was "Hales Tours," where spectators entered mock railcars, and watched, on a screen at the front of the car, a penetrating, dromoscopic camera tour of exotic places.[10]

But cinema soon outgrew the travelogue, as films such as D.W. Griffith's 1915 *The Birth of a Nation* established the popularity of plot-driven cinema. Since then, architecture in film has usually been overshadowed by narrative, actors, and dialogue; the introduction of talkies in 1928 would force cinematographers off the streets of cities and into studio soundstages,

7. Rudolf Arnheim, *Film as Art* [1933] (Berkeley: University of California Press, 1957), 85–86.

8. Katherine Shonfield, *Walls Have Feelings: Architecture, Film, and the City* (London: Routledge, 2000), 55, 59.

9. Tom Gunning, *D.W. Griffith and the Origins of American Narrative Film: The Early Years at Biograph* (Urbana: University of Illinois Press, 1991), 41–42.

10. Raymond Fielding, "Hales Tours: Ultrarealism in the Pre-1910 Motion Picture," in *Film Before Griffith*, ed. John Fell (Berkeley: University of California Press, 1983), 117.

further reducing the presence of real places in movies. Not until the rise neo-realism after the Second World War would directors move back to location shooting. In its hundred-year history, then, film has showcased architecture in various ways, from studio simulacrum to extensive location footage. In commercial films, establishing shots of architecture are used to provide a sense of place. In artistically ambitious films, architecture is used to suggest the visual intricacies of the built world and to reflect the emotional intricacies of characters. Experimental cinema often challenges our perceptual expectations of architecture and urban space. And a unique genre, the city symphony, turns the elements of architecture and urbanism into the narrative of a movie.

Last Year at Marienbad, by Alain Resnais emphasizes mise-en-scène over story or dialogue. In this 1961 movie Resnais constructs a series of non-linear episodes that challenge a viewer's attempts to make sense of what is happening, and when and why. He sets the action in a grand architectural environment—the grounds and spaces of a baroque palace, now an exclusive hotel—that powerfully informs the narrative. From the first tracking shots of vaulted ceilings in the palace, the film glides languorously across salons, along corridors, up and down staircases. The film ventures outdoors, taking us onto broad terraces, around fountains, and along the paths of formal gardens (exteriors were shot at the Nymphenburg and Schleissheim palaces outside Munich). The script and dialogue are based on a text by Alain Robbe-Grillet; early on the narrator announces his architectural preoccupations: "I walk on, once again, down these corridors, through these halls, these galleries, in this structure—of another century, this enormous, luxurious, baroque, lugubrious hotel—where corridors succeed endless corridors—silent deserted corridors overloaded with a dim, cold ornamentation of woodwork, stucco, moldings, marble, black mirrors, dark paintings, columns, heaving hangings—sculpted door frames, series of doorways, galleries—transverse corridors that open in turn on empty salons."[11]

Throughout the film, the narrator, known only as "X," pursues a woman, called "A." The mise-en-scène "is obviously a kind of geometric tomb into which the man keeps trying to lure the woman, to wander about forever, alone with him,"[12] comments film historian Peter Harcourt. The camera's movement through the mysterious spaces of the palace/hotel tracks the memories X

11. Alain Robbe-Grillet, Last Year at Marienbad, trans. Richard Howard (New York: Grove Press, 1962), 17.

12. Peter Harcourt, "Alain Resnais: Toward the Certainty of Doubt," Film Comment 10 (January-February 1974), 27.

raises. Repeatedly, Resnais sets taciturn human encounters against the expressive drama of architecture. In one shot, taken from a terrace overlooking over the garden, he frames a group of immobile characters between the pyramidal and circular bushes of a topiary. Eerily, only the human figures seem to cast shadows. In this contrived landscape, it is the guests who seem ornamental, while the buildings and landscapes seem to move—to emote. In another remarkable scene, the camera proceeds toward a tapestry at the end of a corridor. The tapestry depicts an exterior view of the gardens, and the camera's motion confuses us—we seem to be approaching the palace itself. As it reaches the tapestry, however, the camera turns ninety degrees to look down a narrow empty hall, further confusing image with reality. The camera then continues into a colonnaded room crowded with guests; here, too, the people are motionless, as if they were figures woven into the tapestry.

The baroque palace/hotel of Marienbad is the principal character of the film. Its complex spaces and ornamentation underscore the lack of human drama. Indoors, along curved, light-colored surfaces and around the lavish frames of mirrors, the camera follows the tendrils, arabesques, and cartouches of the low-relief rococo ornament—dreamlike crescendos and diminuendos that trail off into a void. Outdoors, the camera lingers on the taut muscles and limbs of stone statues, sculpted heroism, unnervingly lifelike. Several times, X comments on the similarity between words and ornament, both forms of communication, of persuasion, in which the genuine and the false can be difficult to tell apart: "a sentence, once begun, suddenly remained in suspension, as though frozen by the frost. . . . It was always the same conversations that recurred, the same absent voices."[13]

If baroque and rococo ornamentation can be said to naturalize architecture, softening and even melting the hard surfaces and rectilinear forms, then the formal garden, with its strict geometries, can be said to make nature architectural. And like the rooms of the palace, the spaces of the garden lead us in circles. Resnais's camera traces the path of lifelike ornament as it develops and dissolves; conversations among characters loop endlessly; and the geometric gardens lead nowhere, to stagnation. The camera continually glides toward some destination that it never will reach.

The baroque settings of *Last Year at Marienbad* are, ultimately, a critique of more than postwar bourgeois ennui; Resnais is taking aim at the

13. Robbe-Grillet, 90.

From *Last Year at Marienbad*, director Alain Resnais

European idea of civilization as it was developed in court society. In baroque palaces and their formal grounds, at the dawn of the modern era, the European aristocracy ceased being warriors and became courtiers. Training in the art of war was replaced by training in etiquette, taste, and manners, practiced along the enfilades and garden paths, in the halls and salons of palaces. The film argues, however, that this highly wrought civilization, as well as the bourgeois society it produced, has lost its essential vitality. The civilizing process has lead nowhere. The paradoxical patterns of baroque design—the statuary that seems animated, the gardens that seem lifeless—immobilize the moderns, the formally attired and perpetually indecisive guests of the hotel. Promenading endlessly down corridors and passages, the nameless characters seem to wilt and whither amid the sensuous spaces, with their chimerical figures and surfaces.

By heightening the role of architectural mise-en-scène, *Last Year at Marienbad* presents filmgoers with an engrossing view of architecture and landscape. Here architecture is not a backdrop for dialogue and plot; Resnais has cast architecture in a leading role. By animating building and landscape, Resnais challenges customary notions of architectural stillness. In direct experience, we move around buildings; we must make the physical effort to explore their spaces and details. In film, the camera does the moving for us; architecture moves while we remain stationary. Especially in *Last Year at Marienbad*, the camera thrusts architecture into the dramatic role of storyteller. And unexpectedly, this sort of enhanced sensitivity to architecture makes the film seem closer to everyday perception than do the conventions of plot-driven movies. Films that explore architectural landscapes encourage viewers to see the built world anew. As architectural historian Anthony Vidler has argued, "a theoretical apparatus was developed that at once held architecture as the fundamental site of film practice, the indispensable real and ideal matrix of the filmic imaginary, and, at the same time, posited film as the modernist art of space par excellence—a vision of the fusion of space and time."[14]

In the 1920s, as Vidler points out, the art historian Elie Faure recognized the potential of a close affiliation of film and architecture. In *The Art of Cineplastics,* Faure states that architecture should cease to be an art of immobility, and hence detachment, and become a practice of what he called

14. Anthony Vidler, "The Explosion of Space: Architecture and the Filmic Imaginary," *Assemblage* 21 (August 1993), 46.

"ensemble in action." Faure understood that industrial engineering—the design of ships, trains, and automobiles—had begun to explore the possibilities of form in movement. The challenge Faure poses for modern architecture is not the merging of art with industry, of ornament with structure, archetypal concerns of modern architects. Instead, he challenges architects to set their designs in motion, to develop what he calls "cineplastics" as the dynamic and spiritual basis for building and city making. Cineplastics can be understood as a kind of merger between architecture and film, in which film would transcend plot, and architecture would be more than static object. Faure's cineplastics envisions film as a visual symphony of moving architecture, a sensual journal created from form, amid buildings and landscapes. To Faure, film, alone among the arts, is "plastic drama in action, occupying time through its own movement and carrying with it its own space."[15] The space of a film, its surfaces and forms, and even its human characters are, in a sense, its architecture. Faure exhorts architects "to build edifices that are made and broken down and remade ceaselessly—by imperceptible passages of time and modeling that are in themselves architecture at every moment,"[16] and thus to release architecture into shifting assemblages of cinematic motion.

Writing after Faure, in the 1930s, the art historian Erwin Panofsky notes how film uses buildings and cities as the foundational, structural, and decorative elements of its own constructions. Each of the arts employs elements to create compositions—painting and writing use abstract elements (paint on canvas, letters on paper); architecture uses articulated elements (bricks, I-beams); film uses the most complex elements of all—images of people, buildings, and cities—to create cinematic art. "The medium of the movies is a physical reality," writes Panofsky, "the physical reality of eighteenth-century Versailles . . . or of a suburban home in Westchester."[17] A succession of shots in a film is at once a succession of architectural landscapes and an artistic composition—a work of cinematic art built up from images of architecture. Through the medium of film, the largest and most immobile works of art can become flexible and abstract elements of artistic composition. The perception of architecture on film can be a powerful and evocative experience, for often as not, what we are seeing is something entirely new and, at the same time, something we have seen again and again.

15. Elie Faure, *The Art of Cineplastics,* trans. Walter Pach (Boston: The Four Seas Company, 1923), 32.

16. Ibid., 40.

17. Erwin Panofsky, "Style and Medium in Motion Pictures" [1934], in *Film Anthology*, ed. Daniel Talbot (New York: Simon & Schuster, 1959), 31.

ESTABLISHING SHOT

Plot dominates commercial movies and determines their architectural settings. Most movies emphasize dialogue, action, and sometimes music—whatever moves the narrative forward. Although cityscapes and landscapes often figure more prominently in outdoor scenes, the focus of the camera and spectator is primarily on the action and only secondarily on the setting.[18] Things that move—people, animals, machines, weather—draw the attention of the camera and of filmgoers, while fixed structures and surfaces recede into the background.

Sometimes, however, to establish a sense of place, directors project architecture into the foreground. As early as 1910, D.W. Griffith used the San Gabriel Mission in Los Angeles in the making of *Thread of Destiny*. As film historian Lewis Jacobs points out, Griffith "photographed the Mission in great detail, with its weather beaten walls, decorative interiors, stairways, choir loft, and cemetery—shots which were not called for in the plot but which, when carefully edited, created an atmosphere and background that greatly reinforced the narrative and action of the story. No one, not even Griffith himself, had as yet taken shots of the various details of a setting to build a scene."[19] Since then, building exteriors, streets, and cityscapes have been key features in countless movies, sometimes upstaging the actors, and showcasing architecture in a range of shots from the long-range vista to detailed close-up. In the simplest of cases, brief establishing shots of building exteriors are used to set up the action and atmosphere of a scene that will take place within a building; in this way the style and status of a building become part of the plot. In more complex situations, a multi-shot establishing sequence helps not only to set up a scene but also to help structure the ideas of the film. And in some movies, images of buildings and cities are integral to the narrative, creating a continuous architectural subtext. The evocation of location can range greatly—from the studio-created New Orleans in the 1951 *A Streetcar Named Desire* to the ubiquitous Nebraska landscape of *About Schmidt*, released in 2002. In this film, the camera puts on show the First National Bank Tower in Omaha, and the city's neighborhoods, restaurants, shopping centers, and highways; and it shows us as well such roadside attractions as Pioneer Village and the Great Platte River Road Archway. Alexander Payne's

18. Donald Albrecht, *Designing Dreams: Modern Architecture in the Movies* (New York: Harper & Row, 1986), 58.

19. Lewis Jacobs, "D.W. Griffith: New Discoveries," in *The Emergence of Film Art*, ed. Lewis Jacobs (New York: W.W. Norton & Co., 1979), 49–50.

film turns these mundane places into an intriguing landscape, one that enriches the story of a middle-aged man mourning his lost chances.[20]

The most common and least engaging use of architecture in movies occurs in establishing shots. Establishing (and reestablishing) shots are intended merely to identify the place in which the drama (usually filmed on a set) will unfold. Typically, the first such shots show an entire building or large part of a building in a long view. Then the film might cut to characters entering the building or dissolve into an interior space, where the action begins. Establishing shots usually lead from outside to inside, from public to private realm, from the whole of the city or community to some part of it. Sometimes they provide a sense of place through panoramic views of a cityscape, taken from a crane or helicopter. Invariably, in such zoomscape experiences, the camera brings impressive technological mobility to the perception of built environs, allowing us, in seconds, to traverse hundreds of feet of space and to occupy diverse vantage points.

Directors also employ establishing shots to render the complexities of a place or building. One technique is to develop an idea of a place from composite images. The opening scenes of *Citizen Kane*, released in 1941, show in quick succession many images of historic architecture—these establish the artistic legacy and monumental scale of Xanadu, the estate of Charles Foster Kane, the movie's complicated hero. In this sequence, director Orson Welles interspersed photographs of medieval castles, baroque churches, and formal gardens with dark, distanced shots of Xanadu—or rather, with the model of Xanadu, for an exterior set was never built. These images tell us that Kane's new palace is grander and more monumental than these older buildings— "the cost," we are told, "no man can say." To construct a puzzling sense of interior space, directors sometimes use establishing shots that do not fit with the ensuing scenes. At the beginning of Jacques Tati's 1968 *Playtime*, an establishing sequence sets a surreal mood. A camera pans across blue skies with puffy clouds, pauses at a glass-walled high-rise, then cuts to a glazed corridor where two nuns are walking; it then follows the nuns into a large waiting room, where it becomes apparent that we are in an airport outside Paris. But the height of the high-rise makes us wonder if we can be at a real airline terminal. Through this conflation of building types, Tati transports film-

20. Hans Dieter Schaal, *Learning from Hollywood: Architecture and Film* (Stuttgart: Axel Menges, 1996), 36.

goers into an environment of interchangeable parts. What we might call Tati's "anti-establishing shot" sets the tone of a film that will construct an anti-place, a thoroughly bizarre Paris—Tativille.[21] Tati's opening scenes at the airport contradict the notion that air travel will lead anywhere but in circles, will be anything but a revolving cinematic excursion through sparkling and scrubbed non-places.

Unlike more commercial movies, whose establishing shots are direct and literal, films like *Citizen Kane* and *Playtime* use opening shots to show settings that will resonate throughout the films in complex and contradictory ways. But even in commercial films, establishing sequences can upend our expectations of architectural space. In the 1989 *The Silence of the Lambs*, the establishing shots of two buildings tell us about both the buildings' functions and the film's protagonists. Although different in style and age, both the FBI Academy in Quantico, Virginia, and the state asylum for the criminally insane in Baltimore sprawl over expansive grounds; and both enclose secretive and guarded spaces. Director Jonathan Demme first shows us the FBI complex, where we watch an agent, Clarice Starling, run a training course. When she returns to headquarters, two aerial shots show the modern complex; these are followed by a zoom down to a glass-walled pedestrian bridge and the corridors and elevators leading to the office of Clarice's boss. From the woods to the exteriors and then the interiors, the spaces of the sequence progressively narrow, concluding in a small office where the camera cuts to a bulletin board posted with mug shots of serial killers. In contrast, the establishing shot of the Maryland asylum is taken from the ground, which makes the Victorian Gothic building, with its tower and wings, look foreboding. Thus Demme prepares us for a tortuous journey through the asylum's dim halls with their locked gates, a claustrophobic sequence that leads to the maximum-security dungeon that holds the serial killer Hannibal Lecter.

The final scenes of *Silence of the Lambs* work an intriguing variation on what has become a commonplace of establishing shots: the view of a pleasant-looking residential street. Toward the end of the movie, we see such a street, lined with tidy wood houses. The tidy wood house that Demme zeroes in on, however, is no ordinary house; it conceals the basement chambers where a serial killer has tortured and killed young women. Earlier horror

21. Anthony Easthope, "Cinécities in the Sixties," in *The Cinematic City*, 133.

films, such as *Halloween* and *Nightmare on Elm Street*, had been set in suburbia, turning zones of domestic security and comfort into sites of anxiety and
terror. Demme is subtler. He echoes the spatial progression of evil developed
earlier in the film, in which exterior shots of large, complex buildings preceded
views of their labyrinthine interiors. At the end, views of the ordinary exterior
of the serial killer's house are followed by scenes of its dark and even
Piranesian interiors.

Aside from teenagers violating curfew or thieves robbing houses, people normally enter buildings through doors on the ground floor. This is not
necessarily so in the movies. Early on, filmmakers realized that establishing
sequences could be more exciting if filmed from the air. In *The Crowd*,
released in 1928, director King Vidor establishes, in a scene that begins on
a boat in the harbor, that the protagonist, John, has moved from a small town
to New York City. The camera gazes at the Manhattan skyline, zips down to
the docks, and then moves into the maelstrom of the city. From a high angle,
we see crowds of pedestrians, and streets clogged with cars, buses, and elevated trains. Smoke spews from stacks atop skyscrapers and from tugboats in
the harbor. Gradually the camera ascends to encompass the exhilarating
scope of the city, intensifying its drama by rotating in a dizzying turn.

Before taking filmgoers into the building where John will work, Vidor
shows a sequence of skyscraper views that progressively shift perception from
a human to mechanical mode, from ground to air. Beginning at street level,
Vidor tilts the camera and travels up the surface of the Equitable Building—
an acute and disorienting view, but not uncommon in large cities. Then, turning abruptly, he focuses on the facade of another skyscraper. But now the
camera has left the ground, and we gaze at windows high above the street.
Tilting again, the camera treks vertiginously up the building, almost to the
cornice. What follows is one of the most impressionistic tracking shots ever
filmed. Cutting to a long-range view of another skyscraper—this one a
model—the camera swivels to face the building straight on. It then moves
toward the building, glides through a window, and (after an imperceptible dissolve) enters an immense room filled with row upon row of identical desks.
The camera has turned filmgoers into aerial voyagers of Manhattan's downtown canyons.

220

In this extraordinary sequence, which lasts less than a minute, Vidor introduces a daunting contrast: that between the thrilling views from the sky and the crushing monotony of office life. Before John takes his job, filmgoers see buildings gliding through empty space and solid matter, and in panoramic views from high places. Once he starts working, the views become as earthbound as his own limited perspectives on life. The camera assumes the position of a man in the crowd. Some shots are even taken below eye level; these create the impression of hovering, crushing interiors. With its artful cinematography, *The Crowd* shows how film can use architecture to create dramatically different moods. As Kester Rattenbury has observed of film in general, its "synthesis of observed architecture with time and character, background and mood, plot and meaning, gives potent expression to ideas latent in architecture—and usually missed by the majority of its viewers; and it expounds these ideas non-verbally."[22]

The films of Alfred Hitchcock play upon a filmgoer's viewpoints and expectations, often creating exhilarating moments of visual power, and leading audiences into exciting and dangerous places. The director's 1960 *Psycho* opens with an aerial pan of downtown of Phoenix before closing in on a small hotel. Hovering in midair, the camera focuses on a window whose blinds are drawn; after a brief dissolve, it moves inside. The continuous tracking motion continues, and we see a couple, partially clothed, lying in bed. In seconds, we have been transported from the expanse of the city to the shadowy hotel room. This dizzying sequence prefigures the psychological horrors that will follow, as the movie's adulterous heroine, Marion, the woman on the bed, flees Phoenix with a stash of stolen money, and checks into the Bates Motel, where she meets its insane owner, Norman. There, just as the camera had earlier spied on her lunchtime tryst, Norman peers at Marion from a peephole in the wall, watching her undress, in preparation for a shower. What follows is one of the most famous and horrific scenes in cinema history—the brutal murder of Marion in the shower. In *Psycho*, the voyeuristic transgression of walls and boundaries leads inexorably to trouble, to madness and death.

Establishing shots do not always move from a location-shot exterior to a soundstage interior. In some films, footage shot on location is carefully

22. Kester Rattenbury, "Echo and Narcissus," *Architectural Design*, Profile 112 (1994), 35.

intercut throughout an otherwise set-bound story. A movie shot mostly on studio backlots can attain cinematographic distinction through the careful use of potent location photography. In *Force of Evil*, from 1948, director Abraham Polonsky brackets the drama of a New York lawyer who tries to make one million dollars in one day with opening and concluding location sequences that deepen our understanding of its moral. The opening shot frames not only a specific building and district but also the larger problem of greed in modern society. From an upper story of a downtown skyscraper, the camera looks across to Trinity Church, wedged in among the offices of Wall Street—a reminder of spiritual power amid the center of worldly power. Polonsky then tilts the camera down at an acute angle to view an intersection filled with hurrying pedestrians and cars. A dissolve leads to the lobby of a building, and then to an office, where the drama begins.

The conclusion of *Force of Evil* takes place far from the towers of Wall Street, uptown in Washington Heights. The lawyer-protagonist, whose corrupt actions have by now led to the murder of his brother, has taken the train uptown from his office; the film shows brick apartment buildings along Riverside Drive. From the heights of the Drive, the lawyer looks down at the Hudson River. Then, in a precipitous descent that echoes the opening sequence, he hurries down a monumental set of stairs and reaches the base of the George Washington Bridge. The music swells as the lawyer poises under the bridge that spans the river to the American continent beyond, symbolizing, perhaps, his hopes of breaching the troubling chasms of his own life. But the music turns ominous and the movie concludes darkly, as the lawyer moves to the river's edge, where he sees, on the rocks, the corpse of his brother. Shots of architecture and landscape—a church spire, office towers, a bridge, and the edge of a river—trace the hero's rise to the commercial heights even as he falls from spiritual grace.

Force of Evil is film noir; *The Sound of Music* might be called film blanche. But here, too, architecture and landscape are used to deepen a drama of social disintegration. Directed by Robert Wise, the 1965 movie begins with an aerial voyage above the Austrian Alps, the camera gliding above mountains and valleys, above a baroque church and a castle on an island in a lake. The scene is stirring, and the heroine, Maria, climbs up a steep meadow and begins to sing the first song of Rodgers and Hammerstein's well-known score. Soon the panoramic prelude moves from the mountains to Salzburg, the camera slaloming around the monuments, churches, and palaces of the baroque city.

The film's sense of free flight soon ends. The mood changes imperceptibly as we notice uneasy juxtapositions of architecture and nature: steeples and domes alternate with mountains, walls of cut stone and elaborate ornament with granite cliffs, formal dining rooms with spacious meadows. Such comparisons become the visual theme of the movie, for while the architectural spaces of the film are grand and sometimes beautiful, they are also, we come to see, constricting. And they underscore the drama of the film, of Maria and the von Trapp family's flight from the confines of Nazi-occupied Austria. Indeed, as the film progresses, the lovely cities and great houses look increasingly menacing, their spaces sullied with swastikas, their occupants complicit. In *The Sound of Music*, high architecture is foreboding. It is in the high peaks of the Alps that the characters find freedom, not just metaphorically, but actually; the final scenes of the film show Maria and the von Trapp family fleeing Austria on foot, crossing the mountains to Switzerland.

Many moviegoers watch *The Sound of Music* for its melodrama and its music, but those who look closely at the settings will observe an ongoing visual dialogue between liberating nature and stultifying architecture. In the movies, architectural and landscape types frequently signify more than place or identity; they can become a visual language. Tenements, row houses, split-levels, and mansions establish social categories and landscapes. Hallways, fire escapes, rooftops, and sidewalks convey the confinement of the inner city.[23] Lawns, cul-de-sacs, and wide driveways speak the language of the suburbs. A cut from a high-ceilinged, wood-paneled men's club to a sleek downtown loft can signify one social order giving way to another. Images of towers, walls, doors, windows, stairs, escalators, or bridges imbue the events of plot with the associations of these elements and types—height, separation, entrance, opening, vertical and diagonal movement, connection. A depiction of a bridge can indicate not only a span over water but also the joining of landscapes and characters.[24] Glances up or down staircases can prefigure the transition between public and private realms. Sequences leading from rooftops to streets and sometimes to subterranean places like sewers can

23. Patricia Kruth, "The Color of New York: Place and Spaces in the Films of Martin Scorsese and Woody Allen," in *Cinema and Architecture: Méliès, Mallet-Stevens, Multimedia*, ed. Francois Penz and Maureen Thomas (London: British Film Institute, 1997), 71.

24. Alain Silver, "Fragments of the Mirror: Hitchcock's Noir Landscape," in *Film Noir Reader 2*, eds. Alain Silver and James Ursini (New York: Limelight Editions, 1999), 108.

establish a filmic topography leading from the holy to the damned. In many dramatic films, such symbols move plot as forcefully as does dialogue. Yet as the director Andrey Tarkovsky warns, the use of such symbols can become heavy-handed and formulaic: "No mise-en-scène has the right to be repeated, just as two personalities are never the same. As soon as a mise en scène turns into a sign, a cliché, a concept (however original it may be), then the whole thing—characters, situations, psychology—becomes schematic and false."[25]

The Pawnbroker, directed by Sidney Lumet and released in 1965, explores the nature of confinement, both social and architectural. Its mise-en-scène is endlessly inventive; the interior and exterior settings establish, develop, and even resolve the dramatic action. The film's establishing shots are so frequent and complex that they can hardly be distinguished from the established settings. The 1965 movie is set in a Spanish Harlem pawnshop, a warren of rooms, each enclosed by chain-link and bars; the spaces call to mind a prison cell, and in this they express the mentality, the memories, of the pawnbroker, Sol Nazerman, a German-Jewish survivor of the Holocaust. Nazerman talks to customers through holes in the cage, slits wide enough for him to do business with people down on their luck but too narrow for meaningful communication. Outdoors, Lumet shows us streets shadowed by elevated trains and the high pockmarked walls of buildings; these fortify the exploration of Nazerman's sense of perpetual incarceration, years after his liberation from Auschwitz.

The only happy scenes in *The Pawnbroker* occur in the past. The opening scenes are pastoral. A boy and girl are running through a meadow, trying to catch a butterfly; their Jewish family is vacationing by a river in the German countryside. Filmed in slow motion to heighten the expansiveness of the summer afternoon, the scene ends abruptly, with shots of the faces of the characters, which look fearful. The next scene, which takes place twenty-five years later, is set in Long Island. The camera looks down at a postwar housing development. Here there is not a river but an expressway, running noisily in the background. The camera zooms down to a backyard, and cuts to a medium shot of a man lying on a chaise longue. He is the boy from the picnic, Nazerman, now middle-aged. The suburban environment, with its uniform

25. Andrey Tarkovsky, *Sculpting in Time: Reflections on the Cinema,* trans. Kitty Hunter-Blair (New York: Alfred A. Knopf, 1987), 25.

From *Il Grido*, director Michelangelo Antonioni

cramped lots, suggests the character's ongoing emotional captivity. At one point, the camera traps Nazerman in a trapezoidal frame created by a fence post, a telegraph pole, a steel utility stanchion, and a leafless tree.[26]

Later, as Nazerman drives to Harlem, the camera tracks the cityscape from his car, showing groups of people on the sidewalks and bundles of merchandise in front of stores. Lumet's camera lingers on an abandoned store, where a heap of old shoes press into the window—an allusion to the shoes, glasses, and suitcases taken from prisoners as they arrived at the Nazi camps. Later in the day, he sees a violent fight in a chain-linked lot, and flashes back to the death camp and the memory of an inmate being killed as he climbed a barbed wire fence.

Near the end of the film, Nazerman, who has walled himself off from people and places, discovers that his business depends not just on money laundering but also on prostitution. Dazed, he walks through the nighttime streets of Harlem, past brightly lit stores, theater marquees, and neon signs. The lights, the crowds, the dazzling sparks of the elevated trains provide an ironic backdrop for his emotional collapse, for his unbearable isolation. By dawn he reaches a new housing complex near Lincoln Center, the home of a woman who had earlier offered him friendship. Outside on the terrace, we see the first expansive views of the film, as the camera pans out toward the Hudson River, the West Side Highway, and Lower Manhattan. Temporarily out of confinement, Nazerman begins to speak of the past, but soon pulls back, unable at this stage to escape his grim past. The final view is chilling: we see Nazerman's slumping figure and, in the distance, freight trains and smokestacks.

LONG LOOKS

Many film genres depend heavily on the atmosphere of architectural mise-en-scène. Film noir sets the mood in shadowy interiors, with the blinds half down, and on rain-spattered sidewalks under blinking neon signs. Neorealism situates its tragedies in the grim streets of postwar Europe—Berlin reduced to rubble, Rome less eternal than desperate. One cannot imagine historical films or costume dramas—set in ancient Egypt, feudal Japan, or courtly Europe—without painstakingly crafted sets and carefully edited location footage. Nor would a Western be a Western without vistas of cowboys on horseback riding through

26. Frank Cunningham, *Sidney Lumet: Film and Literary Vision* (Lexington: University Press of Kentucky Press, 1991), 159.

the desert, and of lawmen walking along the dusty streets of frontier towns. In these and other genres, the director's attention to the details of building and city not only reinforces the narrative; it can also promote the independence of the visual from the narrative, making us shift attention from the intrigues of plot and character to the cinematic construction of place. Some shots of buildings do more than just establish scenes. They become scenes in themselves.

Important works of architecture, especially when their forms are startling or brazen, can dominate our impressions of a movie. Tour-de-force architectural cameos appear throughout the movies. In *Back to the Future*, released in 1989, the Gamble House in Pasadena by Greene and Greene, with its fusion of Arts and Crafts and Japanese sensibilities, makes an exotic laboratory/manse for Doc Brown, the eccentric inventor. Frank Lloyd Wright's Ennis Brown House in Los Angeles has starred in many thrillers and science fiction fantasies, including *Blade Runner* and the 1989 *Black Rain*, both by Ridley Scott, largely because its evocation of Mayan pyramids makes it look intriguingly futuristic. In *Body Double*, released in 1984 and directed by Brian de Palma, a peeping Tom peers out at his stripteasing neighbor, who is doing her act in John Lautner's Malin House, which hovers like a spaceship over the San Fernando Valley.

Architectural style can give a movie great distinction. Style depends less on the unique or strange than on the exquisitely appropriate. Guy Hamilton's *Goldfinger*, of 1964, the third of the James Bond series, sets one of its most famous scenes at the Fontainebleau Hotel in Miami Beach, designed by Morris Lapidus. The modernist curves of the hotel are a fitting backdrop for the debonair spy, but the sleek spaces and sybaritic pool are enjoyable to watch in themselves. Richard Neutra's Lovell House, in the Hollywood Hills, appears in Curtis Hanson's 1997 *LA Confidential*, where it not only suggests the nouveau-riche aspirations of its owner, who runs a prostitution ring, but also titillates the audience with its swooping spaces. In *Manhunter*, released in 1986, Michael Mann inserts views of landmarks of modernist airport architecture, including Eero Saarinen's TWA Terminal in New York and Minoru Yamasaki's Lambert-St. Louis Air Terminal. Also in the film, Richard Meier's High Museum in Atlanta becomes the setting for a maximum-security prison; its spiraling tubular steel, white panels, and glass walls, with their calculated coolness, effectively suggest the architecture of incarceration.

Architecture becomes still more independent of plot in films with little plot. In the 1950s, the French film theorist André Bazin began to champion cinematic realism, a method of filmmaking that favors narratives about ordinary people and that employs long takes of the everyday city. The long take usually features slow camera movements that concentrate on mise-en-scène. As shots become scenes, filmgoers have time to observe details of the environment. Describing Luchino Visconti's postwar semi-documentary *La Terra Trema*, about Sicilian fishermen, Bazin praises the lengthy (three- to four-minute) shots, the views of stark scenery that convey the hardness of life. "Neorealism," he writes, "knows only immanence. It is from appearance only, the simple appearance of beings and of the world, that it knows how to deduce the ideas that it unearths. It is a phenomenology."[27]

Among the filmmakers analyzed by Bazin is Michelangelo Antonioni. The Italian director's films are usually set in urban places, from Renaissance plazas to modern housing estates. Occasionally Antonioni uses well-known buildings; *The Passenger*, of 1975, for instance, shot partly in Barcelona, uses the buildings of Antonio Gaudì. Usually, though, his disturbing dramas take place in the sort of vernacular buildings and landscapes where most people live, work, and travel—which makes them even more unsettling. Many of his films are silent for long stretches, when long takes of buildings, cities, and roadsides tell the story. An early Antonioni film, *Il Grido*, made in 1957, is set in the Po River valley. (Its depiction of foggy melancholic landscape has inspired filmmakers such as Tarkovsky, Wim Wenders, Theo Angelopoulos, Béla Tarr, and Alexander Sokurov.) *Il Grido* tells the story of Aldo, a refinery mechanic, who, after being dumped by his girlfriend, wanders around the dreary industrial landscape. For most of the film, Aldo roams the foggy banks of the river with his young daughter, looking for work, finding a lover, moving on to the next town. Antonioni's camera follows Aldo in long panning shots that expose the barren landscape and often end with views of distant cities. Antonioni makes us see the monotony of poverty, the flimsy wooden shacks, the greasy restaurants and gas stations. This landscape, with its river and

27. André Bazin, *What is Cinema?*, Volume II, trans. Hugh Gray (Berkeley: University of California Press, 1974), 64.

road that seem to lead nowhere, is the central visual metaphor of the film—postwar Italy, reduced to grim survival. Another powerful image brackets the drama at beginning and end. At the start, we see Aldo atop a water tower as his girlfriend happily calls him to lunch. At the end of the film, Aldo, lonely and disillusioned, kills himself by jumping off the tower. The single high vantage in a story that most of the time slogs along the low river and road, the tower promises perspective and offers, finally, escape.

In a quartet of remarkable films from the early 1960s—*L'Avventura*, *La Notte*, *L'Eclisse*, and *Red Desert*—Antonioni mixes the working class and the haute bourgeoisie, industrialized Italy and the resorts of the rich, old monuments and new modernist projects. The credits of *La Notte* announce that architecture will be more than a backdrop in the film. From a shot of a noisy street, a sudden cut transports us skyward to the roof deck of the Pirelli Tower (designed by Gio Ponti, and the tallest building in Milan). From the tower's summit, in a bird's-eye view, the entire city is visible. But as the camera descends its sheer walls, it looks in rather than out, at the building's glass and steel surfaces. This cinematographic posture creates an analogy between cinema and architecture, the frames of a filmstrip paralleling the stories of a building. Midway down the building, the camera pans ninety degrees and looks toward the city. This shot is divided between views of the city and views of the city reflected in the Pirelli building. The modern perception of the city occurs through the cinematic lens.[28]

Throughout Antonioni's quartet, place plays a leading role. But the director's sense of place is ambiguous. Long segments show characters wandering through the semi-deserted streets of Milan's business district, or through an abandoned town founded in Fascist days, or on the polluted ground near an oil refinery. Such long takes facilitate Antonioni's exploration of the fragmentation of the modern metropolis and the rootlessness of its inhabitants. As the camera dwells on a space, we notice that characters are ill at ease, disoriented by the industrial and commercial forces that are shaping urban form and infrastructure. The long take, as opposed to the fast cut, makes us concentrate on the awkward movements of people within the mechanized, anonymous city. We see their bodies dwarfed by tall buildings and power stations, by enormous, empty plazas and streets. We see their efforts

28. Mitchell Schwarzer, "The Consuming Landscape: Architecture in the Films of Michelangelo Antonioni," in *Architecture and Film*, ed. Mark Lamster (New York: Princeton Architectural Press, 2000), 199.

to communicate with each other thwarted by interceding columns, sliding glass doors, car doors. The textures of Antonioni's modern city are equally discomforting. Asphalt-paved avenues and plate-glass walls are shown in monochrome flatness, then in blinding contrasts of sunlight and shadow, then in pale moonlight and lightning flashes. Interiors are often packed with unheeded possessions, while city streets and suburban landscapes are barren. One might think that the alienation of the modern city had forced emotional life indoors. But this is not Antonioni's point. Indeed, the interior lives of his characters are as empty as the surrounding environments.

Antonioni chose industrializing Italy as the setting in which to explore contemporary alienation; Alain Resnais found an even more extreme setting. *Hiroshima Mon Amour*, of 1958, takes place in the first city hit by the atom bomb. Early on, a man and a woman lie in bed at the Hiroshima City Hotel. The woman, Elle, who is French, talks about the bomb, while the man, Lui, who is Japanese, hardly speaks. *Hiroshima Mon Amour* has little plot; it consists mostly of voice-over monologues and images of the city, both immediately after the blast and in the late 1950s. As Elle soliloquizes, Resnais shows us period footage, including an aerial pan across the destroyed city, with its endless blocks of rubble and crumbling buildings. Most of the views, though, are of reconstructed Hiroshima, as the camera roams through the rebuilt streets. At one point it steadies on the Peace Memorial Museum, a careful sequence of shots taking us through the grounds and then inside to the displays of artifacts and representations of the blast. And yet neither the images nor Elle's monologues do justice to the catastrophe they seek to understand; the blast, Resnais seems to be saying, is beyond description and comprehension.

A powerful scene of five static shots follows the museum visit, picturing what is now called the A-Bomb Dome, the mangled but preserved ruins of the Hiroshima Prefectural Building for the Promotion of Industry. At first, the camera looks through a chain-link fence at the fragmented walls that somehow survived the blast. Then it closes in on the cracked walls. The third shot, taken from a high point, looks down at the floors of the building that pancaked to the ground on August 6, 1945. The camera then wheels around to look up at the framework of the dome. The dome no longer encloses the building; its framework leaves it open to the sky, from which destruction once rained. For centuries a symbol of the heavens, an architectural evocation of sky, the dome now speaks of death, of the hellish destruction of total war.

Another scene in *Hiroshima Mon Amour* uses the technique of parallel editing, which allows filmmakers to depict multiple geographies (and temporalities) in the same scene. Here the depictions are of Hiroshima and Nevers, France, the town Elle comes from. The juxtaposition seems strange at first. But Resnais is arguing that war affects not only those places that were destroyed but also those left seemingly intact, and that the effects of destruction are registered not only through observation but also through remembrance. The sequence shows not just two cities, but two modes of visual consciousness. We see the neon lights of Hiroshima, illuminating the new buildings of the rebuilt city, which look thin and insubstantial compared with the old stone structures of Nevers. In the French city, we see the thick walls and iron gates of old buildings shrouded in wintry fog. In striking contrast to the Japanese city, the French city seems to have no new architecture, as if it had been frozen in time. Seen in parallel, new Japan and old France offer complementary perspectives, and indeed, they even begin to blur together, the glow of Japanese neon blending with the glare of French sky. This sort of sequence of parallel images illustrates one of the central arguments in Giuliana Bruno's *Atlas of Emotion*, which is that film conflates architecture and emotion. Throughout *Hiroshima Mon Amour*, Resnais goes back and forth from Hiroshima to Nevers, from past to present, from one love affair to another; and then in the parallel city sequence, he suggests the convergences of bodies and buildings. "As their physiognomies blur, the distant topographies blur with them: one lover turns into the other; the city of today turns into the city of yesterday."[29]

Film can reveal to us architectures that exist only in the mind, architectures composed of sensation but also memory and imagination; and such film architecture yields insight into the perception of real architecture. Through changes in viewing distance and height, in the shape and size of the field of view, in the movement of a camera through space, and in the duration of scenes, cinema constructs alternative worlds. Because it can marshal various technologies of the zoomscape—panning like a train, tracking like an automobile, staring down from the sky like a plane, condensing lived experience

29. Giuliana Bruno, *Atlas of Emotion: Journeys in Art, Architecture, and Film* (London: Verso, 2002), 40.

into dense image like a photograph—film is the medium that best allows us to explore the perceptual transformations of the modern age. To Walter Benjamin, writing in the 1930s, it was apparent that the visual dynamics of film were contributing to the rise of a modern consciousness. For citizens of the modern metropolis, cinematic mise-en-scène functions as a form of surrogate, often therapeutic travel. Film, he writes, "on the one hand, extends our comprehension of the necessities which rule our lives; on the other hand, it manages to assure us of an immense and unexpected field of action. Our taverns and our metropolitan streets, our offices and furnished rooms, our railroad stations and our factories appeared to have us locked up hopelessly. Then came the film and burst this prison-world asunder by the dynamite of the tenth of a second, so that now, in the midst of its far-flung ruins and debris, we calmly and adventurously go traveling. With the close-up, space expands; with slow motion, movement is extended."[30] Benjamin understands the workings of the camera—its rises and falls, breaks and isolations, extensions and accelerations, and enlargements and reproductions—as the features of a mechanical eye that can help us comprehend modern life. All those hours at the movies help us intuit the changing meanings of architecture, which otherwise might be overwhelming, too various to comprehend. The structured and specific sights of architecture, likewise, help us understand the human condition. And cinema uses architecture as a visual language, one both intimate and sensual, instructing us in the complexities of visual consciousness, even as both film and architecture were transforming that consciousness

The films of Yasujiro Ozu are extraordinary investigations into how we experience architecture. From the 1930s to the 1960s, Ozu scrutinized ordinary and monumental places in modernizing Japan, focusing on relationships of scale, material, texture, and space. Ozu's sense of style depends on neither peculiarity nor perfection, and only occasionally does he use famous architecture. The shots range over traditional and modern buildings, from wooden houses to high-rise apartments to vast factory complexes. Like the narratives of Antonioni and Resnais, Ozu's tales of family life depict distance more than closeness, gestures more than communication. They explore the personalities of place as well as people; Ozu's scenes of buildings and cities

30. Walter Benjamin, "The Work of Art in the Age of Mechanical Reproduction," in *Illuminations: Walter Benjamin*, ed. Hannah Arendt (New York: Schocken Books, 1968), 236.

are compelling. Film historian Noel Burch, in *To The Distant Observer*, analyzes Japanese cinema by focusing on Japanese modes of perception. Of Ozu's shots of buildings and cities, Burch writes, "it is the tension between the suspension of human presence (of the diegesis) and its potential return which animates some of Ozu's most thoughtful work, making these shots anything but decorative vignettes."[31] Similar to photographs, Ozu's shots of domestic and urban space are a visual analogue to his ideas about order, rupture, isolation, and community.

For these "pillow shots," as Burch calls, them, Ozu's camera lingers on architecture. Using a static camera, especially in his later films, he constructs many scenes as successions of still lifes. In interiors, Ozu places the camera only two to three feet above the ground, which reflects the Japanese custom of sitting on the floor, and exaggerates the height of the room, accentuating light wells, ladders, and stairways. He positions the camera perpendicular to the principal walls of house and street. The main points of view look in toward the interior (and backyard garden) or out to the front door and street. Space seems conspicuously geometric and planar.[32] Doors and windows look like solid surfaces. Rectangles predominate. Tonalities and textures merge into a two-dimensional pictorial rendition, rather like a painting. But Ozu also deploys the Japanese practice of creating spaces that expand or contract with the closing and opening of doors and screens. Many shots of back gardens, for instance, depict a striking compression of space through a succession of framed openings and shoji screens. These effects are also achieved in shots that look toward a house's front door, where the space before the portal is made ambiguous by intermediate partitions and screens. It is often difficult to tell where the house ends and the street begins. Multiple planes substitute for a fixed architectural background. In *Floating Weeds*, from 1959, a shot from the interior of a barbershop divides into two views: a glass-and-wood sliding door, and the wood and stone surfaces of the building across the street. In such depth-of-field compositions, the space of a garden, with pounding lines of rain, or a street, with billowing fog, can be as textured as building materials.

Ozu explores the buildings and spaces of Japanese cities, too. Shooting train stations, harbors, and streets in small towns and burgeoning cities, he

31. Noel Burch, *To the Distant Observer: Form and Meaning in the Japanese Cinema* (Berkeley: University of California Press, 1979), 161.

32. David Bordwell, *Ozu and the Poetics of Cinema* (Princeton: Princeton University Press, 1988), 86–87.

emphasizes their archetypal qualities. Some sequences focus on cylindrical structures such as smokestacks or lighthouses, others on elements of connection like bridges and stairwells. In this way Ozu links the modern city to the traditional home and its artifacts—bowls, table, mats, screens. But while the home is a condensed universe of discrete planes of space, the city is an encompassing space of large objects and dense infrastructure. But even here, amid the perplexing contortions of factory complexes or train corridors, Ozu reveals underlying order.

In *Late Spring,* from 1949, Ozu surveys the ancient cities of Kamakura and Kyoto. A tea ceremony at one of Kamakura's temples opens the film. No establishing shot precedes the interior view. The ceremony establishes the scene, its perfect order providing a gateway to the world outside. The next images set up various counterpoints—a staircase at a train station, tracks and signal lights, and then the tiled roof of the Kenchoji temple and close-ups of a drainage ditch, flowers, and bushes. After another view of the tea ceremony, the scene concludes with a long take of a thickly wooded hillside. Despite its apparent randomness, the outer world, Ozu is suggesting, might actually be as finely ordered as the tea ceremony. The Kyoto sequence reverses the trajectory, as we now move from views of the exterior world to a commentary on filmic perception. From a long shot of the tower of a pagoda piercing the rim of a mountain, and through progressive moves inward toward its bracketed supports, Ozu takes us to the Ryoanji Zen Garden. At first glance, the walled garden appears to consist of dispersed rocky forms floating on a sea of gravel. But Ozu shows us the garden from multiple perspectives. The scene begins to evoke diverse places, things, and ideas—islands in the sea, art in a void, a dispersed family, the harmony that can exist among discrete and isolated elements. These evocations correspond to a series of deeper, overlapping levels of order, Ozu is telling us, that can help us to read the seemingly unruly appearance of the modern built environment. Ozu's portraits of built environments exemplify Walter Benjamin's understanding of film as visual instruction into the modern social and architectural condition.

The long takes championed by Bazin and used by Ozu and Antonioni make us concentrate on architectural settings we might overlook in daily life. But if such concentration can inspire revelatory insights, it can lead also to disorientation and tedium. Most of the time, movies satisfy our appetite for suspense and story; when architectural mise-en-scène dominates, we inevitably scramble for meanings and experience frustration. What's going on? Why are we lingering on this strip of roadway or that part of the cathedral? What will happen next? When will the action return? The absence of plot places great demands on filmgoers, as if we were lost in a strange place with no map. Of course, that is precisely the point. Sometimes, looking closely at the built world can be excruciating or even harrowing. Sometimes there is too much architecture to stare at, for too long. The oversize images on the screen can seem overpowering, even uncanny, as we sit in the dark. But when we are captivated by the images, we want them to go on and on. And in the cinema, unlike in real life, we can see places a second or third or tenth time, the buildings and streets always the same, changing only through the powers of our perception, possessed of no future but that which we give them. The director Peter Greenaway is noted for his fantastical constructions of architectural environments in films such as *The Draughtsman's Contract*, *The Belly of the Architect*, and *Prospero's Books*, which make one wonder whether he prefers film to real architecture. As Greenaway writes, his grand vision would consist of "a series of architectural sets, ten gallery spaces around the world to hold a deliberation on the mutability of film, where the cheat of the false perspective, the disorientation of invented scales, the curse of having always to make a choice, the wish to use thirty light-readings on one architectural view, the wish to see an architectural facade ten times throughout its history of decay—all these and more, without the limiting necessity of the anecdotes of plot and the vanity of actors will be made explicitly. . . and then the camera can restfully contemplate the excitements of architecture to its heart's delight."[33]

DISORIENTATION

In recent years, movies have gassed up with high-octane action, a trend that, as film historian Peter Wollen argues, has led increasingly to spatial dislocation.[34] The cinema, he argues, creates interchangeable non-places, celluloid versions of the Las Vegas Strip, of the globalized shopping centers and entertainment districts analyzed by French anthropologist Marc Augé, in *Non-Places*. Rather than immersing filmgoers in the details of a place, action

33. Peter Greenaway, "Photographing Architecture," in *Site-Work*, 85–86.

34. Peter Wollen, "Architecture and Film: Places and Non-places," in *Paris Hollywood: Writings on Film* (London: Verso, 2002), 213.

movies offer a kind of hyperkinesis. Such films mimic the headlong rush of automotive dromoscopy, but at a delirious pace, with aerial zooms and tracking shots as well as ultra-fast editing. Much of this is nothing new. Filmmakers have long sought to merge the mechanical movement of the camera with the emotional dynamics of a moviegoer's perception. Automobiles and airplanes have made possible fast camera speeds and aerial perspectives. Dollies and jib-arms enable cameras to glide steadily up, down, sideways, and diagonally. Camera zooms, by changing the focal length of the lens, can alter the angles of view and apparent size of objects. The Steadicam, a gyroscopic camera invented in the 1970s, merged the smooth sweep of the dolly with the flexibility of the handheld camera; the camera eye could now float through space seemingly unfettered by gravity or materiality.[35]

But beginning with movies like *Star Wars*, in 1977, special effects have played an increasingly large role in movies, especially big budget ones. Early on, special effects technicians used models, matte paintings, and blue screens, in combination with camera motion controlled by computers. Beginning in the mid-1990s, digital animation has created even more astonishing and improbable sights, turning movies like *Speed*, *The Matrix*, *Black Hawk Down*, and Star *Wars II: Attack of the Clones* into fast-action spectacles. The cuts are quick, the scenes short, the plots simple—and the special effects tantalizing. The cineplex lights dim, and our seats turn into cockpits, the action whirling and blaring all around us. We become gyroscopic observers of mobility, as action heroes survive precipitous drops, whoosh through tunnels in advance of fireballs, and leap between tall buildings. Amid the mayhem, the architectural mise-en-scène hemorrhages, morphing into strange hybrid shapes. From disconcerting angles, at supersonic speeds, and through splattering montage, buildings and skylines appear and vanish, sink and swing, merge and explode. The action sequences are part of a formula, of course, whose plot proceeds from tranquility to violation to vengeance to the restoration of tranquility, and whose mise-en-scène moves from soothing views of ordinary places to scenes of chaos and than back again to the comfort of the ordinary. Both action and architecture return, eventually, to normal.

Experimental filmmakers have long been fascinated by—if not addicted to—speed and disorientation. Dating back to early silent films like Edwin

35. Jean-Pierre Gevens, "Visuality and Power: The Work of the Steadicam," *Film Quarterly* 47 (Winter 1993–94), 16.

Porter's *The Great Train Robbery*, of 1903, filmmakers have long strived to recalibrate perception. D.W. Griffiths pioneered the used of montage; he used parallel editing, and also employed multiple shots of decreasing length to create the impression of acceleration in a scene.[36] According to film theorist Jean Mitry, "editing (or montage) is not so much the effect of matching images according to a logical continuity as of giving the images a meaning beyond that of the information presented in them, creating a new power deriving from the juxtaposition of two or more shots which then assume a value they could never have outside that association. Through montage, shots in a sequence behave in the same way as words in a sentence where subject, verb, and object only begin to have meaning when they are related to each other."[37]

In the 1920s, Soviet filmmakers used montage to dramatize revolution. In his 1927 *October*, Sergei Eisenstein shoots buildings to symbolize their status in postrevolutionary Russia, as either proletarian or ruling class. Images of statues of Czarist rulers, of the empty hallways of palaces, and of cathedral domes represent the decadence of the aristocracy. Across the dialectical divide, images of industrial machinery and crowds of workers striding down boulevards signal the vigor of the proletariat. Works of architecture, then, are seen cinematically as parts of class struggle; buildings have political meanings. In "Montage and Architecture," of 1940, Eisenstein argues that cinema can foster a revolutionary consciousness by constructing a new visual consciousness. He puts it this way: "In themselves, the pictures, the phases, the elements of the whole are innocent and indecipherable. The blow is struck only when the elements are juxtaposed into a sequential image."[38] Montage consists of the splicing together of separate shots—from separate places and even times—to construct a new visual landscape. A formal precursor of the fast cutting of Hollywood blockbusters, Soviet montage was not meant to be entertaining; it was intended to propagandize political and social revolution. Instead of showing the space of the city as constructed by the ruling classes, Eisenstein's montage unveiled a new and edifying pictorial space.

Surrealist cinema, in the work of directors like Luis Bunuel or Maya Deren, conveys a sense of perceptual liberation through disorienting and often dreamlike montage. Interested not in politics but psychology, Bunuel's films—

36. André Bazin, *What is Cinema?* (Berkeley: University of California Press, 1967), 24.

37. Jean Mitry, *The Aesthetics and Psychology of the Cinema* [1963], trans. Christopher King (Bloomington: Indiana University Press, 1997), 68.

38. Sergei Eisenstein, "Montage and Architecture," *Assemblage* 10 (December 1989), 126.

An Andalusian Dog, of 1928, *The Golden Age*, of 1930—expose the fantastic in the real through the use of fetish objects like seashells. In *Meshes in the Afternoon*, made in 1943, Deren shoots hallucinatory sequences in the stairway of a house, which here symbolizes the transition from consciousness to dreams. Such experimental films pursue new alchemies of vision, seeking to create fresh depictions of the world. And yet their visual dislocations often occur within recognizable places. In *Metaphors on Vision*, published in 1963, Stan Brakhage argues that the aim of cinema is to reveal the variety of the world, unclouded by learned patterns and habitual ways of seeing. For Brakhage, films can uncover the aberrant within the familiar. "By deliberately spitting on the lens or wrecking its focal intention, one can achieve the early stages of impressionism," he writes. "One can make this prima donna heavy in performance of image movement by speeding up the motor, or one can break up movement, in a way that approaches a more direct inspiration of contemporary eye perceptibility of movement, by slowing the motion while recording the image. One may hand hold the camera and inherit worlds of space. One may over- or under-expose the film. One may use the filters of the world, fog, downpours, unbalanced lights, neons with neurotic color temperatures, glass which was never designed for a camera, or even glass which was but which can be used against specifications, or one may photograph an hour after sunrise or an hour before sunset, those marvelous taboo hours when the film labs will guarantee nothing."[39] Many standard Hollywood techniques can be exaggerated to challenge our usual viewpoints; these include rapid-fire changes in camera focal length, partial reframings with mattes that expose open borders, and unusual camera speeds and angles.[40]

Innovative filmmakers have mechanized vision beyond human capacities. As in the establishing shots of Vidor's *The Crowd* and Hitchcock's *Psycho*, a tracking camera on a crane or helicopter can propel our sight across great distances. Orson Welles's 1958 *Touch of Evil* opens with a continuous tracking shot during which the camera travels four blocks of a Mexican border town, viewing architecture from the street, and then ascends on a crane to pass over the tops of buildings. In Mikhail Kalatozov's *I am Cuba*, a 1964 docudrama about the Cuban revolution, several acrobatic tracking shots exploit the perceptual discrepancy between views of architec-

39. Stan Brakhage, *Metaphors on Vision*, ed. P. Adams Sitney (New York: Film Culture Inc., 1963), n.p.

40. Maureen Turim, *Abstraction in Avant-Garde Films* (Ann Arbor: University of Michigan Press 1985), 52.

ture within human capacity and those beyond. Early on, Kalatazov's camera transports filmgoers to the rooftop of a high-rise hotel in Havana. Fashion models strut on a runway; in the background is the city's skyline of modernist buildings. Following the pirouettes of the models, Kalatozov's camerawork becomes bold. The camera approaches the edge of the roof, peers down at a swimming pool, and then continues to move, descending the side of the building like Spiderman, all the while gazing at the gleaming city and the sun-bathers by the pool.

Later, in another gravity defying tracking shot, Kalatazov's camera follows a funeral march for a martyred student; and here, too, it transcends the human perspective. Climbing up the wall of a four-story building, it reaches the roof, passes through an iron grate, and flies across the street to the roof of another building, where it enters a large room (where workers are rolling cigars), and then slides through another window into a glide above the street, from where it continues to track the funeral cortege from the air. The startling vertical movements and aerial glides constantly alter the horizon, projecting it out and then down or up. Floors, walls, and ceilings seem interchangeable, as windows become doors, and corridors turn into space. The sky becomes architectural, walling the screen in unexpected places, seeming more sub-stance than space.

Something even more disconcerting happens in Ernie Gehr's *Side/Walk/Shuttle*, of 1991. This short film depicts San Francisco from atop Nob Hill, close to where Muybridge photographed his panorama. But while Muybridge unifies the city into a composition of continuous geography, Gehr focuses at only a few places in the city, just east of Nob Hill. Twenty-five shots that average one-and-a-half minutes offer ungrounded city views. Streets, buildings, and sky tumble together. Gilberto Perez describes Gehr's flowing, spinning camera: "It can set whole buildings in apparent motion, vary their speeds relative to one another by subtle panning, halt their motion while the rest of the city slides by, or in one striking instance, reverse the direction of motion without a discernible cut as a tall building tilted downward stands sus-pended in midair. It can disorient us and reorient us by rendering the city from various arresting, shifting angles, up, down and sideways, upside down and right side up, unaccustomed mobile positions that keep giving us pause, the

From *Side/Walk/Shuttle*, director Ernie Gehr

sky sometimes at the bottom and the streets sometimes at the top, the traffic surprising us in some shots when we start to notice that, for a bit now, it has been going backward."[41]

The perceptual jolt in *Side/Walk/Shuttle* comes not only from its mechanization, but also from its resemblance to human vision. Gehr films from the exterior glass elevator of the Fairmount Hotel, as it moves up and down the building—his point of view suggests that of a passenger in the elevator whose body had somehow begun to turn around and around. Yet because viewers do not know the camera's location, the aerial experience feels more liberating. Viewers know they are looking at the city from some mechanized contraption. The glass elevator exaggerates but parallels the views of the city available from elevated railcars, freeways, helicopters, and airplanes. "This connection of elevator and railroad is emphasized," notes the film historian Scott MacDonald, "by the frequent trolleys we see moving along California Street during *Side/Walk/Shuttle*—and especially by the fact that Gehr often frames his imagery of San Francisco so that the trolleys seem to be moving vertically, at virtually the same pace as we are moving in the elevator."[42]

Across the San Francisco Bay in Richmond, California, Bruce Baillie films another city street in the 1966 short *Castro Street*. Baillie states his goal: "To use a street as a basic form rather than a narrative or any kind of storyline. And so I really did start the film at the beginning of the street, and ended it on the red barn at the end."[43] Baillie's Castro Street is not the gay mecca of San Francisco, but a little-known industrial thoroughfare in Richmond, northeast of San Francisco. Until the 1960s, railroad-switching yards lined one side of Castro Street, oil refineries and industrial buildings the other side. Baillie's *Castro Street* is an energetic mélange of rolling, crossing, and floating images, a mix of diverse impressions with an audio track consisting of rail and industrial noises recorded on site. Baillie shows us Castro Street as we might see it when walking or as it might be viewed from a train or car— but all at the same time. The ten-minute film brims with images that would usually be experienced over days or weeks. Superimposed trains glide in opposite directions. Smokestacks appear within floating irises. Men walk up ramps, looking ghost-white due to Baillie's use of inter-negatives. *Castro Street* shows us the familiar images of an old industrial corridor, but it alters

41. Gilberto Perez, "Film in Review: Ghosts of the City, Films of Ernie Gehr," *The Yale Review* 87 (October 1999), 182.

42. Scott MacDonald, *The Garden in the Machine: A Field Guide to Independent Films about Place* (Berkeley: University of California Press, 2001), 204.

43. Richard Whitehall, "An Interview with Bruce Baillie," *Film Culture* 47 (1969), 17.

those images with various photographic processes. Using optical printing,
Baillie projects one film onto another that has already been printed; the filmed image is thus refilmed, allowing for superimpositions, new zooms, blurring, refocusing, and out-of-focusing. He combines vehicular tracking, panning, and fast montage. He uses mattes that almost seamlessly align different images, textures, and colors in a single frame.[44] The city street and its diverse features become pieces in a recombinatory graphic experiment. The infrastructure of railroad and refinery has been thus abstracted and reworked into something new. In ten minutes, viewers see a street larger, livelier, and more lustrous than it appears in real life.

Experimental films extend, alter, and hence question the normal workings of vision. They capture and often create unruly sights, the peripheries and oddities we have learned not to see. In a film by Gehr, Baillie, or Michael Snow, film technologies complicate, truncate, and disturb the normal workings of vision so that our eyes may do more, see more. Some films can even create a sense of movement through space without camera movement. In the forty-five-minute *Wavelength*, Michael Snow produces diverse spatial impressions through a series of zooms within a New York City loft. Every few minutes, by changing its focal distance, the camera zooms the space of the loft into a new configuration. Snow reformulates architectural space, turning it from an environment for experience into an evolving experience of its own. Of the 1967 film, art theorist Annette Michelson writes, "Waiting for an issue, we are 'suspended' towards resolution. And it is as if by emptying the space of his film (dramatically, through extreme distancing, visually by presenting it as mere volume, the scene of pure moments in time), Snow has redefined filmic space as that of action."[45]

In *Wavelength*, we compare the brightness of light in the day and at night; we notice a few people; and a murder happens. Street and building noises fill the soundtrack. But the zooming exploration of dwelling space takes precedence. Snow positions his camera at one end of the loft, and throughout the film it looks across its eighty-foot depth toward a wall with four windows. The film begins with a very wide angle that shows the largest possible volume of space, a perspectival impression of floors, walls, and ceiling leading toward a horizon at the midpoint of the windows, where a photograph of a

44. Lucy Fisher, "Castro Street: The Sensibility of Style," *Film Quarterly* 29.3 (Spring 1976), 20.

45. Annette Michelson, "Toward Snow," *Artforum* 9 (June 1971), 32–33.

beach scene is fastened to the wall. The camera then begins to zoom in, and the angle progressively narrows. Each zoom deletes some space and surface from the view. The architectural elements of the loft lose their identity; the floors and walls become planes of color, changing from earth tones to gray and white tones as evening approaches. By the end, the space has narrowed and flattened to the point where the camera is so close to the photograph that it is all we see. The view of the space of the loft has become the view of a picture of ocean waves. Paradoxically, this last shot contains the deepest and most imaginative space of the film. Here Snow shows us not the space of the loft, but rather architectural space transformed into photographic space.

Throughout the film Snow's camera is stationary, looking from the same distance. The zoom channels and compresses space. Here human perception changes not because of bodily movement but because of mechanized optics—the quintessence of the zoomscape. It is technology, not physiology, that moves us through the space. "This viewer is only moved through a series of framings," writes film theorist Maureen Turim. "The moments of holding a given lens position emphasize the artificiality of what earlier seemed to be a movement through space. These moments of waiting, of looking, as well as the insistent, extended duration of the mechanically achieved advance, compel one to contemplate the work of restructuring involved in the film."[46]

Challenges to spatial perception link film with architecture. In the modern era, a building's encircling glass curtain walls or free plan work to resist confinement, akin to cinematic shots that use depth of focus and wide angles; similarly, a tall building's elevated vistas resemble the craned or aerial tracking shots of the movies. Later, influenced by structuralist philosophy, avant-garde cinema, like avant-garde architecture, has transported viewers into spaces whose appearance demonstrates the formal and theoretical techniques of the medium. Instead of building a film around acceptable notions of spatial succession or formal appearance, films turn architecture into a set of random and unusual experiences, situations where meaning emerges anew through each encounter.

46. Maureen Turim, "The Displacement of Architecture in Avant-Garde Films," *IRIS* 12 (Spring 1991), 36.

Lev Kuleshov, in his 1929 "Art of the Cinema," recognizes the extent to which cinema propagates original visual experience through technology. The Russian film theorist is famous for his explanation of montage—"the Kuleshov effect"— that states that two images shown in succession will be interpreted by filmgoers as relating to the same event. Kuleshov also realized that unusual vantage points could heighten the new synthetic reality appearing on screen. As he argues, "the filmmaker takes the viewer as if by the scruff of his neck and, let's say, thrusts him under a locomotive and forces him to see from that point of view; thrusts him into an airplane and forces him to see the landscape from the air, makes him whirl with the propeller and see the landscape through the whirling propeller."[47]

Kuleshov's ideas are reflected in Dziga Vertov's *The Man with the Movie Camera*, a 1929 film composed of briefs shots of virtuoso cinematography unified by montage editing. In Moscow and other Russian cities, Vertov photographs moving trains, the tops of smokestacks, and high bridges. He employs an array of effects: close-ups, long views, freeze frames, head-on shots, angled vistas, and camera movements that mimic machine movement—slow motion, fast rushes, angles up or down, staccato rhythms. Focusing on a cameraman filming the city from a moving automobile, Vertov makes explicit what is usually concealed: that we are watching a work of art, a transformative construction. In this way, too, he makes us feel as if we are participating in the construction. *Man with a Movie Camera* has often been called a film about film. It is also a film about how a city is constructed on film.

Film extends human perception via mechanical operations—it can make us see from the viewpoints of engines; it can show us sights and sounds once limited to fantasies or nightmares. For many filmmakers, this creative potential is realized most fully in the city. Indeed, the city itself, with its buildings and infrastructure of streets, transit, elevators, and moving walkways, can be understood as a kind of vision machine. The film genre known as the city symphony explores the power of this machine. In a city symphony— which can be an entire film or part of a larger narrative—the city and its architecture take center stage. Instead of plot and dialogue, actors and sets, the city symphony uses buildings, streets, bridges, and vehicles, showing us how cities rattle and rush, stream and plod, awake and settle down.

47. Lev Kuleshov, "Art of the Cinema" (1929), in *Kuleshov on Film: Writings by Lev Kuleshov*, ed. Ronald Levaco (Berkeley: University of California Press, 1974), 59.

The first city symphony was Charles Sheeler and Paul Strand's 1921 *Manhatta*, a seven-minute exploration of the island of Manhattan. Consisting of sixty-five shots and, like a symphony, of four movements, *Manhatta* shows the diversity of urban form and development. The film begins on the Staten Island Ferry, the camera looking toward Manhattan, letting us marvel at the tall buildings; and as it proceeds, it exhibits skyscrapers being built, railroads shuttling along, and steamships sailing. The film ends with a view of the busy harbor and Hudson River taken from an upper floor of the Equitable Building in Lower Manhattan.[48] Fifty-eight years later, Woody Allen began the narrative *Manhattan* with a four-minute city symphony in black and white, set to the music of George Gershwin. *Manhattan* is not like *Manhatta*. Sheeler and Strand's experimental film shows us a city in the throes of construction and movement; Allen's New York is a city of nostalgic set-pieces: the blinking neon sign of the Manhattan Hotel, the 59th Street Bridge, Lincoln Center, the interior of the Guggenheim Museum, Yankee Stadium, Central Park at dusk. The first views, shot from the East River, display the Midtown skyline, with the Chrysler and Empire State Buildings crowning the residential towers along the East River. The mood is wistful. This is postindustrial Manhattan, not a galvanizing machine, but a romantic backdrop to upper-middle class strivings.

The structure of Allen's city symphony—its progression from morning to nocturnal fireworks above Central Park—recalls Walther Ruttmann's *Berlin: The Symphony of a Great City*, made in 1927 (and discussed in an earlier chapter). Ruttmann's *Berlin* is often credited with being the first city symphony.[49] This is debatable, for there were predecessors: not only *Manhatta* but also René Clair's 1923 *Paris qui dort* and Alberto Cavalcanto's 1926 *Rien que les heures*. But *Berlin: The Symphony of a Great City*, along with *The Man with a Movie Camera*, was the most influential, the most ambitious and comprehensive effort to capture the dynamism of a city on film. It was also the least concerned with character development. *Berlin* displays objects, people, buildings, and sites as anonymous elements of an urban machine.

Like the day, *Berlin* begins at dawn, taking us on a train ride from the Brandenburg countryside to the city's Anhalter Station. An aerial sequence follows, moving from panoramic views to urban details—the silhouette of the cathedral, a baroque palace, long straight streets, a city block, a factory, and a tower whose clock reads five a.m. At first, the camera shows vacant streets,

48. Jan-Christopher Horak, "Paul Strand and Charles Sheeler's Manhatta," in *Lovers of Cinema: The First American Avant-Garde, 1919–1945*, ed. Jan-Christopher Horak (Madison: University of Wisconsin Press, 1995), 271.

49. William Uricchio, "Ruttman's Berlin and the City Film to 1930" (Ph.D. dissertation, New York University, 1982).

Advertisement for *Berlin: The Symphony of a Great City*, director Walther Ruttmann

the morning light spreading over roads and buildings. The city slowly awakes. A man walks a dog. A cat scurries along a building wall. Morning papers arrive at kiosks.

From here on, Ruttmann no longer shows us expansive vistas. He immerses us in Berlin's vital parts, its circulation arteries, myriad functions, and countless buildings. In close-up and medium-range views, we see details of buildings—window patterns, ornamental language, cladding materials. We see wavy telephone wires, machines on a factory floor, mannequins in a store window, elevated trains, elegantly dressed people, products in store windows, horses standing on streets. In hundreds of shots, lasting from one to six seconds, Berlin emerges as both orderly and frantic. The camera hardly moves; the portrait is created through individual shots, which interconnect and create curious patterns within standardized categories. The day unfolds through the movie's four movements, which correspond to transit, work, domesticity, and recreation.

Berlin: The Symphony of a Great City mechanizes the city, its architecture and society. Ruttmann makes us see the coordination of the urban life, how its disparate parts work together. Through repeated shots of similar actions, we watch Berlin move through a day. Crowds of commuters file through rail stations, up stairways, and over bridges; soldiers march in formation; elevated trains flash left and right, coursing above and below one another. The succession of images links together the parts and people of the city. At one point, we see smokestacks, then lightbulbs, bottles, and loaves of bread produced in factories. We see the metal grates of the factory rise, its doors, shutters, and windows open. Much like their products, factories come to life through the rigor and order of assembly-line processes. The same can be said of other buildings, of apartments and stores. We notice blankets laid out on balconies; people are awake. Shutters are rolled up and casement windows flung outward; people are ready to go out. Shopkeepers unlock their doors and merchandise is again on display. The city is open for business. The shots are too numerous for any to dominate. What matters is the Kuleshov effect, the accumulation of interconnected images, some of which are comical—a mannequin followed by a still woman, a rotund policeman succeeded by fat swaying dolls. "The strict rhythmic style of editing indicates that Berlin doesn't wait or pause for anything, as film historian Jay Chapman observes, "and that rhythm is the very essence of the city."[50] The most beautifully choreographed images are the night shots that conclude the film—images of brightly lit trams, illuminated store windows, flashing neon signs, all flowing together. The last image shows a searchlight beaming over the now darkened metropolis.

Even the occasional disorderly sights—a street fight, a suicidal jump off a bridge, a disorienting view of apartment facades from a roller coaster—do not disrupt the relentless order that Ruttmann's editing has imposed upon Berlin. A scene of dogs fighting gives way to images of hands dialing telephones and people circling through revolving doors—it is all part of the structural workings of the city. Editing subsumes irregularities, making them flow together into meaningful sequences. Montage links trains and pedestrians, buildings and streets, machines and humans, and animals and people. *Berlin* underscores how cinema differs from architecture in its construction of urban order. Architects work to organize the forms and spaces of cities, achieving partial success at best. A filmmaker can transform a city. Almost any set of urban images can be edited into a cinematic journey more logical than any we might take in everyday life. Ruttmann filmed Berlin just as Germany was recovering from severe economic depression—and yet his film displays a prosperous and energetic city. Decadent cabaret, radical art, and religious and political turbulence are nowhere evident in this view of Weimar Berlin. Four years after Hitler's beer hall putsch, the German capital is presented as stable, a model of urban decorum. Less than two decades later, of course, much of the city we see in *Berlin* would no longer be standing.

Most later city symphonies are neither as uniform nor as rational as *Berlin.* Joris Ivens's *Rain*, of 1928, takes a poetic look at Amsterdam during a rainstorm. *A propos de Nice*, directed by Jean Vigo in 1930, contrasts the summertime leisure of the upper classes along the Cote d'Azur with the routines of the working-class city. In *Up and Down the Waterfront*, made in 1946, Rudy Burckhardt shows the quotidian life of the New York waterfront. Sacrificing mechanism for chance, mass objectivity for individual stories, these films find the city's stories more in deviation than coordination.[51]

In the 1960s, Jean-Luc Godard approached Ruttmann's relentless objectivity by shifting the focus of urban logic from production to consumption. If the metaphor of the city as machine was no longer resonant, what about the

50. Jay Chapman, "Two Aspects of the City: Cavalcanti and Ruttmann," in *The Documentary Tradition: From Nanook to Woodstock*, ed. Lewis Jacobs (New York: Hopkinson & Blake, 1971), 39.

51. Scott MacDonald, "The City as the Country: The New York City Symphony from Rudy Burckhardt to Spike Lee," *Film Quarterly* 51 (Winter 1997–98), 13.

metaphor of the city as an emporium? Like other city symphonies, *Two or Three Things I Know About Her*, made in 1966, takes place in a single day. Godard's "her" refers partly to the human protagonist, a housewife who supplements her husband's income by moonlighting as a prostitute, and partly to the urban protagonist, the new postwar Paris.[52] And just as the woman is prostituting herself, so, too, is Paris—eviscerating itself to accommodate the new consumer society. Godard sets the story in the suburbs, at the Sarcelles housing estate, built in 1954. Historical Paris, famous Paris, is seen hardly at all. Like Tati's *Playtime*, *Two or Three Things* shows a Paris neither urbane nor soulful, a Paris defined not by monuments and boulevards but by merchandise, expressways, and high-rise slabs.

Like Ruttmann, Godard recognizes the centrality of transportation to any city portrait. By the 1960s, of course, the railroad and trolley had been superseded by the freeway and automobile. And while *Berlin* showed the smooth and ceaseless flow of urban mass transit, *Two or Three Things* displays vehicular transitways as congested, ceaselessly under construction, the source of constant frustration. *Two or Three Things I Know About Her* opens with a static shot of the unfinished Parisian beltway, the Periphèrique—a central component of postwar Parisian master planning. Subsequent views show the shadows cast by the elevated structure on the ground plane of the city, which looks both wiped clean and left dirty by the intrusion of the motorway. The accompanying succession of sounds—roaring traffic, utter silence, neighborhood noises, and the whispered voice-over of the director—intensifies the sense of uneasiness. Godard favors images of roads covered in scaffolding, blocked by gridlock, and abruptly truncated. The camera lingers on the curve of an unfinished highway ramp that hangs in the air. It takes us to a site along the Seine where a new bridge is being built, and observes piles of concrete slabs and reinforcing bars, trucks dumping dirt. Never does the film show fast movement on an expressway.

In *Two or Three Things*, public space dies so that privatized consumption may live. In this early critique of modernist urbanism, Godard argues that the superblock, high-rise city has failed to make good on its utopian promises. By eliminating small streets and blocks, architects and urban planners had hoped to open up space for parklands. In Godard's Paris, the "liberated land" that is not desecrated by automobiles is shown to be vacant, sterile. He positions

52. Alfred Guzzetti, *Two or Three Things I Know About Her: Analysis of a Film by Godard* (Cambridge: Harvard University Press, 1981), 37.

From *Two or Three Things I Know About Her*, director Jean-Luc Godard

characters in front of high-rise buildings, and their words seem to be absorbed by the mesmerizing window grids. In one back-and-forth panning shot, the film surveys a group of colorless apartment towers atop a large plinth, a desolate zone. The most stunning shot in the film is a full-circle pan of the housing estate, showing us balcony and window patterns; we see the astounding scale of the complex, which dominates our field of view and which seems unnervingly self-contained. The modernist suburbs of outer Paris are bleak environments, their landscapes dreary residual spaces that residents must somehow navigate. Except for traffic jams, the new city on the periphery shows no signs of life; the most interesting objects are some colorful and shapely gasoline pumps, and the giant red letters of a sign jutting above a building.

The life of the city has moved indoors, to living rooms filled with the blare of radios and televisions, to billboards and magazines filled with celebrities and advertising, and to stores filled with alluring products. A society obsessed with consumption has no time for public life, no place for public space. From afar, the modernist buildings can look like cardboard boxes. And the last shot of the film shows boxes of Ajax, Java, Dash, and Omo, arranged on a lawn, like little buildings.

James Benning's *Los*, made in 2001, completes the trajectory begun by *Berlin: The Symphony of a Great City* and continued by *Two or Three Things I Know About Her*. From the city as efficient machine to the city as consumptive container, we have come now to the city as postindustrial residue. In thirty-five static camera takes, each lasting two-and-a-half minutes, Benning chronicles Los Angeles as an expansive, noisy place whose inhabitants seem unnecessary, almost ornamental. Here we enter no interiors, see virtually no homes, offices, or shopping malls. The only image of a private residence is taken from the sidewalk and depicts a gardener mowing a lawn. This Los Angeles is a city of huge spaces curiously devoid of people.

Benning's Los Angeles is as stripped-down as Godard's Paris. The public spaces are vacant; historic, tourist, and civic spaces hardly appear; nor do the region's famous beaches. A billboard above a parking lot shows a bit of Sunset Boulevard, but the parking lot could be anywhere. Almost every shot emphasizes infrastructure and industry, the colossal fluctuations of landscape that characterize Los Angeles, that define its environment.

Los is the second film of a trilogy that begins with *El Valley Centro*, a meditation on the agricultural lands of the Central Valley, and concludes with *Sogobi*, an ode to California wilderness. *Los* opens with a view of the Los Angeles aqueduct, and follows with shots of a power plant, power stanchions, the port, a commuter train and station, a garbage dump, a wrecking yard, an oil derrick, and a sand hill where trucks gather earth. Benning's city consists of gigantic machines and systems that pierce, pound, and crush; concrete networks for the movement of water, gas, electricity, automobiles, and pedestrians. Within the oscillations of mammoth infrastructure, however, one notices unexpected things. As in cinema vérité, events in *Los* are captured but not controlled, and the mise-en-scène seems open to circumstance. In one scene, the camera looks down from an overpass atop the Golden State Freeway at dusk, watching twelve lanes of fast traffic. It looks uniform at first, but we soon start to notice random differences, cars darting out of their lanes, cars without their lights on. A shot of a median strip on San Vicente Boulevard in Santa Monica is dominated by a row of jacaranda trees. But slowly we notice groups of joggers, suggesting the interchangeability of the moving parts of the city.

The Los Angeles of *Los* finds its essence in infrastructure. In the extended static takes, the framed spaces look like the eerie residue of other spaces, not shown in the film, which might extend for hundreds of miles. Since so much of the energy within each frame radiates from off-screen sources, the spaces within the frame seem empty, or scarred, or depopulated. In film, writes Noel Burch, "the longer the screen remains empty (of plot and characters), the greater the resulting tension between screen and off-screen space and the greater the attention concentrated on off-screen space."[53] Benning shows the city as vestigial space, a landscape sacrificed to the anonymous and remote workings of global capital. All the parking lots, junkyards, billboards, graffiti-scarred walls, and half-deserted streets strewn with the "homes" of the homeless point elsewhere, to systems and processes beyond their control. The identity of urban space and architecture thus emerges from what is not visible or even present—from the aqueducts, power grids, rail yards, airports, and oil ports.

The soundtrack is the soul of the film. Off-screen sounds often indicate actions that will soon occur on-screen or actions that influence the places we see. Before we know we are looking at Los Angeles Airport, we hear the roar

53. Noel Burch, *Theory of Film Practice* [1969], trans. Helen R. Lane (Princeton: Princeton University Press, 1981), 25.

of plane engines. We hear the sounds of cars, ambulances, airplanes, birds, voices, radios, and all sorts of large machines, and these sounds give the film, which has no narrative, its sense of continuity. In the long takes, filmgoers look and listen, and are given time to peruse the spaces of the frame and ponder their relationships to each other and to the world unseen.

Benning films Los Angeles as a beautiful wasteland; he romanticizes industry and transportation as much as he critiques them. The succession of shots has less to do with didactic points about the urban condition than with his desire to create rhythms of formal complexity and energy. One almost has the feeling that *Los* could be experienced in reality, by researching its locations and positioning oneself in its various vantage points. But it could not, of course. For in this film, as in others that construct new architectures, the views constructed by camerawork and editing transcend the views available to the human eye. In a movie theater, with the film director orchestrating our view, we never know what will follow next. Released from the need choose where to move, or where to look, we filmgoers can watch the visual field more closely. Like passengers in a train or car, we are there for the ride. And if we feel little of the exhilaration of choice that drivers or directors feel, we can be as attentive to the smallest detail as a direct observer. And we can go places he or she never dreamed of going.

From *Los*, director James Benning

CHAPTER 6

TELEVISION

IN 1927, IN A WAREHOUSE in San Francisco, Philo Farnsworth transmitted an image of a line onto a fluorescent screen lit by cathode ray tubes. Farnsworth's invention, which he called an "image dissector," would lead to the greatest medium of mass entertainment in history. Introduced to the public at the 1939 New York World's Fair, broadcast television became a business in the postwar years, when the National Broadcast Corporation began to air variety shows, the World Series, presidential speeches, and the Howdy Doody Show. By 1951, in the United States, there were more than 100 television stations and more than twelve million households owned television sets. A decade later, a TV set had become commonplace—almost a necessity. Eventually Americans would spend on average, between three and five hours a day watching the box. Andy Warhol's 1975 sentiments seem prophetic: "A whole day in life is like a whole day of television. TV never goes off the air once it starts for the day, and I don't either. At the end of the day the whole day will be a movie. A movie made for TV."[1]

A drive at night through a suburb, past the flickering blue glow in countless windows, reveals the omnipresence of television. This powerful medium has transformed our relationship to the built environment. More than any other technology, TV has brought entertainment into our homes; a large part of the social life of the street has moved indoors, and public entertainment districts have dwindled considerably. Why go out at night if you can watch TV?

Of course, television watching also takes place in semipublic spaces. Early on, many people watched TV in taverns and stores. Televisions have long been a fixture in hair salons, waiting rooms, train stations and airports; recently, they have been installed in taxicabs. But television is ultimately a medium of private mass spectatorship. By the early 1950s, most TV watching had migrated from the corner bar to the living room. Television sets grew in stature from an appliance to a signature piece of living room furniture—the visual hearth of the postwar family. Eventually television viewing split families apart, as the number of sets per household multiplied, and TVs popped up in bedrooms, kitchens, dens, and even bathrooms. "Television recapitulated," says cultural historian Richard Butsch, "the phases of radio audience development: from communal to domestic viewing, from rapt attention to use of television as a background, from family hearth to individual use."[2]

1. Andy Warhol, *The Philosophy of Andy Warhol: From A to B and Back Again* (New York: Harcourt Brace Jovanovich, 1975), 5.

2. Richard Butsch, *The Making of American Audiences: From Stage to Television, 1750–1990* (Cambridge: Cambridge University Press, 2000), 237.

Wherever it is present, television often substitutes for human contact. Television is the ever-present alternative to social experience in the home, or outside. Ubiquitous, affordable, and popular, television determines what millions of people will watch every day, and in prime time, too. An increasingly large part of contemporary society's exposure to architecture occurs while watching TV programs and movies aired on television. The tube puts on view a sprawling built landscape, as stations beam tens of thousands of images of architecture, of streets and skylines, hour after hour, or half hour after half hour. The visuality of television is cinematic, energized by tracking, panning, tilting and zoom shots, slow-motion interludes, and brisk editing. The variety of buildings and urban environments streaming across the screen is encyclopedic, representing every part of the globe. Armed with a remote, we have only to sit down and choose the place we want to experience. But of course, television places differ considerably from real places. Does TV follow life or does life follow TV? Television historian Margaret Morse suggests an answer: "What was once television is becoming life itself, wrapped with metaphors in light and sound, a world without edges or end, a space without place, where planes overlap and intersect without boundaries or frames."[3] Does television follow architecture or does architecture follow television? On television, incredibly diverse architectural environments follow one after the other. In a twenty-second commercial we might see twenty different buildings in twenty different places. In a single evening, watching with remote control in hand, we might see more faraway places than in a lifetime of travel.

        But how wide is the range of what is available to watch? Until the 1980s, a few networks and local stations dominated the airwaves. The proliferation of cable networks since then has expanded the number of options, but not the diversity of what we see. Even with scores of programs to choose from, millions of viewers, week after week, tune into the same police dramas, the same situation comedies, watching the same gritty streets, the same studio sets. Never in history have so many people watched the same thing, at the same time, over and over again.

        Television's architectural environment has inherent drawbacks. The small size of the screen (although it is growing every year) and its low level

3. Margaret Morse, *Virtualities: Television, Media Art, and Cyberculture* (Bloomington: Indiana University Press, 1998), 98.

of definition (although that, too, is improving) limit the visual quality of television. This has encouraged more reliance on close-ups in television programs
than in film. Most programs consist largely of shots of people engaged in dialogue. Personality and celebrity overshadow mise-en-scène, and architecture
is relegated to the role of backdrop. What's more, most shows are shot on
soundstages. It is usually hard to tell where the program is taking place, and
usually, it doesn't matter. Even when TV ventures outside, it pays relatively little attention to place, frequently cutting back to studio interiors, conflating
real place with its own non-place. Like the view from a fast train, the architecture seen on television often seems distant, out-of-focus, fleeting.

Nonetheless, some television environments become well known, even
familiar. Night after night, week after week, and year after year, the opening
credits of hit shows popularize certain buildings and urban settings—they
become part of the show. Some TV architectures have become part of collective and popular memory—the drive to Minneapolis that opened *The Mary
Tyler Moore Show*, for instance, and the swanky South Florida featured in
Miami Vice. Certain shows, like the melodrama *Providence* and the soap
opera *Savannah*, have generated new interest in their titular cities—making
TV an unintentional partner in urban revitalization. *The Sopranos* has led to
surprising interest in industrial New Jersey, largely because of its heady
blend of glamour and grit.

The opening credits of *The Sopranos*, which HBO debuted in 1999,
use a fast-cut sequence of architectural images to situate this drama about
a Mafia chief and his family in time and place. Filmed on location by cinematographers Alik Sakharov and Phil Abraham, the lengthy sequence follows
the progress of an SUV driving from New York City to suburban New Jersey;
cigar-smoking mobster Tony Soprano is at the wheel. The first shots are
underground, blurry views of the ceiling tiles of the Lincoln Tunnel, under-
scoring the ambiguity and blurriness of this underworld drama. Tony's car
emerges into daylight on a toll plaza of the New Jersey Turnpike. We see the
skyline of Midtown Manhattan out the side window. Aside from a glimpse of
the Statue of Liberty, juxtaposed against a plane taking off from Newark
Airport, the rest of the ninety-second sequence takes us through the industrial landscape of the Garden State. Tony is on is way to his sprawling nouveau-

riche house in an upscale suburb. But as the credit sequence makes clear, his turf, as mob capo, is old Jersey, the Jersey of the Pulaski Skyway, of the Meadowlands, of Polish and Italian immigrant towns.

The Sopranos combines various location shots to show the trip from New York to the Jersey suburbs. The scenes were shot in diverse places in north Jersey—Tony Soprano's televisual drive has no real-world counterpart. Viewers can get a sense of the journey through road signs—Exit 13 Elizabeth, Two Miles; South 440, North 149—but these roads actually lead in different directions. Like most shows, The Sopranos constructs—or concocts—a fictional world by editing together images of real places. Because of the extensive use of actual locations we are persuaded that we are seeing not only real places, which we are, but also a real sequence of place, which we are not. Watched week after week, Tony Soprano's drive epitomizes television's capacity to fabricate urban geography. If we have learned over time to talk like TV characters, we have also learned to see places through the mediation of TV space.

Tony Soprano's drive combines the visual experiences of a real drive—the penetrating perception of the automobile driver, the distanced perception of passengers gazing out side windows—with the mobile sights of camerawork and editing. From the start of the drive, the videographers are attracted to the highway and its landscape, with the passing trucks, the oil refineries and gas tanks. A blur of trees, chain-link fences, steel posts and girders, filters the distant landscape—the smokestacks, cranes, wetlands, old housing, church spires. Occasionally, the camera looks straight ahead at the roadway and signage, showing us Tony's view. But instead of maintaining either dromoscopic or panoramic perception, the television viewpoint constantly shifts, leaping in and out of the car, treating audiences to a range of perceptions. Interspersing the camera's mechanical viewpoints with the automobile's mechanical viewpoints, the show creates a complex and captivating experience. Like the editing of location footage into televisual geographies, the mix of modes of sight offers audiences a new way of understanding urban form and space.

In The Sopranos, the distortions of the driving experience take many forms. Sometimes the videographers mimic the movements of a handheld camera, jerking back and forth and up and down. They use jib-arm shots of the passing cityscape reflected off the hubcaps of Tony's SUV, and zooms toward distant structures that break the sense of automotive enclosure. When Tony's Chevy Suburban crosses a bridge, the camera zooms up for a close-up of the steel trusses, and then zooms back down to survey the undersides of a nearby railroad bridge. At another point, positioned just outside the car, the camera shows us the steady repetition of overhead streetlamps. Later, attached to the front of the car, it reveals the roadway's blurring asphalt and converging white lines. Made with quick cuts and jazzy editing, the architecture of *The Sopranos* is not a physical place but a syncopated montage of images.

Midway through the credits, Tony exits the expressway onto city streets, and the camera scans old downtowns. It passes Pizzaland, a tiny building with a huge sign, and Satriale's Pork Store, with its fake stone siding and statue of a pig on top. Here the pace of the editing slows as we drive by modest prewar houses. As Tony nears home, the houses get newer, the lots larger, the landscaping lusher. The Soprano family's hulking home, looking at bit like a tacky supper club, is the first contemporary structure we see. Up until now, we realize, the sequence has focused on older architecture—on the sort of architecture we have come to associate with mobster dramas. Not a single big-box store, strip mall, tilt-up office park, or condominium complex break the romantic illusion of Tony's drive

The Sopranos' credits, and individual episodes as well, display many older city settings that take viewers back in time—the Sit-Tite Loungette in Jersey City, the South Beach Amusement Park in Staten Island, the boardwalk at Asbury Park. One episode features a drug dealer being thrown off a cast-iron bridge in Paterson into the Great Falls. Another has Tony's nephew, aspiring to be "made," shoot a worker in a bakery whose décor dates to the 1950s. The infamous Bada Bing club—actually a real strip club in Lodi, surrounded by dented guardrails and dumpsters—looks straight out of the early 1970s. The typical settings for conspiratorial conversations and gangland murder are a weed-strewn lot under the Pulaski Skyway and a cobblestone street near a boarded-up factory.

Much of *The Sopranos* is set, of course, in contemporary environments—the arty and urbane office of Tony's therapist, the up-to-date

From *The Sopranos*

Soprano home, shopping malls, hotels, senior citizen communities. The characters move between places that evoke different time periods, and by implication, different value systems. The mise-en-scène is an intriguing mix of old and new, brick and Dryvit, industrial decay and postmodern affluence. Much of the visual gravity of the show results from its interweaving of architecture of different eras into dramatic events. In a single scene, we might observe characters dressed in contemporary fashions, mouthing '70s lingo, stealing '50s suits, standing beneath a '20s bridge, and debating eighteenth-century Mafia codes of *omerta*. In the first episode, to the music of the Beach Boys, the mobsters sit outside Centanni's Meat Market, whose 1920s architecture has been updated with fake-brick siding, a red shingle roof, and old round paper signs in the window that could date from the 1960s. In *The Sopranos*, architecture is a leading character, transposing our sense of place and time. Viewers watch a screen environment as richly flavored as one of Carmela Soprano's ricotta cheesecakes.

The show's stylized settings resemble the overall television environment. One of the signal characteristics of television viewing, after all, is its inevitable conflation of time—channel surfing, we flip between '50s Westerns, '60s comedies, '70s detective shows, and the latest reality shows; after a while, we might forget what year it actually is. Even within a particular show, we are suspended between its purported era, the year it was filmed, and the time we are watching. "Television produces a sort of 'present continuous' that confuses the immediate time of the display of the image with the time when the events shown actually took place,"[4] writes Sandy Flitterman-Lewis. The use of location shooting further complicates the picture. For one must add the time when the buildings were built (or the era they represent) to television's multifaceted chronological puzzle. Architecture, too, produces this sort of "present continuous." The perception of buildings mixes the moment of viewing with all sorts of associations that might involve the building's style, history, setting, and use.

For all their obvious dissimilarities, television and architecture are alike in many ways. They are each limitless environments. Architecture, of course, extends over much of the earth; it is our ever-present environment.

4. Sandy Flitterman-Lewis, "Psychoanalysis, Film, and Television," in *Channels of Discourse, Reassembled*, ed. Robert C. Allen (Chapel Hill: University of North Carolina Press, 1992), 218.

Television is another sort of ever-present environment, a medium that has, by now, infiltrated most spaces, endlessly available and usually on. To surf from station to station is to range across architectural landscapes, from the Gobi Desert on the Nature Channel to war-ravaged Stalingrad on the History Channel, from the contemporary Chicago of *ER* to the '70s Chicago of *The Bob Newhart Show*. Travel across architectural and televisual landscapes can even become conflated. Arriving in a new city, turning on the set in a hotel room, one encounters new arrays of channels, new television geographies alongside the new architectural landscapes.

Television and architecture, because they are so continuously present, are often viewed casually, distractedly. Most people do not think much about the architecture that surrounds them every day—it's there, in the background. And most people do not carefully watch the programs that flicker across the screen. Sitting in a living room watching NBC or HBO is such a mundane activity, such an easy one, too, that it requires little choice, or self-awareness. Both our living rooms and television programs are the products of complex historical, cultural, and artistic forces, but it is hard to see them as such. They are simply too much with us.

In little more than fifty years, television has built a massive viewing environment of streaming imagery. More than any other medium, television, with its ability to simulate and reconstruct architectural setting, infringes on architecture. The video artist Dan Graham, who has explored architecture and perception, argues that television has constructed a public-private space that threatens to replace the influence that architecture has traditionally exerted on perception. "As cabled television images displayed on wall-sized monitors connect and mediate between rooms, families, social classes, public/private domains, connecting architecturally (and socially) bounded regions, they take on an architectural and social function," Graham wrote in 1979. "Video in architecture will function semiotically speaking as window and mirror simultaneously, but subvert the effects and functions of both. . . its initial use might tend to de-construct or re-define existing social hierarchies."[5] More than twenty-five years later, Graham's prophecy has been borne out. Our understanding of the built environment, and our relationships within it, are increasingly televisual.

5. Dan Graham, *Video-Architecture-Television: Writings on Video and Video Works, 1970–78* (Halifax: Press of the Nova Scotia College of Art and Design, 1979), 64.

Television is big country, a universe of comedy, drama, documentary, news, sports, games, variety, talk, music, and commercials. Each of these features abundant architectures, and various attitudes to architecture. Many of us first became aware of architecture as we watched television. Many of us know buildings and cities because we have seen them on television. The architectural historian Ernest Pascucci describes a common experience when he writes, "My first knowledge of modern architecture and 'the city' came through television. . . . Every weekday morning through the summer I would await the train ride that brings That Girl into Manhattan, superimposes her face on its skyline, and delivers her to the glass and steel architecture and neon Broadway lights that are taken in through her wide eyes and gaping mouth. This was my introduction to New York as much as hers. It was inconceivable without her, without that relationship. An intimate relationship, a visual relationship, moreover a televisual relationship."[6]

The most deliberate explorations of architecture on television occur in documentaries. Documentaries scrutinize buildings at length, in long-range and close-up shots, roaming over landscapes, panning along facades, and tracking through rooms. These shows, which have been infrequent, have ranged across the globe and through history. There have been programs focusing on individual works, such as the Eiffel Tower, the Kremlin, or the Great Wall of China. There have been shows on architectural events, such as *World of Tomorrow*, aired in 1984, which told the history of the Futurama exhibit at the 1939 New York World's Fair. And there have been ambitious series, such as *America by Design*, a serial documentary that covered the history of the American built environment. Hosted by Spiro Kostof, *America by Design*, which aired in 1984, examines American architecture by looking at building types—houses, workplaces, public places, monuments, and landscapes. One episode details the construction of streets, sidewalks, sewers, and storm-drain design. The series is comprehensive and academic—often the narrator looks at the buildings instead of the camera—and as such it highlights the challenge of the format. How can the still and weighty art of architecture be made animated enough for the splashy, breezy, action-filled medium of TV?

6. Ernest Pascucci, "Intimate (Tele)visions," in *Architecture of the Everyday*, eds. Steven Harris and Deborah Berke (New York: Princeton Architectural Press, 1997), 46.

More popular documentaries have favored action over analysis. In *Pyramid,* from 1988, hosted by David Macaulay and based on his book, animation and live-action sequences show (instead of tell) the story of the planning and construction of the pyramids of Giza. In *Secrets from Lost Empires: Inca,* shown in 1997 as part of the *Nova* series, architectural historians and Quechua Indians cut stone blocks using ancient tools; they then haul these blocks across flimsy bridges that span harrowingly deep ravines. Such reenactments are, to be sure, hokey, and they blur the line between documentary and docudrama.

The most commercially successful documentaries have pivoted on personality. *Pride of Place: Building the American Dream*, shown in 1986, featured the prominent architect Robert A.M. Stern as host. Stern leads us on a tour of high design in America, past to present. One segment focuses on postwar resort architecture in Florida, including the hotels of Miami Beach and the resort complex of Disney World. Often Stern interviews other famous architects, and in this lively and indirect manner, audiences are exposed to erudite design and theory, as well as to obtuse argument, witty satire, and catty observation.[7] Another documentary, Ken Burns's *Frank Lloyd Wright,* is four hours of hero worship. The 1998 show, whose various interviewees include Robert Stern, devotes most of its time to narrating the melodramatic events of Wright's personal life, including his several marriages. Audiences learn much about Wright's dreams of grandeur, but not much about his buildings and practically nothing about how they relate to architectural culture.

More popular yet are shows like Michael Palin's *Great Railway Journey*, produced by the BBC in 1999, which take viewers at a fast clip through assorted international buildings and cities. Palin, a star of *Monty Python's Flying Circus,* keeps the mood light with frequent dashes to the W.C., and amazing perseverance. Shown in 2001, *Great Streets,* another exercise in personality, takes us on driving or walking excursions with celebrities—Halle Berry on the Champs Elysées, Emmylou Harris along the Royal Mile of Edinburgh, and Randy Newman as he drives his convertible along Sunset Boulevard. As expected, the stars are more interested in food and shopping than architecture or urbanism, although Newman stops on the Strip to interview Ed Ruscha.

7. "Architects' Varied Response to Public Television's 'Pride of Place,'" *Architecture* (June 1986), 10–11.

The most common format for showcasing buildings on television is the "house and garden" approach—architecture as personal habitat and consumer product. While some programs present quirky buildings (straw-bale or rammed-earth construction) or even historic styles (the Arts and Crafts Movement is especially popular), most feature houses under construction or renovation, supplying viewers with handy tips and how-to advice. *This Old House*, begun in 1981, showcases ongoing projects, and lets us watch a carpenter hammer away at floorboards and install period wainscoting. *Martha Stewart Living*, on the air since 1993, dispenses with tools and two-by-fours, preferring the less strenuous business of selecting décor and buying furniture and bric-a-brac; with brisk skill and cunning, Stewart encourages us to admire architecture, and then purchase endless products for it. So popular has this format become that in 2000 an entire network, Home and Garden Television, was introduced, with programs catering to diverse tastes and budgets; this is where viewers learn about gut rehabs and how to use vegetables to make a colorful dining-table centerpiece. Not all home and garden programs cater to reality or possibility. Robin Leach, on the popular 1980s show *Lifestyles of the Rich and Famous*, takes viewers to the fabulous homes of movie stars, guiding millions of fame voyeurs beyond considerations of architecture to those of lifestyle.

Most architecture seen on television, however, is not part of programs devoted to the subject, but visible incidentally, in the course of watching comedies, drama, and especially, the news. Round the clock, television news uses buildings and places of all types in the coverage of events, framing them in colorful borders, underlining them with clever logos, accompanying them with information boxes and bars, and often subjecting them to the dominant foreground presence of reporters. When anchors file a live report, television functions as telecommunication; by linking places together, it fosters a sense of presence over distance. But televisual presence, especially when multiple places are contained within a shot, is diffuse. As media historian Lev Manovich argues, "We might be shown an image of an announcer sitting in a studio; behind her, in a cutout, we see news footage of a city street. The two spaces are connected through their meanings (the announcer discusses events shown in the cutout), but visually they are disjointed, as they share neither the same scale nor the same perspective."[8]

8. Lev Manovich, *The Language of New Media* (Cambridge: MIT Press, 2001), 150.

Usually news stories feature architecture as part of a larger narrative, the physical presence that makes a story more immediate, more real. Occasionally, a news report focuses on architecture per se—for instance, when prominent buildings open, receive major renovations, or are threatened with the wrecking ball. More frequently, though, television uses architecture to heighten the drama of a new story. News broadcasts lead with crime and politics. Shot from a helicopter, police chases (along with traffic reports) show audiences the transportation infrastructure of a city. Sometimes they even capture an event in real time, as when, in the mid-1990s, news teams filmed O.J. Simpson, then under suspicion for murdering his ex-wife, driving his Ford Bronco on the freeways of Los Angeles. More often, television reports on events in their immediate aftermath or as they unfold, and here architecture figures centrally as well. In local, national, or international crises, reporters read the news as they stand in front of representative buildings—a city hall, an office building, the White House. The building in the background, usually seen in long-range and partial view, is understood to be the scene of the action. Just as often, a view of a building functions as a visual metonym, symbolizing persons in the news; a view of the Pentagon, for instance, can suggest the activities of the secretary of defense. In such sequences, cameras usually focus on a building's most notable feature—a tower, a prominent entrance, the shape of the Pentagon glimpsed in an aerial view.

Television news regularly ventures to the thresholds of buildings in which important events are happening, and where access might temporarily be barred. Reporters file stories on jury trials as they stand on the courthouse steps. Covering an execution, they position themselves at the gate of a maximum-security prison. Following a local crime, the can be found near the scene, talking with residents of the building where the suspect lives, or where the crime occurred. In such cases, the architecture itself seems imbued with the significance of the story—the courthouse might look particularly dignified, the prison gloomy and menacing, the apartment building a bit shady or pathetic.

Television news is tenacious in its coverage of catastrophe, and here, too, the images of architecture and cities are deployed to enhance the interest or pathos of the story. After a hurricane, there cannot be too many views of beachfront houses being swept away or lying in heaps of debris. Television news will find the charred ruins of buildings after a fire, the hotel evacuated after a viral infection, the collapsed highway after an earthquake, cities reduced to rubble by heavy bombing. That this sort of reporting can be as voyeuristic as it is valuable was especially apparent on September 11, 2001. The terrorist attack on the World Trade Center made for horrific yet mesmerizing television. Already famous for their height and an earlier terrorist bombing, the twin towers became the most recognizable buildings in the world, as images of their destruction were broadcast ceaselessly, for days. Hundreds of millions of viewers watched the endlessly replayed footage of the jet planes flying into the buildings and exploding into flames. The news networks replayed footage of the towers collapsing, disintegrating into dust; as they enveloped the cameras, the clouds of debris plunged viewers into the disaster, even as they watched from afar. The collapse of the 110-story buildings was terrifying because of the many lives lost and because of the shockingly sudden transformation of an orderly and seemingly permanent work of architecture into toxic disarray. For days, the images filled the airwaves and our viewing fields, until they seemed to become all that we could see.

In reports on events in progress, the news is more spontaneous. Such news segments are usually composed of long takes and even lengthy static shots, as the television eye searches for powerful images and larger meanings. Most of the time, however, news segments consist of multiple concise shots. It is not enough for television news to depict buildings; buildings themselves rarely animate the view. It is more effective to use architectural images as parts of a lively, larger whole. Television producers can generate a sense of suspense by filming a building from different angles and interspersing these shots with other arresting images. Many images shown together can create a sense of urgency, even when there is not much to show and not much happening. Increasingly, on television news, architectural images stream by as information, implicated in events, and just as ephemeral. And because of the urgency attributed to every news event, the flow of news clouds our memories of prior stories and prior imagery. The state of presentness and transience on the news undermines reflection and lasting meaning.[9]

From MSNBC News, September 11, 2001

Although the news presents a great deal of location footage, over time these scenes of architecture come to resemble the non-place of the TV studio.

The individual images of a news story—or any other program for that matter—rarely seem to matter; what matters is the succession of images, what has come before and what will come next, and this succession occurs not only within programs but also from program to program. The viewing frame of television finds its peculiar energy not in image but in imaging, in what cultural theorist Raymond Williams has called flow. In *Television, Technology, and Cultural Form*, Williams defines flow as "the replacement of a program series of timed sequential units by a flow series of differently related units in which the timing, though real, is undeclared, and in which the real internal organization is something other than the declared organization."[10] Instead of the elements of an individual image, the organizing principles of television space are the speed of cutting, the order of shots (and segments), and the variety of images shown.[11] Instead of looking merely at the "timed sequential units" in a program, we look at the flow of images, within and among programs—and including commercials.

Williams was writing on the brink of a television revolution. In 1981, the cable network MTV debuted a music video called "Video killed the Radio Star," by the British group, The Buggles. Setting images to music, MTV changed the pace and look of television flow. Visual images began to stream alongside music, and visual perception was calibrated to melodic lines and rhythmic beats. Music videos are short, fast, and hallucinatory. As Steve Reiss and Neil Feineman note, "The video has to be densely textured so it can hold up over repeated viewings. It has to be edgy enough to be noticed, but palatable enough to satisfy the often divergent demands of the performers, the record company, and the public."[12] Music videos typically display performers in bizarre makeup and costumes, cavorting around dreamlike spaces; setting these scenes in downtown streets and lofts, and shooting them in rapid-fire cuts from acute angles, add to the effect. For the first time in television history, videographers began to use architecture to create stunning and strange visuals. An R.E.M. video shows members of the group standing on the ramps of a freeway interchange— the gyrations of the music heightened by the structural dynamics of the

9. Mary Anne Doane, "Information, Crisis, Catastrophe," in *Logics of Television: Essays in Cultural Criticism*, ed. Patricia Mellencamp (Bloomington: Indiana University Press, 1990), 228.

10. Raymond Williams, *Television, Technology, and Cultural Form* (New York: Schocken Books, 1975), 93.

11. Ibid., 105.

12. Steve Reiss and Neil Feineman, *Thirty Frames Per Second: The Visionary Art of the Music Video* (New York: Harry N. Abrams, 2000), 11.

road. A Björk video shows the singer in the streets of Manhattan, her bodily contortions playing off the walls of buildings. A Rolling Stones video displays the band enlarged to the scale of buildings; at one point, Charlie Watt plays not his drums but a set of rooftop water towers. MTV's three-minute videos have introduced speed and surrealism into television's viewing environment. Like the dizzying views from a fast car on an elevated freeway, the architectural landscapes seen in the broadcast environment have become more breathtaking than ever. In *Televisuality*, John Thornton Caldwell recognizes MTV's influence on the television landscape. TV visuality, as Caldwell writes, uses the Steadicam and other devices to create high-tech artifice: "They automate an inherently omniscient point of view and subjectify it around a technological rather than human center. . . . The televisual image no longer seems to be anchored by the comforting human eye-level view of the pedestal mounted camera, but floats like the eye of a cyborg."[13]

In recent years, commercials have pioneered new visual frontiers on television. Commercials employ sophisticated special effects and considerable narrative irony. Sponsors, of course, do not want their advertisements to be subsumed within the flow of TV. Commercials need to be noticed; they need to pop out and grab us. In *Visible Fictions*, film and television historian John Ellis modifies Williams's idea of flow, arguing that news shows and other television sequences strive for autonomy—and hence recognizability. Ellis finds this especially pronounced in commercials. "Advertisements on TV cannot be scanned or ignored like the page of a newspaper; they demand short bursts of attention, producing an understanding that rests at the level of the particular segment involved and is not forced to go further, is not made to combine as a montage fragment into a larger organization of meaning."[14]

Advertisers have thus worked hard to create attention-grabbing vignettes, many of which feature shots of architecture and landscape. In a Lexus commercial, the Guggenheim Museum in Bilbao is presented in a cascade of shots at varying distances and angles, making the car and building meld into a flash of form. A twenty-second BMW commercial constructs a night drive through a city in almost 100 shots, using fleeting images of buildings to

13. John Thornton Caldwell, *Televisuality: Style, Crisis, and Authority in American Television* (New Brunswick: Rutgers University Press, 1995), 81.

14. John Ellis, *Visible Fictions: Cinema, Television, Video* (London: Routledge & Kegan Paul, 1982), 118.

evoke the rush of driving. A single car commercial might feature several places—might take us on a thirty-second drive across the United States, the landmarks and landscapes signaling a minivan's power and spaciousness. In such segments, multiple and dispersed shots of architecture hammer home the message that the automobile can take its owner anywhere, anytime. The built environment morphs from a continuous place of limited experience into a wide-open zoomscape of succession. In *The Rise of the Image*, the historian of journalism Mitchell Stephens remarks on TV's transformation of viewing time into dense fields of information, exemplified by MTV and commercials. "We frequently bemoan the shrinking of attention spans," says Stephens. "We almost never celebrate its corollary, which is the expansion in the amount of information or impressions that can be taken in in a short span of time."[15]

Architectural landscapes convey a lifestyle—and sell the product. Dramatic landscapes and cutting-edge buildings appeal to our sense of adventure, flattering us that we are intrepid in spirit. Images of traditional kitchens or living rooms comfort us with their familiarity, suggesting that a certain cereal or soda will remind us of home, and youth. Architectural styles themselves push the image of a product. A monochrome setting, a gray room or blank concrete wall, tells us that we are looking at something rarefied, exclusive, arty. Crowded and colorful scenes, like shopping malls, target a mass audience. Camera movements, too, can connect the product to the consumer. Slow-motion pans and close-ups of building elements—the buzzer by a door that signals a UPS delivery, the grooves in a linoleum floor as a dog frisks toward a bowl of food—can make the places seem almost tactile, and pleasantly assuring. Rapid cutting and zooms signal the arrival of something new and thrilling. Such presentations are, by now, carefully calibrated: commercials with many images that flash by quickly are pushing change and novelty; those with only a few images, shown at a leisurely pace, are trying to convince us of a product's timeless value or resistance to trends. Thus has architecture become part of a multibillion-dollar marketing campaign to sell goods through the visualization of lifestyle scenarios.

15. Mitchell Stephens, *The Rise of the Image, The Fall of the Word* (Oxford: Oxford University Press, 1998), 154.

SETTING THE SITCOM

The situation comedy is arguably the most important television genre. It is also the most studio-bound. Sitcoms confine most action to a single environment, a set that resembles the stage of a theatrical play. From season to season, this principal space stays the same—Lucy and Ricky's living room, Archie and Edith's living room, Jerry Seinfeld's living room. Viewers get used to the same furniture and features, and to the same patterns of movement around the set.[16] Because of constant exposure on cable networks like Nick at Nite or TV Land, sitcom sets can be more familiar to us than some actual places we once dwelled in. The familiarity of the sitcom set has also influenced domestic architecture. The set is by necessity one big room—partly because many comedy shows are filmed live, and need a multipurpose stage set. This big room might have popularized the ubiquitous "great room" of post-1970s housing, the big space where everyone in the family can be together at once, doing different things. In the 1950s, Lucy's big room was merely a formal living room; in the 1970s, the Bunker's big room featured a dining room table near the living room; by the 1990s, Jerry Seinfeld's big room consisted of living, dining, and cooking areas—the components of the great room, albeit on a smaller urban scale. Watching television from decade to decade, we have seen TV living environments become ever more casual—even as we have been influenced by these TV environments to make our own places look more and more like those we watch.

Besides encouraging informality, sitcoms promote staying at home—not only because we want to watch them, but also because they exhibit a rich social life, indoors. In many shows, the big room resembles the square of a small town; people come and go, and the door is never locked. These fluid social interactions account for much of the sitcom's popularity. The TV screen has become yet another portal to the sitcom big room. Millions of viewers, watching at home, feel that they, too, are participating in the action on-screen. They also readily leave the room—the room they are in, and the room they are watching—either by getting up or changing the channel. With its many programs, TV constructs a vivacious, welcoming, and undemanding space of social interaction. It acclimatizes us to abrupt perceptual

16. David Barken, "Television Production Techniques as Communication," in *Television: The Critical View*, 6th edition, ed. Horace Newcomb (Oxford: Oxford University Press, 2000), 171–175.

changes, as when we turn from the set to our own architectural environment, or when commercials interrupt the show, or when we change the channel. Like driving, watching television is a restless activity; both are impelled by movement through changing scenery.

One of TV's common transitions on television shows is from exterior establishing shots to scenes filmed on sets, from views of real places to TV places. In early television, most sitcoms featured little location footage. None of the thirty-nine episodes of *The Honeymooners*, first broadcast in the mid-1950s, show exteriors of 327 Chauncey Street in Bensonhurst, the apartment building where Alice and Ralph Kramden lived, although the Brooklyn locale mattered to the show. In TV's first decade, after decades of listening to radio shows, audiences were used to imagining the settings they could not see.

But television soon began to realize the visual possibilities of the medium. In the mid-1950s, some comedies sought to create a sense of architectural place through shots of the exterior of a house, especially of the front door. Even if these establishing shots rarely coordinated with the interiors, they were effective images. *Father Knows Best*, which aired from 1954 to 1962, was of the first shows to use establishing shots. At the start of each show, a brief static shot showcases the Anderson Home, a two-story house with a gabled roof and three dormers. Trees shade the house, a white picket fence frames the front lawn, and trellised columns flank the front door. The frontal shot of the house is clearly intended to convey a mood of comfortable domesticity, a pleasant middle-class environment that was part of the inevitable order of postwar American life, timeless and curiously placeless. Its inhabitants, the Anderson family, were understood to be a typical American family—white Anglo-Saxon Protestants, happy, conforming, unaware of historical change and social diversity. *Father Knows Best* leaves nothing to chance, not even the address—607 South Maple Street in Springfield, Ohio. Maple is the fifth most common American street name (after Park, Main, Oak, and Pine), and Springfield the most common city name.

A few years later, another sitcom family, the Cleavers of *Leave It to Beaver* took up residence at 485 Maple Drive; their house, too, had a white picket fence, although the town was not Springfield but Mayfield. In the middle of the series, which ran from 1957 to 1963, the Cleavers moved to Pine Street, but they suffered no downward mobility. The new house is as reassuring as the Andersons', with a brick path leading to the front door, flanked by shrubs and wrought-iron benches. Other establishing shots of the home reveal an ample front lawn, planter boxes in the windows, and a driveway leading to a separate garage in the rear. The house is tidy and the lawn is clipped, suggesting another idealized setting for an idealized American family.

During the 1950s and early 1960s, the domestic settings of sitcoms promoted an image of manicured and uniform domesticity. Unlike the architecture of certain melodramatic films of the period—by directors like Nicholas Ray or Douglas Sirk—in which suburban homes are seen to be threatened by all sorts of dangers,[17] the sitcom home looks smaller than life. It is the still center of a middle-class suburban world that displayed no poverty, no disorder, no ethnic or racial difference, no role for women beyond that of homemaker.[18] Exterior images of houses, with their spacious lots and driveways, acknowledged the nation's postwar affluence and burgeoning car culture. But the houses are as conservative in style as the shows are in demography. We see no modern house designs or much modern furniture. Sitcom design avoided any association with contemporary art movements or any whiff of individual eccentricity. Like the generic names of the communities, the physical settings of the suburban sitcom aimed straight down the middle.

The first sitcom attuned to the changing social mores of the postwar years was the *Dick Van Dyke Show*, which ran from 1961 to 1966. Most of the show's scenes took place not in the home, but in Rob Petrie's New York office. The opening credits show Rob and Laura Petrie's open-plan living room, and we learn that they live in the New York suburb of New Rochelle. But we are never shown an exterior of the house. Perhaps the producers could not agree on its architectural style, or perhaps they understood that it was safe to leave it vague. Or perhaps, the Petrie's "class status must be gleaned," as television historian David Marc writes, not from an architectural exterior, but from "subtle connotations of interior decoration: their contemporary sectional sofa; their quasi-modern objets d'art; their breakfast

17. Roger McNiven, "The Middle-Class American Home of the 1950s: The Use of Architecture in Nicholas Ray's 'Bigger than Life' and Douglas Sirk's 'All That Heaven Allows,'"*Cinema Journal* 22.4 (Summer 1985), 39–40.

18. Mary Beth Haralovich, "Sitcoms and Suburbs: Positioning the 1950s Homemaker," *Quarterly Review of Film and Video* 11 (1989), 74–75.

counter; their elaborate but unused woodstove fireplace. In this way, the
Petries' living room transcends the traditional sitcom standard of family comfort, introducing notions of personal taste."[19]

One of the most complex and realistic exterior sequences was, surprisingly, on one of the zaniest shows of the period, *The Beverly Hillbillies*, which aired from 1962 to 1971. In the first episode, after hearing the announcer say, "This is Beverly Hills and here come the Beverly Hillbillies," viewers see a jalopy driving down a wide street lined with lavish houses and towering palms. Closing in on the car, the camera watches the Clampett family, fresh from the boondocks, as they marvel at the splendor of Beverly Hills, America's residential dreamland. The camera then cuts to a view of their brand-new Renaissance-style mansion, complete with iron gate, entrance court, and crowning pediment. In flashbacks, we see how far the Clampetts have come—their home in the backwoods was a wobbly shack. The Clampetts rise in wealth as far as "Americanly possible," and it is suggestive of the changing times that their home—actually located in Bel Air—should have exceeded all standards of television domesticity. Earlier comedies used affluent and sanitized images of suburbia to emphasize the moral seriousness of their stories; *The Beverly Hillbillies* used images of high and low architecture to unravel the moral and architectural order of the comedy show, the extremes of dirt poverty and fabulous wealth replacing the archetypal middle-class home. In search of novelty and a larger market share—the hunt for which inspires so much creativity in American culture—television embarked on a bold new adventure in architectural setting.

Novelty is often followed by imitation. The success of *The Beverly Hillbillies* led to *Green Acres*, another comedy about rural hicks and city slickers, which ran from 1965 to 1971. Here the dynamic is reversed: wealthy, Harvard-educated Oliver Wendell Douglas abandons his Park Avenue penthouse for a farm in Hooterville and the romance of rustic life. The show, like *The Beverly Hillbillies*, explores environmental extremes—in this case, the opposite worlds of sophisticated Manhattan and rural America. In the credits we see a farmhouse, bales of hay, and cornfields, and then a barn with "Green Acres" painted on the roof. Next, a sequence of parallel

19. David Marc, *Comic Visions: Television Comedy and American Culture* (Oxford: Blackwell, 1997), 83–84.

views contrasts farm with city, or more pointedly, hard work with hard shopping. In exploiting the longstanding tension between city and countryside, *Green Acres* and *The Beverly Hillbillies* disrupted the smooth homogeneous suburban environment of American television. The television landscape of the 1960s, in its satirical way, eased into depictions of cultural diversity, individual desire, and class and political confrontation.

Beginning in the mid-1960s, it was the romance of the city, not the country, which became the dominant theme of TV comedy. During the next quarter-century, numerous sitcoms would be situated in Manhattan and its environs, far out of proportion to the region's population or the nation's demographic trends. Reversing a trend begun with *I Love Lucy's* move from Manhattan to Connecticut in 1957, *That Girl*, which ran from 1966 to 1971, rekindled television's romance with New York. In the opening credits, the heroine, Ann Marie, leaves the small city of Brewster, New York, bound for the big city. We see her traveling in a train along the Hudson River, her face superimposed over the skyline of New York (photographed from New Jersey, as she takes one of television's circuitous yet panoramic journeys). In Manhattan, wearing a smart suit and a pert white hat, she looks up as a montage of landmarks whisk by—the Empire State Building, the Museum of Natural History, Columbus Circle, the Chrysler Building, the Statue of Liberty, Broadway and Times Square. We see Ann Marie walking in Central Park and Lincoln Center, and then flying a kite on a pier off Lower Manhattan, the East River and the Brooklyn Bridge in the foreground. For the aspiring actress, and for millions of American girls, the tough and challenging island of Manhattan was now a playground in which to explore changing definitions of femininity. Television's depiction of Ann Marie's solo journey around Manhattan was something new. Setting up one's own household in the big city had not been done by young single women on television. Ann Marie might have emboldened countless young girls of the mid-1960s. "Her mission," as Ernest Pascucci writes, "to boldly go where no un-chaperoned girl has gone before."[20]

Other 1960s comedies, too, saw Manhattan as the setting for a glamorous and enviable lifestyle. In *Family Affair*, which aired from 1966 to 1971, the title sequence shows a sepia-toned view of the Manhattan skyline

20. Ernest Pascucci, "This City Belongs to That Girl," *ANY Magazine* 12 (1995), 51.

from the Empire State building, encompassing Midtown from the Pan Am Building to the Chrysler Building to the United Nations. The sequence then cuts to a shot of the residential tower where the hero, a wealthy widower, and his butler and adopted children live. Slowly, the camera tilts up to view the modern facade, indicating that not only is the family ensconced amid the monuments of Manhattan, but they also occupy a high enough floor to peer down at these landmarks. A few years later, *The Jeffersons,* which ran from 1975 to 1985, was set in posh Manhattan as well, but the African-American family of the title had to work its way up—in fact, George Jefferson had been Archie Bunker's neighbor in Queens. In the credits, George gets out of a cab and enters a building, which has a doorman. To a jingle, "moving up to the East Side," the camera tilts up and ascends an early 1960s high-rise even taller than that in *Family Affair*. Once again, the towers of Manhattan symbolize the social goals of wealth and success. And in *The Jeffersons*, a nation of viewers watched a black family achieve these goals. Black people, especially professionals, had not been seen much on television. Only seven years before *The Jeffersons*, the sitcom *Julia* had been the first show to feature an African-American who was not a servant. But Julia, a nurse in Los Angeles, was safely middle class. The Jeffersons rose higher—both economically and architecturally.

The Jeffersons also featured television's first interracial couple. A few years earlier, *Bridget Loves Bernie,* which lasted only a single season, from 1972 to 1973, had used Manhattan architecture to express and explore a mixed marriage. The premiere episode began with a scene of a cab driving along Park Avenue. Bernie, the Jewish cab driver, spots Bridget, an Irish-Catholic, her hand out, hailing a cab. The ride results in romance, and a year of comedic tension between the couple's Jewish and Catholic families. A New York mise-en-scène accentuates the course of this uptown-downtown pairing. The streets of the city allow for a chance encounter between two people who otherwise might never meet. Can love in the big city conquer centuries of religious and social division? The credits show images that contrast Bridget's and Bernie's architectural worlds. We see the couple strolling the streets of Midtown and Central Park, the towers of the San Remo and Plaza Hotel providing a romantic backdrop. But then we move downtown to

From *All in the Family*

Steinberg's Delicatessen—a small store with old signage in a working-class neighborhood. The camera cuts to views of Bridget's home—an imposing town house on a tony block. Somehow the dialectic works, and after a few wistful walks in Central Park, the opening sequence concludes with Bridget and Bernie embracing along the East River. Only then does she ask him the obvious question: What's your last name?

By the early 1970s, Manhattan was so important a visual icon that even comedies set in the boroughs or suburbs showed it in opening sequences. In *All in the Family*, which aired from 1971 to 1983, after Edith and Archie sing, "Those Were the Days," the credits cut to an aerial view of Midtown Manhattan. Then they shift back to the Bunkers' neighborhood in Queens, where we see a block of modest, two-family houses. The sequence concludes with a shot of the Bunker House and a zoom to its door. Inevitably, the view of the old-fashioned house would be followed by a scene in which Archie would offer one of his backward opinions. The opening sequence's contrast of Manhattan and Queens prepares us for the show's ongoing clash between now and then, progressive ideas and stubborn prejudice.

Maude, which ran from 1972 to 1978, is set in suburban Tuckahoe, New York, but its credits, too, begin in Manhattan. Maude, an occasional character on *All in the Family*, is as opinionated as Archie Bunker. Her opinions, however, veer to the left, and here Manhattan suggests the locus and incubator of her social progressiveness. Audiences see an aerial track of the Midtown skyline from the Chrysler Building looking toward the East River; afterward, the credits follow Maude's drive north to Tuckahoe—the West Side Highway and Henry Hudson Parkway, the approaching towers of the George Washington Bridge, a view of the span of the bridge, and finally a parkway that leads to the suburb (somehow Maude makes it back over the Hudson River to Westchester County). At first, the residential street is lined with small Cape Cod houses, but soon we see a larger two-story house with a screened porch. Maude's reassuringly conservative residence, not much different from the Anderson or Cleaver house, was no doubt carefully calculated. The show's controversial content—wife swapping, abortion, menopause, and alcoholism—was somehow domesticated in this familiar setting. Here, as in America in general, personal liberalism was not accompanied by aesthetic progressiveness.

The theme of social and geographical change was the inspiration for a popular show set not in New York but in the Midwest. *The Mary Tyler Moore Show*, which ran from 1970 to 1977, opened with a long and revealing credit sequence. As the theme song asks, "How will you make it on your own?" we see a car on an interstate, Mary Richards at the wheel. In *That Girl*, Ann Marie takes a train to nearby New York. A few years later, the more liberated Mary drives herself to her new home in an unfamiliar city. We soon learn her destination. A directional sign hovers over the roadway, arrows pointing to Minneapolis and St. Paul. Images of the Twin Cities appear—the expressway along the Mississippi River, and the Minneapolis skyline. Soon Mary plunges into the heart of Minneapolis. The experience is new to her, and we sense her exhilaration. Watching *The Mary Tyler Moore Show* on Saturday nights in the 1970s, the viewer could feel inspired to hit the road, to break out of the rut and make a new life in an unknown place. *That Girl* intimates the pleasures of a single girl in the city. *The Mary Tyler Moore* Show, more realistically, follows a slightly older woman making a real life in a city in the middle of the country. Mary's arrival in the Twin Cities could even call to mind the story of the frontier— but this time the frontier is not wilderness but the yuppie lifestyle then emerging in American cities.

The views of architecture in the credits establish that Mary's horizons are now urbane, various, and sophisticated. In wintry Minneapolis, she is photographed walking by a frozen lake wearing a short fur coat, popping in and out of a downtown crowd in front of Donaldson's department store, riding an escalator in the atrium of a high-rise. The sequence concludes, of course, with an exuberant Mary throwing her beret in the air, amid a downtown of strangers, laying claim to her place in the city. In another first among sitcoms, frequent establishing shots reference the show's two principal settings. Scenes in her studio apartment are preceded by shots of a three-story Victorian house on Kenwood Parkway. Scenes in Mary's office, at the WJM-TV studio, are heralded by images of an urban street and the modernist Snyder Building. Mary's new life is split between the coziness of her apartment and the cool uniformity of the downtown office. Her emergence as an independent woman looks, in an architectural sense, both to the past and present.

From *The Mary Tyler Moore Show*

Another show of the 1970s that divided its settings between home and office was *The Bob Newhart Show*, set in another Midwestern city. Bob is a psychologist—an urban occupation, to be sure—and his wife a teacher. The show takes place in Chicago, and the architectural settings are up-to-date. The opening follows Bob from his downtown office to his Edgewater apartment. Encompassing far more scenery than any real-life commute, Bob's trip is a mini-tour of Chicago. After a brief shot of Bob in his office, the camera zooms away to show off a modern high-rise. As Bob walks on a bridge over the Chicago River, the camera zooms out to show the Wrigley Building in the background. Later, the aerial camera tilts and pans for a view of the river and its bridges, the Marina Towers Apartments, Wacker Drive, and the industrial landscape to the west. After Bob boards an el train, the camera once again zooms back to show the expansive cityscape. The final shots show the el rolling away and Bob walking to his lakefront high-rise. An alternative ending features Emily walking toward the same high-rise, and depicts the building along Lake Michigan. Unlike Mary, caught between past and future, Victorian studio and high-rise office, the Hartleys are ensconced in architecture of recent vintage. *The Bob Newhart Show* was one of the first to use contemporary architecture for domestic as well as work settings. The Chicago locale perhaps explains the architectural emphasis and the stress on high-rises. Some of the greatest moments in the history of the skyscraper occurred in Chicago—the invention of the steel frame in the late nineteenth century, the development of the Miesian glass-and-steel box after the Second World War. *The Bob Newhart Show*, which chronicles the life of a childless couple, connects the potential of that life with the grand spaces and heights of a major metropolis.

Chicago's illustrious architecture is on more limited view in another Windy City sitcom of the era, *Good Times*. *Good Times* was about an African-American family in the Cabrini-Green housing project. By the 1970s, such projects had become notorious, their dilapidated buildings the scene of much violence. In fact, they had come to represent the failure of public housing in America—and as such they were hardly suitable images for the credits of a sitcom. Good Times begins with an aerial view that pictures, instead, the Chicago River and McCormick Place as well as the John Hancock tower and

Gold Coast apartments. Approaching Cabrini-Green, the camera cuts to an
interior view. Only at the end does the show offer any exterior shots of the
projects, and these are safely brief.

By the late 1970s, the aerial overview had become a standard format
for sitcom credits—it was almost as if the sequences had been supplied by
municipal tourist bureaus. Running from 1978 to 1982, *WKRP in
Cincinnati* presented an extended tour of Cincinnati. Beginning with a close-
up of a car radio and set to the constant rumble of changing stations, the
sequence shows the Cincinnati skyline, including Riverfront Stadium, the
Carew Tower, and the Roebling Bridge. After tracking the flight of a pigeon,
the camera focuses on the Tyler Davidson Fountain and its dedication "to the
people of Cincinnati." The opening to *Laverne and Shirley*, broadcast from
1976 to 1983, featured views of the Shotz Brewery where the girls work, as
well as a dramatic zoom toward the City Hall tower, emblazoned with a sign
"Welcome Milwaukee Visitors." Brooklyn, New York, was introduced by a
sign in *Welcome Back Kotter*, shown from 1975 to 1979. The show began
with the sign on the Verrazzano Bridge that reads: "Welcome to Brooklyn/4th
Largest City in America." The sequence includes no images of familiar
Brooklyn landmarks such as Coney Island, the Brooklyn Museum, the
Brooklyn Heights Esplanade, or the triumphal column in Fort Greene Park.
Instead, it focuses on Bensonhurst, the neighborhood where the show is set,
and includes such urban-gritty elements as subway and elevated lines,
streets crowded with pedestrians and store merchandise spilling out onto the
sidewalk. Unlike other contemporaneous sitcoms, which showcased new
buildings, *Welcome Back Kotter* was nostalgic. Just as architectural culture
was embracing postmodern revivalism, so, too, the television landscape was
becoming a place that recalled the past. The protagonist, Kotter, had gone
back to the place of his childhood; TV viewers were encouraged to go back
with him to a simpler time. The show's images of working-class Brooklyn
display no recent buildings. Watching architecture and urbanity on television, by the late 1970s, had become a form of time travel.

Some television shows turn real places into nostalgic never-lands.
Designing Women, which aired from 1986 to 1993, featured a group of
female friends in the New South, interior designers who work together in a

rambling Victorian house in Atlanta. The establishing shot of Sugarbaker Design Firm displays a real house—the 1881 Villa Marre (which is actually in Little Rock, Arkansas). With its Second Empire ornamental excess, the house was a fitting setting for a quartet of Reagan-era Southern belles, described as "sweet smelling, coy, cunning, voluptuous, voracious, delicious, pernicious, vexing, and sexing." The homes of other characters are suggested by shots of revivalist architectural elements, such as the colonnades of the Arkansas Governor's Mansion. The producers of this Atlanta-in-Little Rock show were clearly trying to evoke Southern gentility, but as Ethel Goodstein points out, they mainly called to mind the generic suburbs. "Rather than emu- lating an old Southern architecture or trying to create a new one, calculated- ly choosing the Villa Marre for the 'trendy' Atlanta interior designers might be read as an evasion of regionally specific codes in favor of a hegemonic sym- bol of home," she writes. "If one of the hegemonic effects of television is the negotiation of oppositional ideologies, the consequence might well be places that are neither urban nor suburban, neither Southern nor Northern."[21]

By the 1980s, few shows used images of real places with any fre- quency or visual complexity. Shown from 1982 to 1993, *Cheers* quickly cut from a view of cars driving down Beacon Street in Boston to the sign entrance to the bar, where most of the action happened. *Full House*, aired from 1987 to 1995, featured shots of San Francisco as a tourist attraction— hardly a new reading of the city. The introductory visuals of comedies set in New York highlighted standardized shots of landmark skyscraper or couples walking in a park. *Different Strokes*, shown from 1987 to 1995, included a single view of Manhattan that pans from the Empire State Building to the Pan Am Building. *Mad About You*, shown from 1992 to 1999, showed the same famous skyscrapers as well as several street shots of the hero and heroine strolling happily through Greenwich Village. *Friends*, which ran from 1994 to 2004, contained only one identifiable Manhattan view, again of landmark skyscrapers, here the Empire State and Metropolitan Life Buildings. Perhaps, after two decades of being used in television credits (and other media), Manhattan had become overexposed. The fresh city of *That Girl* had devolved into a tightly constructed cliché, the metropolitan equiva- lent of the idealized *Father Knows Best*. Vistas of skyline would alternate

21. Ethel S. Goodstein, "Southern Belles and Southern Buildings: The Built Environment as Text and Context in *Designing Women*," *Critical Studies in Mass Communication* 9 (1992), 179.

predictably with views of characters in the park. Rarely would the views have any connection with the lives and struggles of those characters—and indeed, rarely would those characters have real struggles. Manhattan on television had come to seem so smoothly predictable that it might as well have been a soundstage. The sitcom had reverted from an exploration of architecture and place, begun in the 1960s, to the standardization of architecture and place, characteristic of the 1950s.

Situation comedies, of course, leave out much of America's new social landscape. Throughout the 1980s and 1990s, young people trying to figure out life in a big city, New York or elsewhere, were staking new ground; yet sitcoms have not explored the tenement and warehouse geographies of the New York's Lower East Side or Chicago's Wicker Park. America has been transformed in recent times by immigration, primarily from Latin America and Asia. Yet sitcoms almost never feature immigrant families or their neighborhoods—Little Havana in Miami, or the Vietnamese suburb of Westminster in Orange County. And while television has begun to feature gay characters, even in leading roles, gay neighborhoods, like New York's West Village or San Francisco's Castro, have been ignored. TV's new terrain tends to be old terrain—the above-average suburbs of *The Fresh Prince of Bel-Air*, shown from 1990 to 1996, the average suburbs of *Home Improvement*, shown from 1991 to1999, or the below-average suburbs of *Roseanne,* which ran from 1988 to 1997. And perhaps because such sitcoms know they are portraying environments familiar to many viewers, they see no need to use location footage. But the chief reason that television does not highlight the diverse urban landscape is that most programs have shown stereotypical views of class and of class mobility. Depictions of place center around people making it, trying to make it, or not making it— living on the Upper East Side, aspiring to move to Beverly Hills, or stuck in the old neighborhood in Queens. The sitcom has yet to acknowledge that making it in America might mean living in a building or neighborhood that looks quite different from the mainstream—that is neither cookie-cutter suburban nor big-time Manhattan.

One show, however, resisted such standardization. *Seinfeld*, which aired from 1990 to 1998, presented no gratuitous views of New York in its credits, exhibited no images of generic urban lifestyle. This enormously popular show, about a group of comically self-centered and often obnoxious New Yorkers, used carefully selected shots of Manhattan and the New York region. Establishing exterior views show the buff-brick walls and terra-cotta moldings of Jerry's Upper West Side apartment from different angles and distances, and at different times of day. Images of a coffee shop, with an illuminated sign reading "Restaurant"—the real place is on Broadway in Morningside Heights—always precede the friends' frequent gatherings over coffee and sandwiches. Other location shots show places connected to the lives of the characters—the ramps and large bat in front of Yankee Stadium, George's parent's house in Queens, the Midtown building where Elaine works for Mr. Peterman. Other exteriors take us further into Jerry's world—the Long Island Expressway, a shopping mall garage in New Jersey, the exterior of the Del Boca Vista condominium where Jerry's parents live in Florida. The architecture of Seinfeld spirals into the vortex of the show, into Jerry's present-day haunts and childhood memories.

The New York of *Seinfeld* sets up an architectural world of personal and often jaundiced perspectives; here views of the city reflect the amoral plot lines of the show, which is, notoriously, about "nothing." In *Seinfeld*, we view no timeless suburban ideal, no electric metropolis where a person might change and grow; the only generic place is the backlot street used for sidewalk scenes. The Manhattan of Jerry, Kramer, George, and Elaine is a city of quirky and irritable characters, where everyone is out for himself or herself. The interspersed establishing shots are purged of the morality, sentimentality, and sense of discovery that had become tropes of sitcom imagery. Like the show's relentless skewering of social relationships, its establishing shots turn architecture and city into cartoon images as hilariously one-dimensional as Jerry and his friends. In *Seinfeld*, people live in a cardboard city enlivened by outrage, impertinence, and self-interest, a fragmented metropolis of multiple views, meanings, and memories.

Watching *Seinfeld*, we saw for the first time an architectural landscape wholly conditioned by television. By the early 1990s, the first generation raised on TV had come of age and was creating new TV. Jerry Seinfeld, born in the mid-1950s, knew buildings and cities as part of a televisual environment. In *Seinfeld*, urban environments are understood through the one-liners and absurd plot events of early television. Its architecture refers as much to older television shows as to actual New York locales. By the first years of the new century, television's visual universe had become deeply self-reflexive and often premised on self-parody; the nation's visual sights, one might argue, had become equally skewed.

STREETS OF SURVEILLANCE

Unlike film, television offers architecture as an everyday experience. Television shows come into our homes and become part of our lives. On a small screen, audiences watch characters and settings smaller than themselves and their environs. Armed with a remote control, audiences can decide which programs to watch, and which to click off. In rooms where the lights are usually on, where conversation is permitted, and where other activities take place, TV watching is integrated into our daily routine. It should not be surprising, then, that TV programs are more subject to popular trends than motion pictures or artistic photographs. Instead of rarefied experience, television fosters an arena of generalized reflection. In situation comedies, brief establishing shots of architecture and cityscape depict ideas of domesticity to audiences watching in their own homes.

With the police drama, the plot thickens. Cop shows feature an extensive architectural and urbanistic subplot, and the imagery of these dramas can tell us a great deal about our culture's changing ideas of the city. Where the sitcom fears to tread, the police drama is only too happy to go. Alone among television genres, cop shows range over the metropolis, making energetic use of location shooting. In addition to the establishing shot, the long take and extended sequence are commonplace. The stories of unsolved crimes, of sordid big-city doings, of stakeouts, chases, and shootouts, almost always take us out into the city, to its streets, alleys, garages, vacant lots, parks, fire escapes, and rooftops. Cameras venture not only into crack houses but also into opulent houses, where criminal syndicates plan their operations, and to waterfronts, where dead bodies have washed up. Audiences witness the crime and, along with the plainclothes detectives, investigate the site, interview bystanders and informants; they must experience the thrill of the chase, of shootings, and of catching and handcuffing the villain; by now, most viewers could probably read a suspect his rights. "Television's stories of crime and police," writes Thomas Zynda, "have been the spine of its claims to aesthetic realism throughout its history."[22] In the tradition of film noir, police shows provide a front (and safe) seat for viewing action and violence. Viewers can peer into raffish and dangerous worlds, safe to watch but not to enter. Cop shows feature television's most comprehensive and voyeuristic explorations of urban form and space.

Because they use so much location footage, police dramas have become valuable records of the changing appearance of cities. Some long-running shows feature lengthy views of bygone city scenes—of old cars and transit systems, of dated neon signage and street fixtures, of buildings long-since demolished or renovated, even of entire districts that have been torn down or changed beyond recognition. To watch a cop show from the 1950s or 1960s is to enter another era, an era where the cityscape looks different, and where the moral codes are different, too. To watch an episode of *Dragnet*, first aired from 1951 to 1959, is to glimpse the streetscape of a vanished (and in the show, black-and-white) Los Angeles. But it is also to experience how the city can be used as visual evidence of the authority of its moralistic officers; camera views on the city demonstrate, in the words of its hero, Officer Friday, "just the facts." In the opening credits, "as the camera moves slowly over an expanse of urban sprawl, the narrator tells us," writes television historian Horace Newcomb, "that this is the city. We cannot deny our eyes, so his credibility is assured."[23] But of course, the show, created by its star Jack Webb, portrayed Los Angeles not in ordinary circumstances but in seedy and violent vignettes. Most episodes from the early seasons had the word "big" in their title—"The Big Death," "The Big Blast," "The Big Grandma," "The Big Eavesdrop." Although depicting events taken from the police files, *Dragnet* was larger-than-life—television verité that showed life "scripted" at its most shocking and entertaining moments.

Dragnet was revived in 1967; the new show used more extensive location filming, this time in color. The opening credits picture the Los Angeles skyline by day and night, focusing on landmarks like the Music Center and Griffith Park Observatory. We see churches and synagogues as

22. Thomas Zynda, "The Metaphoric Vision of Hill Street Blues," *Journal of Popular Film and Television* 14 (Fall 1986), 101.

23. Horace Newcomb, *TV: The Most Popular Art* (Garden City, New York: Doubleday Books, 1974), 91.

well—reminders that we are watching morality tales. One smoggy view of Los Angeles zeroes in on what was then the tallest building downtown, City Hall, and then zooms out to reveal the white-and-green city, sprawling from mountains to ocean. The expanse of Los Angeles engulfs the municipal building, suggesting the futility of trying to police this metropolitan territory.

One episode, "The LSD Story," highlighted what the police were up against in the countercultural 1960s. The most striking scenes happen on the happening Sunset Strip. Here, instead of the cool documentary views of Ed Ruscha's early-morning photo shoot, we see the drugged-out, outrageous nighttime Strip, with bright signs advertising "The Boss," "The Scene: World's Foremost Hypnotist," and "The Strip Combers," a dog-grooming parlor. The Sunset Strip of *Dragnet* is a quirky and rebellious place. Hippies are shown protesting drug laws, framed by the sign for the Whiskey A Go-Go. The Strip is aglow, and *Dragnet* can be watched today for its earnest portrait of the opposition between "square" police officers and hallucinating hipsters, between the areas of the city under police (and the camera's) surveillance and those marked by the loopy decadence of the times.

Another police drama, *The Naked City*, which ran from 1958 to 1963, presented a more nuanced image of a large city, as place both dangerous and exhilarating. All its episodes were shot on location in New York City. The cinematographic quality—the director of photography was J. Burgi Contner—approached that of film. And in fact, the show had been inspired by a film, *The Naked City*, directed by Jules Dassin and released in 1948; in turn, the film itself had been inspired by a 1945 book of photographs, *Naked City*, by Weegee. The television show fully exploits its locale; in most episodes of this police procedure drama, we watch its heroes, two NYPD detectives, drive through the city, through Central Park and Times Square, over the bridges and through the tunnels, out into the boroughs and onto the harbor; we see bus and train stations, expressways, construction sites, docks, ferries, cemeteries, hospitals, bars, and ethnic and working-class neighborhoods.

An early episode, "Lady Bug, Lady Bug," begins with an aerial shot of Lower Manhattan, cuts to a closer view of downtown, and dissolves into a shot of a crowded downtown sidewalk—the scene recalls *The Crowd* and anticipates *West Side Story*. The next sequence builds upon the tension these views create, that between the serene overview and the violence that lurks on the ground. A wrecking ball savages the crumbling walls of an old building. After this potent image, the scene cuts to Sutton Place and its exclusive homes, to the East River esplanade and serene views of the river and the 59th Street Bridge. Just as suddenly, it moves into a swish pan of racing cars, and then focuses on a mail slot at one of the street's wealthy residences, where a grenade has been placed. A bystander comments that the grenade arrived on a fifteen-cent bus ride from Mulberry Street—the still-notorious Five Points neighborhood—while it took him thirty years to make the move uptown. In the naked city, a life of plenty is no protection against peril.

Naked City shootouts are artfully filmed set pieces. Like Polonsky's Force of Evil, the opening shot of "A Death of a Princess," an episode from 1960, stares down at Trinity Church before cutting to a man on a park bench and then traveling uptown to Morningside Heights. After an angled view up at the tower of Riverside Church, the camera takes us inside a nearby apartment, whose kitchen view is dominated by the church. From this vantage, we see a handgun, hear a shot, and witness the murder of a cop on the street below. The ensuing chase and gun battle takes us on an anxious, highly choreographed tour of the neighborhood, with arresting views of the Riverside Drive Viaduct and its neighboring gas tank. (In 1937, Berenice Abbott photographed the viaduct and tank as a monumental composition of arched space and cylindrical form.) Naked City employs the two structures as focal points of a larger background that encompasses the Hudson River, Riverside Church, and myriad vernacular structures in what was once a wholesale meat district. Some shots zero in on the intricate texture of brick walls or the structure of freight elevators. Others are taken from shifting street and rooftop perspectives that propel the action and reveal the complex urban landscape. At the end of a scene on a rooftop parking lot, after the killer has been cornered and shot, the camera looks again at Riverside Church, only this time the view includes Grant's Tomb. Like a skene in a Greek tragedy, architectural monuments frame the action and deepen its significance.

Time and again, Naked City explores New York's architectural topography, its high bridges, tall buildings, and rooftops. One episode, "The King of Venus Will Take Care of You," pivots around a water tower atop a tenement in Chelsea. It begins with a boy scanning the city through binoculars from a crack in a rooftop water tower and, predictably, witnessing a murder. In the chase that follows, the rooftop, with its piping, stair towers, water drums, and edges overlooking precipitous drops, is central to the action. Uneven surfaces must be crossed. Multiple vertical routes down to the street must be negotiated. A child's kinesthetic understanding of the city emerges. The camera follows the boy as he scampers down stone stairs to an alley filled with trash cans, runs up steel stairs and climbs over a fence, runs down another flight of stairs before entering another building, races through corridors, crawls out of a window, climbs a fire escape, reaches the roof, slips under a gate, and shimmies up a fire escape to the water tower. After the killer is shot near the water tower, the camera shows us a long view of the Midtown skyline—a visual reminder of the show's voice-over narrative, which every week tells us that there are "eight million stories in the Naked City."

Like all police shows, *Naked City* often depicts its characters entering and leaving buildings and vehicles. To accentuate the setting of these movements, the camera often looks up at a building and then tilts down as a car or taxi pulls up in front of it. Another typical sequence might open with a camera tracking a car down a street and following its occupants as they get out and go into some structure or space. Sidewalks feature prominently as the venue for long discussions or moody departures. In these extended scenes, audiences see various apartment facades with their rickety fire escapes and fading signs of long departed businesses. And just as *Dragnet* has preserved the Los Angeles of mid-century, *Naked City* has left us an extensive inventory of images of a New York long gone. Its 138 episodes are one of the best visual records of a city ever created by television. In "A Kettle of Precious Fish," from 1961, a chase scene takes us into the cavernous halls of the old Pennsylvania Station, McKim, Mead, and White's 1910 masterwork. The episode probes the station's sumptuous spaces and myriad nooks. In the first shot, a cab arrives and we glimpse the base of a huge colonnade, with its soot-covered stone. Inside, the camera tracks a suspect through a steel-framed arcade of shops and down an escalator into the main waiting room. In the high vaulted space, there is a model of the Polaris Missile—a reminder of the cold war and the space race. The final confrontation occurs in the vast glass-roofed concourse. We see most of the giant steel piers, some covered by lockers. The scene culminates as the suspect is shot on the steps of the grand staircase. Pennsylvania Station would be demolished four years later, its stone and steel carted off the Jersey Meadowlands. But today, through the fluid camerawork of *Naked City*, we can experience the great station and its sequence of spaces.

Naked City was filmed in an era when works of modern architecture and engineering were remaking the substance and skyline of New York City. Through in-depth visual investigations of the everyday city, the show might have inadvertently contributed to an appreciation for an older New York that was being demolished. Because it suited the show's noir origins and atmosphere, *Naked City* showed less of the emerging steel-and-glass New York and more of the brick-and-stone city. For the same reason, the show ventured less to Midtown and the new suburbs than to the older districts of Manhattan and the boroughs. In some ways, *Naked City* can be seen as visual and dramatic analogue to Jane Jacobs's pivotal antimodernist book, *The Death and Life of Great American Cities*, published in 1961. Both show and text stress the critical idea that a vital city is a diverse city, made up of different sorts of buildings and different kinds of people.

Some television cop shows are set not in the gritty, gray metropolis, but in an azure-skied paradise. For every crumbling Bronx, Chicago, or Baltimore there is a sleek San Francisco, Miami, or Honolulu. Largely because of its palmy exoticism, *Hawaii Five-O* became the longest-running (from 1968 to 1980) police drama to date. Its opening sequence shows a mix of natural and architectural landscapes; except for closing shots of a car on fire and a blue police light, the footage could have been shot by the local tourist office. As the theme music (by Morton Stevens) begins, we see a huge wave breaking over the drama's titles. From here we tour the Waikiki beachfront, enjoying views of Diamond Head, and then the sexy sights of Honolulu, which include the jiggling belly of a hula dancer and the curving metal underbelly of a jetliner.

Responding to the visual pizzazz of the James Bond movies, *Hawaii*
Five-O broke with the visual tradition of the police drama; it rarely featured seedy nightclubs or bars, threatening dark alleys, warehouses, and waterfront piers. Here the crime scenes are lush gardens and tranquil beaches, airport concourses and elegant hotels. Here the backdrop to mayhem is not an aging industrial city, but rather tropical foliage, steep green mountains, and the wild waves of the Pacific Ocean. *Hawaii Five-O* also makes the most of Honolulu's distinctive architecture, its modernist high-rise hotels and older coral-faced buildings. The show's top cop, Steve McGarrett, has his office not in a nondescript precinct house but in the grandest setting in downtown Honolulu, the Iolani Palace. His briefings to the higher-ups take place while strolling through gardens under graceful, tropical trees. Watching swaying palms and white hotels became as much a part of the show's attraction as following its criminal escapades. McGarrett always got his man, and it mattered that he got him in a tropical paradise.

The extensive visuals of *Hawaii Five-O* were responding in part to one of the greatest developments in American transportation history—mass air travel. By the early 1960s, Boeing had improved the range of its intercontinental jet, the 707, allowing for long flights across oceans. In 1968, the year *Hawaii Five-O* debuted, Boeing premiered its large jet, the 747, which could carry three times as many passengers as the 707. The extra capacity lowered operating costs and fares; global tourism was now possible. The jet age made Hawaii a major tourist destination. Shows like *Five-O* were catalysts in this transformation, beaming the visual delight and excitement of the islands into millions of living rooms on the mainland. In selling the show to the governor of Hawaii, its executive producer argued that *Five-O* was the kind of clean, smokeless industry the islands needed.

Five-O's potent mix of exotic nature and modern buildings influenced other shows. It caught the attention of producer Quinn Martin, who had earlier produced *The Fugitive*. Martin's *The Streets of San Francisco*, running from 1972 to 1977, exploited the smashing views, vertiginous cityscapes, and steep social divides of the Bay Area. Since the nineteenth century, because of its physical beauty, remoteness, and large Asian community, San Francisco had had an exotic image. Now, in the early 1970s, after the Beats,

From *The Streets of San Francisco*

Hippies, SDS, and Black Panthers, San Francisco had become even more strange and alluring. By pairing a veteran cop and young college graduate as partners, *Streets of San Francisco* explored the generation gap in the place where the chasm was greatest. And with its mix of older Victorians and modern skyscrapers, the architectural mise-en-scène complemented the social struggle between old and new, between the countercultural folks who inhabited the funky old buildings and the corporate types who held court in the high-rise downtown.

Landscape unifies these streets of San Francisco. In almost every episode, extended tracking shots follow automobiles as they negotiate the city's steep streets. Expansive vistas provide the backdrop for intrigue. In a typical sequence, a car moves through Pacific Heights, with the bay and Alcatraz Island in the distance; a couple embraces in Lincoln Park, the Golden Gate in the background; a man walks through Maritime Plaza, with Coit Tower in view; a dog discovers a body floating in the bay, in clear sight of the Marin Headlands. The show's chase scenes recall classic San Francisco movies like *Bullitt*, from 1968, and *Dirty Harry*, from 1971, taking TV audiences on hair-raising car chases; using dozens of camera angles and settings, the videographers show us the city's vistas in machine-gun-like bursts of scenery.

The credits of *Streets of San Francisco* also show off the city in a stream of glossy images. Against the panoramic skyline, we see a car driving over the Bay Bridge. The camera cuts back and forth from the bridge to the waterfront, and then, the pace quickening, it dashes to the Golden Gate Bridge, stops by Fisherman's Wharf, and winds up at the Civic Center, where white lines zip across the screen to form the show's title. And then we are off again, touring the Pioneer Monument, the Beaux-Arts Civic Center, and finally an array of tourist sites—Coit Tower, the Ferry Building, Chinatown, the Fairmont and Mark Hopkins Hotels, and North Beach at night. Putting the camera gearshift in overdrive, the show hits us all-out with the city. With the funk-jazz rhythms of Pat Williams's theme song, and the syncopation of static shots followed by swish pans and zooms, the sequence plays like an MTV video. Combining the exoticism of *Hawaii Five-O* with the realism of *Naked City*, *The Streets of San Francisco* pointed the way to a new symbiosis of architectural style and dramatic suspense.

From *Miami Vice*

A few years later, *Miami Vice* would treat viewers to this sort of potent mix of danger and design. The *Vice* cops, Crockett and Tubbs, have the moves of a James Bond, the wardrobe of a Giorgio Armani. The station house could be the studio of a trendy architect. Clean, hard lines and cool, pastel light create *Vice*'s distinctive visual atmosphere. In a city of tropical heat and bright sun, the most provocative scenes occur at night, against chilly blue illumination. *Miami Vice* downplays the city's traditional tourist images, its hotels, swimming pools, and day-tripper sites. The show transforms the resort town into the setting for a larger fashion statement that goes far beyond the beach. According to Todd Gitlin, "The hard-edged look echoes the fashion magazine layouts which preceded both MTV and the pulsating car commercial, all meant to break through the clutter, as the advertisers say—the clutter being the profusion of images themselves, of billboards, commercials, and television shows, the unending cornucopia spilling its promises upon the national attention, the noise finally drowning out each of its poor components. *Vice*'s environments of artifice are intended to arrest the attention; self-consciousness is precisely the point."[24]

The new, designer Miami of *Vice* emerges in the credits. After a tracking shot of the Atlantic coast, the usual attractions roll across the screen—pink flamingoes, gray dolphins, sailboats, palm trees, a white Rolls Royce, polychrome parrots, women in bikinis, a jai alai player, and the horse and dog tracks. Midway through, we see views of the city's distinctive architecture—white high-rise hotels at the ocean's edge, then the twenty-story Atlantis on Brickell Avenue, designed by the Arquitectonica, one of the leading postmodernist firms of the 1980s. (*Miami Vice* aired from 1984 to 1989). The televisual image of the Atlantis skycourt, with its single palm and red corkscrew stair, almost single-handedly popularized the design culture of Miami.

When *Miami Vice* debuted, Miami itself had come to seem passé, a torpid, subtropical city with bleached-out buildings. The show's historical importance lies not only in its televisualization of the city, but also in the influence that its imagery has had on the city and its architecture. The wildly popular and prosperous Miami of today began on the small screen, in the

24. Todd Gitlin, "Car Commercials and Miami Vice: We Build Excitement," in *Watching Television: A Pantheon Guide to Popular Culture*, ed. Todd Gitlin (New York: Pantheon Books, 1986), 152.

pastel and neon look of *Vice*. In every show, the stylish vice cops traverse the flatlands of Florida, its roadways and waterways, bridges and beaches. Tubbs and Crockett meet with drug kingpins in steamy discothèques, swagger along Bayfront Park, saunter through the Miami Marina and the lobbies of the Fontainebleau and the Biltmore. In "Duty and Honor," a car chase through the streets and alleys of Miami Beach ends in a typical *Vice* moment. The fugitive's car blows up in front of an apartment house, and the camera lingers on the orange flames and the Art Deco details of the building, making them seem to harmonize. In "Streetwise," a conversation takes place inside a downtown office where audiences see, through floor-to-ceiling glass walls, Miami's tallest building, the First Union Financial Center. Michael Mann, the show's creator, set the scene at night, making the building look as if it were dressed in a slip of blue lights. In "The Dutch Oven," one of Miami Beach's pale stucco buildings is attired in pink and blue flashing neon to become the Dynamo Disco; today, of course, South Beach's Ocean Drive is awash in bright neon. "No Exit" showcases the Spear House in Coral Gables, a 1978 design by Arquitectonica (with assistance from Rem Koolhaas). Seen from Biscayne Bay, the house, with its colorful walls, large windows, and projecting balconies, showed off a posh and forward-looking Miami.

The intersection of architecture and television was fortuitous. In the 1920s and 1930s, blocks of Art Deco buildings had been erected in Miami Beach. Although Deco is an ornamental style, its references are to machine technologies—to the streamlined designs of railroads and steamships. The style's extensive stucco surfaces and crisp corners also link it to mid-century modernism. In the 1980s, Miami postmodernism, as exemplified by Arquitectonica, was similarly inspired by modernism. In fact, it can be seen as a revival of modernism with flourishes from Art Deco and Latin American design. In retrospect, Miami in the 1980s was the perfect setting for a swank cop show. At a time when architecture in most other American cities was mired in historicist confusion, the televised streets of Miami looked like scenes from the future.

Like other cop shows, *Miami Vice* recognized the power of contrast—classy houses and gardens look even swankier when preceded by views of

From *Miami Vice*

barren industrial landscapes. "Evan" begins in an abandoned warehouse, now used as a firing range. Both the interior shots of the cavernous space and the exterior views of the roof profile hint at the mansion that we soon will see. And like the warehouse, the house is spare, modernist, even spartan. Not even artwork and mood lighting, hibiscus and jasmine, keep the house from appearing severe. In *Vice*, the buildings, like the protagonists, are impeccably tailored.

Almost each episode intrudes into the wealthy homes of suspects. In "Forgive Us Our Deb," Tubbs and Crockett dock at a landing in their speedboat. The camera faces them as they open a chain-link gate, a neoclassical mansion in the background, and then pans away from the dowager building as they move toward a skintight modernist palace. The architecture and landscape of such houses are striking, but, as the show goes on, they become as predictable as Crockett's designer T-shirts and linen jackets. Inevitably, the houses are surrounded by jungles of foliage. Living rooms open out onto terraces that feature pools and vistas of the bay or ocean. The massing and fenestration of the houses call to mind the work of modernists such as Craig Elwood and Richard Neutra. Curving staircases relieve the rectilinear severity of high-ceilinged spaces; double-height living rooms are lined by steel-tubular railings and glass-block walls. Color and texture, too, add to the mood. White is *Miami Vice*'s preferred color, but peachy or melony hues contrast effectively with the neutral palette. The minimalist décor usually features artworks, but never a bit of clutter. The hard surfaces of buildings remain a blank canvas for atmospheric lighting—shadows made by window mullions or balustrades, the spark of gunfire. Because so much is filmed at night, when saturating sunlight gives way to muted, dreamy illumination, the houses seem to glow in azure tones. Rarely have television, architecture, and fashion combined to such influential effect.

By 1980, cop shows had a formula: one or two teams of star detectives investigate one or two spectacular crimes and wrap things up by the end of the episode. But television, like fashion, thrives on variety. And like architecture in the real city, the architectural mise-en-scène on television needs to keep changing, too. A couple of years before *Miami Vice*, producers Michael Kozoll and Steven Bochco took the television verité of *Dragnet* deeper into the murk. *Hill Street Blues*, which ran from 1981 to 1987, was in its time the grittiest of the gritty—a look at the pitch-black underside of urban America, with its muggers, rapists, pimps, prostitutes, drunks, addicts, and gangs. Coinciding with the crack epidemic and soaring crime rates, *Hill Street Blues* depicted a precinct where chaos reigns, where many investigations go unsolved, and where the criminal justice system might be rigged. The show never identified its locale, though we know we are in some northern industrial city. In contrast to *Vice*'s fluid camerawork, *Blues* was often filmed with a handheld camera, making the action look even more scrambled and rough. And while *Vice* romanticizes an ascendant, if crime-ridden, Miami, *Hill Street Blues* makes its postindustrial city a vision of hell on earth. The credits open with a static shot of a police car in a garage. The camera follows the vehicle out onto wintry streets, past vacant lots, parking lots, and antediluvian industrial buildings. In the most powerful image of the credits, we see an elevated expressway, rail containers, smokestacks; the sky is heavy and gray. Cities have rarely looked so beautifully ugly.

Hill Street Blues showed generic unsightliness. Cops drive generic "Metro" police cars through a nowhere-anywhere trashed-out city.[25] Careful scrutiny reveals that many scenes are shot in Chicago, and occasionally Los Angeles. The Maxwell Street Precinct house on Chicago's Near West Side functions as the establishing shot for the show's station house. Cars often drive through Chicago's dim concrete tunnels. In one episode, a train pulls into Northwestern Station, and we can see the Chicago River and a Montgomery Ward building in the background. But *Hill Street Blues* avoided the landmarks of Chicago or any other place. With aerial pans of monotonous neighborhoods extending to the horizon, the producers contrive an urban hell lacking any distinct center or upscale districts. This generic quality gave the televisual city greater sociological and geographical weight. These fictional barrens look unnervingly familiar—part of the zoomscape of rail yards, abandoned industry, and decaying housing that many of us drive by everyday. By showcasing the lumpen city as an autonomous entity, television brought into focus the schism that had characterized American urbanity ever since the middle-class flight to suburbia.

25. Zynda, 101–102.

Miami Vice portrays an urban place of white-collar crime amid Floridian luxe; *Hill Street Blues* turns the city into the topic of tomorrow's tabloid headlines. Both shows were self-consciously aesthetic, their visual environments highly crafted. In the 1980s, the crime-ridden city on television became a place in the postmodern landscape. *Vice* and *Blues* epitomized opposing directions in American urbanism. The designer-look Miami reflected the gentrification of the coasts, the rise of a glamorous new urban lifestyle. *Hill Street Blues* was the avatar of anti-style, with its rust-belt landscape that demanded of its characters hard work and hard-won humanity.

During the 1980s, however, gentrification had begun to spread to the rust belt, to cities like Chicago, Pittsburgh, and Baltimore. Baltimore's comeback began along its waterfront when in 1980, the Rouse Company opened a shopping and eating destination called Harbor Place. In the years that followed, the National Aquarium, and the Camden Yards ballpark replaced the harbor's landscape of rotting piers and empty warehouses. Soon after the opening of the new stadium, producer-director Barry Levinson began filming *Homicide: Life on the Street*. Set in Baltimore, *Homicide*, which ran from 1993 to 2000, shows a city teetering between urban decline and urban ascendance. During the years of the show, Baltimore continued its impressive renewal, but it also continued to suffer from poverty and disinvestment. The slow-recovering Baltimore is the star of *Homicide*. The show moves all over city—the tourist playgrounds of the Inner Harbor, the gentrified but still salty Fells Point neighborhood, the labyrinthine precincts of Johns Hopkins Medical Center, and most often, the neighborhoods of distinctive row houses with marble steps. *Homicide* finds style in squalid streets and shuttered grocery stores, places whose gloom is accentuated by tinted camera lenses, and in apartments whose dark empty hallways are made to appear even more sinister by the camera's extreme angles.[26] In "A Doll's Eyes," tracking shots of the ground at a murder site linger on the multicolor chalk outlines drawn by the police around bullet and body fragments, framing them as works of art. In "Every Mother's Son," a gun battle in a back alley between cops and a frightened teenager is dramatically heightened by the camera circling the combat-

26. Norman Klein, "Staging Murders: The Social Imaginary, Film, and the City," *Wide Angle*, 20:3 (July 1998), 86.

ants, turning dirty brick walls and a pile of junked tires into an arena for elaborate violence.

The title sequence makes brilliant use of architecture. It begins with an angled tracking shot of a street of row houses, the tilting of the camera suggesting the instability of the neighborhood. A rapid montage of cityscape follows. In a handheld shot, we first see vernacular, downtrodden Baltimore—an old car driving past a postwar house, a statue of Jesus Christ. These shots of streets and alleys are then intercut with images of city land-marks—a sign for crab cakes, an aerial view of the Inner Harbor. Toward the end of the credits, the camera again files past row houses, their bricks fil-tered orange, their stoops the focus of the camera's slightly out-of-focus gaze. *Homicide*, following several decades of cop shows set in major American cities, had come up with its own time-bound expression of urban visuality. The rediscovery of Baltimore, and cities like it, was based in large part on the distinctiveness of older architecture and neighborhoods, their dif-ferences from suburbia. *Homicide* accentuates these differences through shot selection and succession as well as camera movement. Gone is the police eye that gazed at the city through objective detachment. In its place is a mode of perception meant to immerse the television audience in urban discovery—chance meetings, odd juxtapositions, encounters at street level that feel almost tactile.

As seen on television, architecture and city are implicated in an over-whelming system of display, entertainment, information, and commerce. Compared to a photograph or a film, television is always with us, present nearly everywhere. Its representation of architecture is diverse and diffuse. Photography condenses the meanings of architecture into singular images that can convey significant ideas. Film captures larger, moving aspects of architecture that deepen or amplify narratives or independent visual inves-tigations. The television screen contains channel upon channel of pictures, each presenting a different setting, each constantly changing its settings, flowing through programs and commercials, through the clicks of the remote. A new spatiality of architecture emerges. Neither a fixed flat image nor a moving linear image, television spatiality is more complex, harder to visualize. Unlike the architecture experienced from vehicles, contained if stretched out within three-dimensional space, the televisual zoomscape partakes of a multidimensional world—of live and recorded footage, of location and studio shooting, of new and old programming, of commerce, entertainment, education, art. Contemporary culture's most familiar and accessible visual environment is also its most outlandish and incomprehensible.

The transportation and camera technologies I have discussed in this book are the leading modes of a larger, ongoing transformation of architectural visuality. Elevators, escalators, and people movers allow us to glide through the spaces of buildings or large urban complexes, and similarly dissociate the perception of built space from bodily exertion. Camera recordings play not only on movie or TV screens, but on surveillance monitors, which, in real time, survey huge tracts of the architectural landscape from single rooms. Since the 1980s, computers have become increasingly essential to contemporary life, and they offer a range of new visual environments—websites, virtual reality, video games, interactive installations. Webcams allow us to view places worldwide in real time from any place and for almost any reason. Websites turn businesses, institutions, and individuals into visual landscapes where architecture plays a significant role—photos or video of hotels, restaurants, tourist sites, and other services; reproductions of a museum collection or the spaces of an institution; the personal photos or videos of home parties or travels. At the moment, these developments seem groundbreaking and destined to refashion radically both the design and apprehension of architecture. Yet, as I have argued throughout this book, the moving perspectives of the zoomscape suggest that the technological transformation of architectural perception happens gradually and in a hybrid manner. The page format of websites echoes the mix of photographs and text first used in late-nineteenth-century newspapers and magazines. Video games employ cinematic modes of movement (such as tracking, zooming) to approximate the experience of piloting a vehicle through space. Digital viewing environments will continue to develop these and other perceptual characteristics of the zoomscape—mobility, speed, distance, framing, multiplicity, editing. Zoomscapes have greatly increased our sources of visual information. Zoomscapes have pushed our vision toward a state of almost perpetual transformation. Zoomscapes have estranged and enlightened our understanding of architecture.

Courtesy of James Benning: 253
Carol Buhrmann, photographer: 126, 132, 144, 160
Gusmano Cesaretti, photographer; courtesy of Michael Mann: 296, 299
Courtesy of George Eastman House: 192
Courtesy of Ernie Gehr: 239
J. Philip Gruen, photographer: 60, 85, 120, 138, 150, 268
Peter B. Hales, photographer: 70, 118
Steve Harp, photographer: 53, 75
Todd Hido, photographer: 117, 164, 189
Pad McLaughlin, photographer: 260, 278, 281, 294
Courtesy of Metropolitan Museum of Art: 180, 195
Corinna Nicolaou, photographer: 89
Courtesy of Pacific Film Archive: 36, 206, 213, 224, 245, 249
Keith Plymale, photographer: 93, 103
John Santoro, photographer: 30, 43, 48, 63
Courtesy of Julius Shulman: 184
Bob Thall, photographer: 201